Disciplined Hearts

Disciplined Hearts

*History, Identity, and Depression
in an American Indian
Community*

Theresa DeLeane O'Nell

UNIVERSITY OF CALIFORNIA PRESS
Berkeley   ·   Los Angeles   ·   London

University of California Press
Berkeley and Los Angeles, California

University of California Press
London, England

Library of Congress Cataloging-in-Publication Data

O'Nell, Theresa DeLeane, 1957–
    Disciplined hearts : history, identity, and
depression in an American Indian community /
Theresa DeLeane O'Nell.
        p.   cm.
    Includes bibliographical references and index.
    ISBN 0-520-20229-5 (c : alk. paper)
    ISBN 0-520-21446-3 (pbk : alk. paper)
    1. Salish Indians—Psychology.   2. Salish
Indians—Mental health.   3. Salish Indians—
Ethnic identity.   4. Depression, Mental—
Montana—Flathead Indian Reservation.
  5. Ethnopsychology—Montana—Flathead
Indian Reservation.   6. Cultural psychiatry—
Montana—Flathead Indian Reservation.
  7. Flathead Indian Reservation (Mont.)—Social
conditions.   I. Title.
E99.S2054   1996
155.8'4979—dc20   95-35126
                                        CIP

Printed in the United States of America

1 2 3 4 5 6 7 8 9

The paper used in this publication meets the minimum requirements of American National Standard
for Information Sciences—Permanence of Paper for
Printed Library Materials, ANSI Z39.48—1984 ∞

Respectfully and lovingly dedicated to the memory of Clarence Woodcock, isłaχt u isxʷmimeye'm

Contents

Acknowledgments

Salish and Pend d'Oreilles people living on the Flathead Reservation honor their friendships with gifts. In that spirit, I dedicate this book to the Flathead people, whose countless acts of compassionate hospitality, gentle guidance, and warm friendship nurtured not only me and my family during our stay at the reservation but also the ideas that eventually grew into this treatise. I would like to express my gratitude, in particular, for the generous assistance given to me by members of the Flathead Culture Committee and the Mental Health Program, especially Clarence Woodcock, Tony Incashola, Dolly Linsebigler, Lucy Vanderburg, Germaine White, Myrna Adams, Gyda Swaney, Carol Buck, Kim Azure, and Cheri McClure. Ruby Vanderburg deserves her own special thanks for always being there for me, whether I was in need of a joke, a movie, or a place to stay. I also want to thank the individuals who agreed to be interviewed by me, who patiently tolerated my interruptions and misunderstandings, and who unselfishly allowed me to learn from their experiences. Finally, I want to express my appreciation to the elders of the tribes, most notably, Sophie Adams, Mary Felsman, Agnes Kenmille, Charles McDonald, Louise McDonald, Annie and John Peter Paul, Pat Pierre, Annie Sorrell, and Agnes Vanderburg, for including me in their continuing efforts to teach traditional Flathead ways to the younger members of the tribes.

This book would not have materialized without the unflagging support of my teachers, first among whom are the four people who served as members of my graduate committee in Social Anthropology at

Harvard University: Byron Good (chairman), Arthur Kleinman, Robert LeVine, and Spero Manson. Each has contributed to my thinking in critical ways. I am, however, especially indebted to Byron Good, who has, throughout, gracefully balanced being mentor, role model, and friend. I also want to thank Candace Fleming, who for over a decade has been teaching me about American Indian life in her inimitably gentle and generous fashion. I am fortunate, too, to count my parents, Carl O'Nell and Nancy O'Nell, among my teachers. Words are insufficient to express my admiration for them or my appreciation for their unfailing encouragement and wise counsel.

Without detracting from the debt I owe to the innumerable others who have also contributed to the writing of this book, I would like to single out the following for particularly close readings of sections of my work: John Borneman, Paul Brodwin, Mary-Jo DelVecchio Good, Richard Grinker, Cathy Patrick Harman, Monica Jones, Christina Mitchell, Ilena Norton, Doug Novins, Susan O'Nell, Norbert Peabody, Mary Steedly, and the anonymous reviewers solicited by the University of California Press. I owe special thanks to Bob Desjarlais, whose analytic insight and intellectual honesty in countless conversations have both plagued and propelled me throughout the writing process. My editors, Stanley Holwitz and Michelle Bonnice, too, deserve credit for patiently and skillfully guiding me through each stage of the publishing process and for strategically bestowing much-needed words of encouragement. I also want to acknowledge Spero Manson and Jan Beals, Director and Associate Director of Research, respectively, at the National Center for American Indian and Alaska Native Mental Health Research, for their help in safeguarding my writing time. Thanks also go to Barbara James and Billie Cook for their assistance with various secretarial and word-processing tasks.

Finally, I want to thank each member of my family: Ruth Childress, Isabel Treviño, Carl and Nancy O'Nell, Beatrice and Edward Quintero, and Jim, Melanie, Rachel, Rebecca, Ruth, Heather, Stephanie, Arthur, David, William, Jennifer, Patricia, Susan, Kurt, Hollis, Maureen, and Julie. Without their love and faith, the fertile insights offered to me during my time at the reservation would have fallen on barren ground, and this work would never have been produced. Last, but not least, I want to recognize Bob, my husband, and Andrew, my son. Their patience, enthusiasm, and sustained support have surpassed all reasonable expectations.

Funding for my work has come from a variety of sources. Exploratory fieldwork during the summers of 1984, 1985, and 1986 was supported in part by a Teschemacher Fund Travel Grant and in part by a National Institute of Mental Health (NIMH) predoctoral training fellowship. The NIMH fellowship also provided for two years of graduate training in medical anthropology and special training in psychiatric diagnosis. Eighteen months of field research was supported by a Wenner Gren Dissertation Grant, a Sigma Xi Grant-in-Aid of Research, a Jacobs Research Funds Award from the Whatcom Museum Society, and an award from the National Center for American Indian and Alaska Native Mental Health Research. A third term as an NIMH predoctoral fellow in medical anthropology and the receipt of a Teschemacher Dissertation Completion Award supported the writing of my dissertation, the first version of this book. The final drafting of this book was undertaken during my tenure at the National Center for American Indian and Alaska Native Mental Health Research, a position funded by NIMH Grant MH42473.

This book has been reviewed by members of the Flathead Culture Committee and Flathead Mental Health Program staff. I alone, however, assume complete responsibility for any errors or misinterpretations. All proceeds from this book go to the Flathead Culture Committee, to be used in their important work in the preservation of Flathead cultural ways.[1]

Introduction

The reservation town of St. Ignatius looks different depending on where you stand to view it. Heading north on the two-lane state highway out of Missoula, Montana, St. Ignatius comes into view when the summit of Ravalli Hill is reached. From that perspective, St. Ignatius is Lilliputian, a miniature postcard town of eight hundred people nestled in a green valley over which towers the Goliath of the Mission mountains. As you descend into the valley, St. Ignatius is transformed into an accessory glorifying the Catholic church whose stately red-brick facade commands the surrounding area. With the approach to town, the reality of St. Ignatius changes again. The sights along either side of the highway become more prosaic: off to the left, Col. Doug Allard's Trading Post and Flathead Indian Museum, boasting a gas pump, a 24-hour convenience store, six motel rooms, and a few penned buffalo next to the shop selling Indian books, beadwork, and jewelry; and off to the right, the local drive-in restaurant and the Community Center, a low building painted in the muted institutional gray-pink of the early seventies.

Off the highway, the sights of Main Street are reminiscent of other small rural towns across the nation. The downtown hardware and clothing stores sport recently built cedar fronts and canopies, as well as a wooden boardwalk. Across the street and next to the sewing and fabric store, the TeePee Lounge is visible but not prominent. Several older-model cars and pickups are parked diagonally in front of the grocery store, and a lone car waits at the drive-through window at the

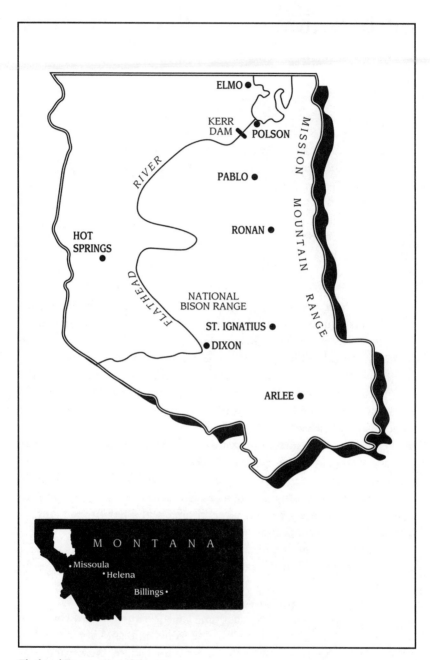

Flathead Reservation, Montana

bank. In the next blocks, the visitor discovers the pharmacy, the laundromat, another hardware store, the video rental store, the one-room library (open two days a week), the corner malt shop, the post office, the school, the barber shop, another bar, several churches, the funeral home, and an old Masonic Lodge that has recently been repainted and restored as a theater house.

From Main Street, St. Ignatius seems to disclaim its location on an Indian reservation. None of the residents—those stopping to gossip as they pick up their mail at the post office, those raising their hands in greeting as they drive slowly through the town, or those carting sacks of groceries to their cars—wears traditional Indian dress. No language other than English is heard on the streets. No signs indecipherable to English speakers appear in store windows. No smells of "exotic" foods waft through the air.

It is not until the small bridge at the south end of Main Street is crossed in the direction of the Catholic mission that minor differences from mainstream rural America begin to appear. Houses are closer together and are more gaily colored, some with tepees set up in the back. Indian children ride their bikes on the side streets, waving or nodding at passing neighbors. Small groups of teenage girls glance without expression at the tourists driving past on their way to visit the church but smile and laugh at relatives and friends passing by in their cars. There, outside one of the homes, the visitor might see an old woman, wearing a bright scarf over her braided hair and a colorful dress drawn at the waist with a beautifully beaded belt, being helped to a car by a young man whose long dark hair is pulled back into a ponytail with a leather strip.

In the summer of 1987, I settled in St. Ignatius with my husband and son to conduct eighteen months of fieldwork on depressive experience and depressive disorder among the Flathead Indians of Montana.[1] Over that period of time, my understanding of "depression" among the Flathead would shift as radically as the appearance of St. Ignatius shifts for the visitor who draws nearer and nearer. And as with the visitor whose perception of St. Ignatius changes depending on whether she views it from the top of Ravalli Hill, from Main Street, or from the side streets around the church, my shifting perceptions about the nature of "depression" would have a great deal to do with the vantage point on which I stood.

In large part, my decision to settle on the Flathead Reservation to conduct my fieldwork was based on the local response to my research

interests. Over the three previous summers, I had made short visits to
the Flathead Reservation to meet with Mental Health Program staff,
members of the Flathead Culture Committee, Tribal Council representatives, and others. In those meetings, I hoped to determine the desir-
ability and feasibility of a research project focused on the issue of culture and depression. Repeatedly, my interests were reciprocated, and,
repeatedly, they seemed to strike a chord among those to whom I
spoke.

At one level, I was not surprised by the response. Although few psychiatric epidemiological studies have been conducted among these peoples, there is, nonetheless, a general consensus in the literature that depressive disorders are of momentous concern for American Indian
individuals, families, and communities. The older studies, dating from
two decades ago, amount to a handful of size-limited or quasi-epidemi-
ological surveys the utility of which is somewhat hampered by out-
dated diagnostic and methodological procedures.[2] Weighing the evidence from those and other studies, however, Spero Manson and his
co-workers (1985) concluded that prevalence rates of depressive disorder among American Indian populations may be up to six times the
rate for the general U.S. population.[3]

In a more recent study, J. D. Kinzie and his colleagues (1992) found
lifetime prevalence rates of 25.2 percent for affective disorders, leading
them to conclude that these disorders are a major mental health problem in the native community where the researchers conducted their
survey. The American Indian village rate is significantly higher than the
17.1 percent for major depression found in a recent national sample
(Blazer et al. 1994; Kessler et al. 1994). But even on its own, the numbers are compelling; using the Kinzie et al. findings, over one in four
persons in the community suffered from a clinically recognizable depressive disorder. This proportion forcefully indicates the magnitude
of the problem of depression not only for individuals but for families
and the community as well.

Other kinds of studies supplement the epidemiological evidence of
the significance of depression in American Indian populations. Investigations of inpatient diagnoses point to depression as one of the most
prevalent problems among hospitalized American Indians (Termansen
and Ryan 1970; Fritz 1976). Mental health service utilization studies
document depression as *the* most frequently diagnosed problem among
American Indian clients presenting for assistance (Schoenfeld and
Miller 1973; Rhoades et al. 1980; Shore and Manson 1983; Kirmayer

et al. 1993). In a recent review of the records of 581 cases receiving a psychiatric referral in the Baffin region, L. T. Young et al. (1993) found that depression accounted for more than one-fourth of the cases.

I entered St. Ignatius with an awareness of the scholarly concern with high rates of depression among American Indian populations. Still, I was unprepared for the extraordinary statements made during my first visits to the reservation. When talking to people I had met about my interest in culture and depression, I was struck by the nearly unanimous concern with the prevalence of depression in the Indian community. Many people told me that depression had been a personal problem and related short anecdotes about ways they had tried to help themselves. More startling than the ubiquity of stories about personal experiences with depression, however, was the repeated comment from many of those with whom I spoke that the *majority* of Flathead Indians were suffering from depression; some claimed figures as high as 70 to 80 percent.

What does it mean when so many Flathead people say that the majority of their people are depressed? Indeed, this became the first puzzle of my fieldwork. First, I wanted to know whether the powerful statements about the prevalence of depression for Indian people, elicited so easily in the context of explaining my proposed work, were also made in other contexts. I soon learned that the concern for depressive-like feelings among the Flathead was evident across many contexts, from the musings of adult children worried about the prolonged grief of their elderly mother to the reflections of parents on reasons why Indian children seem to do poorly in school and the ruminations of many on the painful legacy of discrimination and oppression for contemporary Flathead people.

The breadth of the concern with depression—and the startling assertion that the majority of Flathead people are depressed—evoked in me a sense of widespread personal suffering but begged for further interpretation. Who are the majority who are depressed, and who are the minority who are not? What does being depressed mean for a Flathead person, and what does it mean for the entire Flathead community? How does this putatively ubiquitous Flathead depression relate to psychiatric formulations of depressive disorder?

This book is, in part, an attempt to come to terms with the pervasive rhetoric of widespread Flathead depression, an indisputably powerful and plaintive commentary on contemporary American Indian life. This book is also addressed to the meaning of Flathead depression for individuals who experience profound affective disturbances that pervade their entire psychic lives. For both concerns, I needed to pay strict attention to the language of affect among the Flathead. As for many, if not most, American Indian peoples, English is now the dominant language of the Flathead people. English is used in virtually all settings, both public and private. The exceptions include some ritual gatherings, or when two or more Salish-speaking elders come together. Even in these cases, however, English translations will be offered to anyone present who does not easily understand the native language—a group that includes almost everyone under the age of fifty, save those who were raised by older Salish-speaking grandparents.

Within this context, I learned the handful of Salish words, mostly kinship terms, that pepper contemporary Flathead Reservation English. I also attended beginning Salish classes at the local college, bringing my level of understanding of the native language to that of most young adults. This effort allowed me to greet native speakers, to express my respect for traditional ways to the elders, and to glean the subject matter of some conversations. Most important to the study of culture and depression, however, was a systematic investigation of Salish terms for emotions that resembled depression, most of which was done in consultation with Flathead elders and other native language speakers and which revealed three related aspects of the contemporary language of affect among the Flathead. First, a core set of Salish terms consistently emerged as the closest translations for the English term "depression." Second, these Salish words were *not* commonly known in their native garb to most Flathead people. *But,* third, Salish terms were commonly used in the form of their English glosses. In other words, Flathead use of English emotion terms, such as depression or loneliness, is informed to a large degree by the concepts, categories, and values that structure Salish emotion terms. Thus much of this book is an attempt to make explicit the meanings of key affective terms among the Flathead via an exploration of the various contexts within which such terms arise. Throughout the chapters, then, non-Flathead English speakers need to be very careful about imputing their own meanings to English terms for affect used by contemporary Flathead people—an issue with theoretical significance for cross-cultural research to which I will return throughout the book, but especially in chapter 6 and the afterword.

At the start of my fieldwork, I envisioned a direction for my research that derived from a variety of sources, but two were particularly formative. Having cut my teeth on *Culture and Depression* (1985), the volume of works edited by Arthur Kleinman and Byron Good, I was anxious to reply to a number of the issues that were raised in that provocative set of readings. Of primary relevance was the research indicating important differences in style of expression among various populations.[4] Not surprisingly, hints of variation in the cultural organization of depression had also appeared in research among American Indians.[5] Thus investigating alternative idioms for depressive-like experience and culture-specific explanatory models of depressive disorder in this community was a high priority for me as I set off to do my fieldwork.

Additionally, my interest in depression had been piqued by a desire to elucidate the nature of the links among domination, demoralization, and disordered emotional experience. Numerous studies have documented both the historically high rates of morbidity and mortality among American Indian people and the uniquely oppressive and demoralizing conditions of reservation life.[6] Depression, if understood as a culturally constituted "final common pathway" capable of expressing personal distress (Carr and Vitaliano 1985), seemed to offer a fertile field to investigate the confluence of cultural meaning, oppressive power relations, and personal experience.

This theoretical training led me to be open to the possibility that depression may well be an expression of socially produced demoralization and that depressive-like experience may be expressed through idioms that differ from those presented in psychiatric formulations. Again, however, I was unprepared for the uniqueness of the phenomenology of depressive-like experience and depressive-like disorder among adults at the Flathead Reservation. Thus, in the pursuit of an answer to the first puzzle about the rhetoric of the prevalence of Flathead depression (and to my general concern with culture and depression), I encountered the second puzzle of depression at the Flathead Reservation: rather than strict accounts of illness, reports of depressive experience and disorder reverberated with a sense of the positive value of suffering as a marker of maturity and Indian identity.

On a wintery day, well into my fieldwork, I sat next to a fifty-year-old man on a couch in the Longhouse in St. Ignatius and listened for several hours as he softly recounted the story of his painful experiences with depression. From the start, this man organized his story neither by episodes of depression nor by descriptions of isolated interior feeling states, the directions that my questions might have led him, but instead plunged directly into a moral universe and a set of dramatic life events that were only loosely connected to the formally defined criteria of major depressive disorder. The ego-centered symptoms of depressive disorder, far from being *the* central symbols or themes of the narrative, played a supporting role in a far more significant drama about the self and moral responsibility that was woven around the respondent's attempt to commit suicide some twenty years ago.

I conducted thirty-three such interviews in the course of my work, and without fail, each narrative portrayed depression in ways that were as concerned with moral dilemmas as with the complaints of ego-centered psychological distress. Unlike sadness and depression in formal psychiatric nosology, Flathead depression encircles a broad semantic domain that extends well beyond narrowly defined psychological distress into the realms of moral development, social relations, history, and contemporary American Indian identity. Indeed, Flathead narratives of depression are often poignant tales in which the narrators try to transform personal or collective demoralization into a positive moral charter for modern Indian life.[7]

Depression, as I encountered it at the reservation, reflected far more than a troublesome condition affecting individuals. An essential part of a larger discourse on Indian identity, depression in individual narratives often resonated with one hundred fifty years of loss and betrayal and the moral imagination with which the Flathead Indians strive to make meaning out of that history. After the completion of my work at the Flathead Reservation, the statement that the majority of Flathead people are depressed made eminent sense as a statement about the history and identity of the Flathead people. Similarly, the finding that individual narratives are as much about identity and moral responsibility as they are about psychological distress also made a great deal of sense in this context.

In retrospect, after learning the rich meanings of depression among the Flathead, neither of the puzzles that struck me so forcibly at first seemed particularly puzzling any longer. The third and final puzzle of this project, then, was to figure out why I found the moral, historical, and relational aspects of depressive-like experience among the Flathead so puzzling in the first place and why I found them so difficult to interpret until the final stages of my analyses. I argue that this last puzzle is explicable with reference to the ground on which I chose to try to understand depression in this community. I argue, further, that an important implication of this insight is that cross-cultural researchers intent on understanding depression among non-Western peoples will have to struggle, as I have, with the distinct and sometimes contradictory voices of psychiatry and anthropology and the way each voice translates local conceptualizations of emotion.

I had originally conceived my project as one in which ethnographic and clinical approaches were united to permit a vantage point superior to either one alone. I justified this union in both substantive and methodological terms. I was convinced at one level that the two disciplines could be bridged by a shared concern with understanding particular kinds of human suffering. Then, too, methodologically, the two disciplines seemed to share a tradition of phenomenological inquiry. Along methodological lines, I understood as very similar the meticulous empirical observation by the psychiatric researcher of the signs and symptoms of psychopathology and the detailed and systematic recording by the ethnographer of different behavioral signs of disordered emotion, and of the local interpretations of those behaviors, in a given social and cultural milieu.

From the ground I constructed out of my academic training, I saw depression among the Flathead as amenable to the following kinds of questions: What are the central complaints of depressed Flathead adults? What does the clinical presentation of depression look like? Do the symptoms for depressive disorder as they are formulated in the American Psychiatric Association's Diagnostic and Statistical Manual (DSM) carry expressive force among Flathead people (American Psychiatric Association 1980, 1987, 1994)? What is the relationship between depression as an important affect at the reservation and depression as an important sign of affective disorder at the reservation? Do the key idioms of Flathead depression carry meanings other than that of pathology and illness? What is the relationship between a diagnosis of depressive disorder based on Western criteria and the local definition of being depressed? Does depression among the Flathead Indians carry the same risks that are associated with depression in mainstream society?

As I set off to do my work, I believed that an investigation based on these questions, deriving from both transcultural psychiatry and psychiatric anthropology, would allow me to respond in a single cohesive account to the central issues that each discipline poses to the topic of culture and depression. As my work progressed, however, I encountered a chasm between the two perspectives that seemed more and more unbridgeable. Despite the tradition of phenomenological inquiry in psychiatry, the incorporation of culturally constructed experience into the diagnostic process seemed to be antithetical to contemporary psychiatric thought. Yet, as moral tales that draw on a wide range of meanings, Flathead narratives of depression seem to demand in their analysis the cultural and historical contextualization of psychopathological experience.

What I found as I sought answers to the questions I brought to the field was that the questions contained a hidden division and that the two sets of questions were unable to respond easily and meaningfully to each other. On the one hand, anthropological accounts of the cultural construction of depression seem unable to answer the questions about prevalence or cultural "variation" that derive from the ground of psychiatry. Specifically, if one allows, indeed, searches, for the unique historical and cultural construction of human distress and disorder in a way that permits the very definition of disorder to vary, as interpretive anthropologists do, one is prohibited from answering the paramount questions from the psychiatric perspective as to whether these people were *really* "depressed" and how culture influences or obscures the presentation of depression. In other words, the anthropological perspective that I brought to the field ultimately called into question the primacy of the psychiatric formulation of depressive-like experiences, rendering moot questions about depression as an entity in this cultural setting and focusing instead on locally constructed realities.

On the other hand, psychiatric formulations of how to understand depression in this setting seemed patently unable to answer to the interests of cultural anthropology. From the ethnographer's perspective, what gets lost in the medicalized vision of "depression" from the ground of the DSM is the ability to appreciate the cultural processes whereby unique phenomenologies of self, emotion, and disorder are constructed, to understand the social origins of disease and distress, or to ascertain the impact of history on personal experience. In other words, the psychiatric perspective about the universality, the "givenness," of "real depression" calls into question the primacy of cultural processes in human experiences of disorder, relegating culture to the marginal position of "influencing" the universally recognizable disease of depression.

It was as if Western psychiatric thought had staked out a position on Main Street and could go no further to see the nature of "depression" as constructed by the Flathead people; and as if the ethnographic perspective had crossed over the bridge at the southern end of Main Street and could no longer return to see "depression" from the center of town. My belief, formed from the hilltop position of academic preparation, that the two realities could be encompassed satisfactorily in a single perspective was thrown into doubt. Thus this book is about two distinct "depressions"—a psychiatric depression that accords reality to a putatively universal disease category and an anthropological depression that accords reality to a culture-specific way of understanding normality and abnormality. Each is constructed from a ground that cannot easily accommodate or map onto the reality of the other. As a result, this book is as much about my changing perspectives on how to understand these two "depressions" and my observations on the meaning of this shifting reality for medical anthropology, psychiatric diagnosis, and cross-cultural research as it is about Flathead culture and depression per se.

At a fundamental level, then, this book is about the predicaments and possibilities for the dialogue between psychiatry and anthropology. These are the predicaments and possibilities, however, that characterize cross-cultural understanding more generally. One of the central dilemmas that shapes this enterprise can be seen in the difficulty I have had in finding a language that accords a reality to Flathead depression that does not derive from a psychiatric or Euro-American perspective on human disorder. In the very act of translating my findings about Flathead depression, I have had to use terms that seem to render Flathead depression a "variant" of Euro-American depression. Most assuredly, this is not a position I hold or seek to communicate. Rather, the act of translating produces the appearance that the first reality (Euro-American depression) is the basis for understanding the second reality (Flathead depression).

However, understanding based on translation need not be constrained by such a narrow outlook. Take, for example, the Gestalt-switching illusion in which the image of a goblet shifts to an image of two profiles face-to-face (see fig. 1). Now, if you wanted to help someone to see the illusion, you would start with the image that the person *could* see and then use aspects of the first image to construct a vision of the "other" image. In essence, this is how I have proceeded in my translation of the phenomenal reality of Flathead depression for an academic audience steeped in Euro-American traditions. This hermeneutic process—learning the "new" through a translation that builds on the "old"—characterizes learning to "see" both images in the

Figure 1.   Reversible images illusion

illusion and learning to "see" both Euro-American and Flathead depression.[8]

This analogy, along with the analogy of geographically grounded
perspectives on St. Ignatius, helps to put the language that I use to describe Flathead depression in this book into perspective.[9] Most important, few who have mastered the image-switching illusion would privi-
lege one image over the other as objectively primary. In fact, having
perceived both images, most viewers will achieve a metaperspective
that allows them to recognize both images as related yet independent
of one another and to see either image on demand. Unfortunately,
given the dominance of universalizing perspectives in both psychiatry
and the study of emotion, such relativism is unlikely to prevail when it
comes to issues of emotion and disorder cross-culturally. It is, nonetheless, a vision that I want to encourage, and one that is best accomplished with an awareness of how the act of translation affects the appearance of others' realities. However, neither do I want to suggest
that the two depressions are "equal" in all settings—but that is an
issue that can only be addressed after some of the richness, complexity,
and depth of Flathead history, identity, and affective life have been
presented.

This book is divided into three parts. Part I introduces the charged
context of contemporary Flathead identity, its historical and cultural
shaping, and how moral authority and depressive-like affect are linked
in dominant narrative forms of Indian identity. Part II explores the
ways that loneliness, pity, and responsibility, key idioms in narratives
of depression, are enacted in ritual and everyday settings at the reservation. Parts I and II reveal that underlying many Flathead narratives

and practices is the dramatic moral assertion that depression is the natural and esteemed condition of the "real Indians," those who have "disciplined hearts," those who have transformed their sadness over present and past losses into compassionate responsibility for others. Part III turns to the cultural construction of personal experience and to the relation of loneliness, as a historically situated dialogic product, to depressive disorder, as it has become defined in Western psychiatry. The conclusion explores the parallels between Flathead social histories and personal narratives and contemplates the implications for psychiatry and psychiatric anthropology, as well as for our understanding of emotion and processes of self-construction.

In exploring the role of loneliness in contemporary Flathead lives, this book tells a story about culture and emotion. Moreover, in exploring the shifting nature of "depression," depending on where one stands to view it, this book tells a story about how emotion and affective disorder can be studied cross-culturally. Most striking, however, in describing the moral imagination with which Flathead Indian people weave emotion, history, and contemporary identity together into a tapestry of loss and social responsibility, *Disciplined Hearts* tells a story about the symbolic processes that link individuals, experience, and society.

History and Identity

Part I introduces the Flathead people by way of their storytelling about historical and contemporary encounters with whites. This corpus of stories reveals two issues highly salient to the study of Flathead culture and depression. First, it reveals the self-portraits of the Flathead and the ethnopsychological propositions that are central to Flathead evaluations of themselves and others. Second, it documents a history of exploitation that has produced, and continues to produce, a politics of identity that the Flathead do not themselves completely control. Within these culturally organized narratives, Flathead Indian identity is semantically linked in moral terms to the losses suffered by the tribe over history and to the emotions of loneliness and pity, the two affective terms used in Flathead society that most closely resemble Euro-American depression. Thus, in a very direct way, to understand Flathead depression is to come to terms with the important two-part question, after one hundred fifty years of oppression and domination, how do the Flathead people of today define themselves, and what role does depressive-like affect play in those definitions? It is to the two related aspects of this question that the chapters in Part I are addressed.

Chapter I, "Telling about Whites, Talking about Indians," describes relations between Indians and whites on the Flathead Reservation in the 1980s and then introduces two local discourses about whites that illustrate important ideological links among Indian identity, historical loss, morality, and feelings of sadness and loneliness. The first discourse, an ethnohistorical accounting of three key events in the early years of Indian-white history, evokes images of the Flathead people as tenaciously holding onto their compassionate generosity and deep spirituality in the face of overwhelming loss and profound feelings of loneliness. Repetitive storytelling about contemporary encounters with whites constitutes a second discourse in which affect and morality are linked once again in a similar rhetoric of the moral virtue of the Flathead people.

Chapter 2, "The Making and the Unmaking of the 'Real Indians,' " continues to explore Flathead Indian identity through an examination of two different contexts of Indian identity: formal enrollment policies and informal talk about being a "real Indian." The history of formal enrollment policies among the Flathead tribes is characterized by oscillations between inclusiveness and exclusiveness that have been patterned by the periodic threat of legal annihilation by the federal government. Informal talk about Indian identity is structured by an idea of the "empty center," in which the "real Indians" comprise an esteemed but elusively defined group. Shaped by the same historical and political forces that have influenced formal enrollment patterns, the "empty center" is an idea that seems to withhold from most tribal members a sense of an "authentic" Indian identity. At a fundamental level, Flathead history has produced a situation in which many Flathead people are involved in complex and ongoing negotiations, with others and with themselves, about their Indian identity and their moral worth. The meaning of the terms "loneliness" and "pity," which frequently are called into play for these negotiations, is created in part in these powerful encounters.

Together, chapters 1 and 2 introduce the current social and political climate of the Flathead Reservation, the ethos and self-definitions of the Flathead Indians, and the politically and emotionally charged context of contemporary Flathead Indian identity. In detailing the historical, political, and cultural forces shaping contemporary Flathead Indian identity, Part I also shows the different ways that Flathead depression has become thematized in narratives of tribal and individual identity. These chapters begin to show how claims of depressive-like affect can become claims for moral authority by illuminating dominant culturally shaped narrative practices that link Indian identity, loss and loneliness, pity and moral responsibility. In essence, Part I starts this exploration of Flathead culture and depression by looking at how the meaning of Indian identity is constituted within performative contexts that are structured by the same symbolic, relational, and political forces that structure the narrative construction of self and emotion. At base, this perspective approaches affective experience neither as a natural, precultural fact nor as a cultural category per se, but as constituted and reconstituted in specific narrative performances that are patterned by both symbolic meanings and institutionalized power relations.[1]

CHAPTER ONE

Telling about Whites,
Talking about Indians

Sam Dumont's daughter, Irene, walked into the community Longhouse and, with a quick glance, knew that the critical mass necessary to start the weekly Talking Circle had not yet been reached; there would be time for visiting.[1] After pouring herself a cup of coffee in the back room, she returned to the small office where several of her colleagues from the tribal Mental Health Program, some of the staff members of the Flathead Culture Committee, and I had gathered. After several minutes of small talk, Irene grinned and announced that her father, an elder of the tribes, had been ticketed by a highway patrolman for not wearing his seat belt. Irene paused as we, the listeners, arranged ourselves appreciatively toward her and her story. One of us encouraged Irene to continue with a smile and a simple "Oh?"

Over the next months, I heard oblique references in several settings to Sam Dumont's encounter with the patrolman, and I heard the entire story again in the home of another tribal elder whose daughter was describing the day's events at the Longhouse. At the time of Irene's rendition of her father's adventure, I had already heard the story from Sam Dumont himself when he had narrated his experiences to a small group who, like the group to whom his daughter spoke, had convened before a meeting at the Longhouse.

At a pause in the flow of conversation and with a look of amusement that was directed at no one in particular, Sam Dumont had related how he had been on his way to buy his great-granddaughter

some fried chicken in the small town nearest to his rural home when a
state highway patrolman motioned him over. The officer wrote Sam a
ticket for not having his seat belt or that of his great-granddaughter
fastened. Sam told us how he asked the officer about the legality of
pulling him over and fining him for violating the seat belt law in the
absence of another traffic violation. According to Sam, the patrolman
responded by saying that the action was legal if the vehicle "looked
suspicious." Sam gleefully told the group who had gathered to listen
how he had quipped back to the white officer, "I bet all us Indians
look suspicious to you."[2]

Stories about whites routinely enliven everyday conversations at the
Flathead Reservation. From the amusing imitation of a white woman
singing, with a wide-open mouth and a raging vibrato, to the quietly
disapproving account of a racist act, stories about whites comment in-
cisively on a strange and sometimes unfathomable outsider. Yet, as in
the joking performances about "the Whiteman" among the Western
Apache studied by Keith H. Basso (1979), the overt messages about
whites in these savory conversational tidbits communicate equally important reciprocal messages about what it means to be Indian.[3]

Most stories about whites are funny snippets about the common
foibles of whites that highlight, through implicit contrast, the good etiquette of Indians or some other admirable quality associated with the
Indian way of life. A witty story about whites childishly pacing their
jail cells out of anxiety portrays Indians, in reverse, as able to endure a
wretched but temporary situation without losing composure. A laughing comment about how whites seem unable to enjoy a good card
game questions the sociability of whites and establishes Indians as
companionable. A quick joke about white tourists taking pictures of
Indians at powwows without their permission documents the rudeness
of some whites and illustrates the graciousness of Flathead people,
who, it is well known, courteously provide meals and transportation
money for out-of-town visitors at powwows.

Each vignette underscores an important value in Flathead life,
whether restraint, sociability, or generosity. Often, however, what is at
stake for Indian identity in the telling of these stories is more than a
matter of etiquette. Two kinds of stories about whites, in particular,
seem to reveal more fundamental aspects of Indian identity. Embedded
deeply within a morally charged worldview, storytelling about the
early history of Indian-white relations and storytelling about contemporary encounters with whites are widespread narrative practices in

which the reprehensible behaviors of whites are used to construct, through contrast, a sense of Flathead identity as exemplary. Moreover, an analysis of these kinds of stories reveals important semantic connections among Indian identity, historical loss and sadness, morality and pity—semantic connections that are significant for understanding depressive experience and depressive disorder among the Flathead.

Flathead stories about whites, whether historical or contemporary, reveal the cultural shaping of Flathead experience. They also reveal the obduracy of historical and social fact. While Flathead storytelling establishes that whites are often odd, ignorant, or irresponsible from an Indian perspective, it also reveals that they cannot simply be dismissed. For the Western Apache of Cibecue, who resided in "the most isolated settlement" on their reservation, the interpretive and social functions of their joking portraits of "the Whiteman" were so noticeable, in part, because the everyday reality of whites for them seemed so distant (Basso 1979). In contrast, for tribal members at the Flathead Reservation, whites are a stubborn, unavoidable daily reality. The appeal of storytelling about whites is explained, in part, by the knotted tangle of Indian-white relations and the inescapable importance of whites in the lives of Flathead Indians at the reservation.

CONTEMPORARY INDIAN-WHITE RELATIONS AT THE FLATHEAD RESERVATION

October 23, 1908
The *Missoula Weekly*

"Game warden killed by Flathead Indians"
Word was received in Missoula yesterday morning of the killing of Deputy Game Warden Charles B. Peyton of Ovando by Indians on Sunday afternoon. From meager reports of the affair it is understood that the deputy and his assistant, Herman Rudolph, found a band of flathead [sic] Indians encamped on Holland prairie, about 40 miles northeast of Ovando, and attempted to arrest them for the unlawful shooting of game. In the band were four bucks and three squaws, the latter fleeing at the approach of the officers. When Peyton advised the four bucks that it would be necessary to bring them to Missoula they, with one accord, seized their rifles and fired a close range volley at the officers, who returned the fire dropping two of the bucks. Peyton was struck in the breast, and, as he staggered, called to Rudolph that he was shot, but to keep after the redskins. Peyton dropping on one knee continued to pour a hot shot at the remaining Indians, and as the last of the quartet threw up his hands, the warden fell forward on his face, and, without uttering a groan, died. (Cited in Finley 1956: 7)

Contemporary residents of the Flathead Reservation are heirs to a long and complicated history of troubled relations between Indians and whites. With its references to "redskins," "bucks," and "squaws," the news account quoted above documents the climate of racism in 1908 and the participation of the press in the perpetuation of prejudice against the Flathead Indians. Eighty years later, while newspapers at the reservation no longer served the interests of racism the way they did in the early part of this century, they continued to reflect signs of the tensions between Indians and whites with editorials and articles addressed specifically to race relations or conflicts between the tribes and white interest groups. In 1988, an editorial appeared in one of the area newspapers in which a white resident of the reservation wrote, "The tribes are 'Elitest' in that they want special rights not given to all other U.S. Citizens" (*Mission Valley News*, 20 October 1988). The next week, a front-page article explored electoral opinions about the relevance of the tribal affiliation of one of the candidates for the county commissioner's office (*Mission Valley News*, 27 October 1988). While each example is unique, neither is unusual, and both illuminate the degree to which relations between Indians and whites at the Flathead Reservation remain rife with difficulties.

The problems and tensions of contemporary Indian-white relations at the reservation are played out within an extraordinary context in which tribal members make up less than 20 percent of the reservation population. The Flathead Reservation is home to about half of the approximately 6,000 enrolled members of the confederated tribes. It is also home to over 15,000 non-Indians (U.S. Bureau of the Census 1980). Thus Indian-white relations unfold in a curious situation in which the Flathead Indians are outnumbered by whites four to one on their own lands.

Despite the fact that most Indians and most whites get along most of the time, racism permeates the daily lives of contemporary Flathead Reservation residents. Overt racism comes in the form of an organization known as ACE, or All Citizens Equal, whose stated purpose is to wipe out "discriminatory practices that favor Indians over non-Indians" (*Mission Valley News*, 27 October 1988). The presence of ACE is undeniable at the reservation.[4] Editorials written by ACE members are published virtually every week in the local papers. Members of ACE are also visible politically, often sponsoring candidates for office in local elections. During the period of my fieldwork, the organization sponsored an energetic campaign against a tribal member who was running for county office, claiming that a vote for him was a vote for a "puppet government" under the control of the tribes. According to both Indian and white residents of the reservation, ACE tactics include pointing to the mythic figure of the indigent Indian as an economic drain on local government resources while at the same time promulgating the myth of the rich tribal member whose undeserved wealth derives from the coffers of the federal government.

Overt racism also assumes the form of slighting comments delivered by whites in tones loud enough to be overheard by Indians in stores, restaurants, and other public places. Comments typically refer to popular stereotypes of Indians as dirty ("Look at that messy baby; must be from the reservation"), as shiftless ("How could an Indian own a car that nice!"), or as alcoholic ("That's why they have so many treatment centers, you know"). For the Flathead people, it is an awkward and demoralizing social fact that it is often their own neighbors—the people who live next door, who shop in the same grocery store, and who use the same post office—who are the proponents of these disparaging viewpoints or who are members of ACE.

Aside from the continual agitations of ACE, the major source of ill-feeling between Indians and whites during the 1980s revolved around water rights, with tribal interests in natural resources pitted against the irrigation interests of local farmers and ranchers—few of whom were Indian.[5] Homemade signs lined the highway, proclaiming antitribal positions for upcoming legislation related to the protection of natural resources. Some residents of the reservation, including both Indians and whites, alleged that a fire that destroyed part of the tribal government office complex several years back was set by irrigators in revenge for unfavorable policy decisions. Others talked of barroom fights that nearly exploded into major brawls. While significant violence had not erupted over the issue of water rights, the fear that it could happen was tangible.

Less overt racism takes many forms. For example, a fifth-grade class with both Indian and white students performed a pioneer game task over several weeks in which the children formed wagon trains and planned their trips westward into the "uninhabited" land west of the Mississippi. On the way, they had to contend with various natural obstacles, including a "fierce and warring group of wild Indians," as it was described on a homework sheet. Similarly, the local telephone book map of a small reservation town detailed the street layout only for the northern, predominantly non-Indian, side of town. Like the erasure of tribal people who had lived in the "uninhabited West" in the pioneer game, the nonexistence of the Indian side of town is asserted simply by virtue of its not being represented. As in the presentation of "wild Indians" as just another element of untamed nature, the telephone book map proclaims the Indian side of town to be part of the world of nature that surrounds the town, that is, the world of civilization.

The division of Indian and white neighborhoods in the one small town detailed by the telephone book map is by no means absolute. It does, however, illuminate an important aspect of the larger context for relations between Indians and whites at the reservation: the social geography of the town, in which Indians and whites live on opposite sides, is a concrete manifestation of the social separation of Indians and whites on the reservation as a whole. An Indian friend of mine likes to tell an amusing story about a white schoolteacher at the reservation, a long-term resident, who asked my friend with naive curiosity, "By the way, where *do* the Indians stay?" By pointing out how Indians are often invisible to whites, the story highlights the degree to which the two communities are socially separated.

Most Flathead Indians at the reservation carry out their home lives and work lives within social environments inhabited mostly by other tribal members. The homes of Indian people are often located near those of other Indians, on clusters of family-owned allotment lands, in Indian "neighborhoods" in the numerous small towns on the reservation, in government-subsidized homesites, or in housing complexes for the elderly. Since the majority of job opportunities for Indians are provided by the tribal government, the work colleagues of most Indians are also Indian. Tribal members seeking assistance from the social service, social justice, and welfare programs usually deal with Indian staff, since the tribal government has taken over the administration of many, if not most, of these programs under the new mandate of self-determination.[6]

Thus the lives of the plurality of Flathead Indian people unfold for the most part within contexts peopled predominantly by other Indians. However, the structural inequalities of institutional control over certain facets of life at the reservation force the Flathead people into regular contact with whites. Indian children attend public schools where the teachers and the administrators (and usually the majority of the student body) are white. Groceries, clothing, and durables must be purchased from stores owned and operated, with few exceptions, by whites. Doctors' offices and hospitals, banks, license bureaus, the state courts, and prisons are controlled and their services administered almost exclusively by whites.[7] In contrast, whites on the reservation can and do live in their own neighborhoods and communities, and most do not find it necessary to enter into regular contact with Indian people.

Institutional aspects of the contemporary relations between Indians and whites at the Flathead Reservation are marked in part by the separation of the two communities and in part by the fact that, where the two worlds overlap, whites are in control. Both aspects of the contemporary situation appear to be moving in such a way that there is less contact between the two worlds and less control by whites over the lives of Indians. In the not-too-distant past, though, whites, through agencies such as the Bureau of Indian Affairs (BIA), the Indian Health Service (IHS), and various state welfare offices, controlled almost every aspect of Indian life. Moreover, that control was much more palpable than it is now: requirements for enrollment in the tribes were established by the BIA; Indian children were removed from their homes and placed with white families by state agencies; Indian children were punished by white teachers at their schools for speaking their traditional languages; white welfare agents could enter Indian homes and deny payments on a variety of bases; Indian criminal offenders were arrested, charged, and sentenced not by peers but by whites. In recent years, the tribal government has taken over the administration of many of these programs and probably will continue to administer more and more of them. However, it is the memory of the weighty history of white domination that infuses Flathead perceptions of whites and provides both the backdrop and the mold for contemporary Indian-white relations at the reservation.

A HISTORY OF INDIAN-WHITE RELATIONS AT THE FLATHEAD RESERVATION[8]

Prior to the intrusion of whites into Flathead territories, tribal life had been ordered by the traditional hunting and gathering subsistence patterns common to the Plateau region. According to elders of the Salish and Pend d'Oreilles tribes, the quest for food was an uninterrupted task starting in the early spring and ending in the late fall, even though stores of food sufficient for two years were not unusual. While fishing was important, as it was for most tribes in the Plateau area, annual buffalo hunts east of the Continental Divide in the late fall and winter were also essential to the livelihood of these Salish-speaking people. A variety of gathered foods, including camas root, bitterroot, service berries, huckleberries, onions, and tree moss, was necessary for survival as well. Winter marked a time when the constant search for food came to a halt and the season for visiting, storytelling, and ceremonies began (Flathead Culture Committee 1988: 3).

Precontact life provides the implicit utopian backdrop for Flathead renditions of the early history of Indian-white relations. In storytelling about the past, narrators often evoke the image of precontact life by referring to the subsistence methods and material culture of their ancestors. But the image of this lost paradise of bitterroot, wild meat, moccasins, and tepees transcends the loss of a material way of life and is infused with a moral sense that links material technologies to an ethos marked by piety, discipline, responsibility toward kin, and respectful treatment of others. Precontact life represents an idyllic past in which the ancestors of contemporary Flathead Indians had compassion for the needy, were tolerant of those who were different, and trusted friends and strangers alike.

In a society that honors the ways of its ancestors, to invoke the distant past is to invoke an aura of solemnity and lament that is more than a matter of simple nostalgia. Precontact life provides the moral landscape against which the early history of Indian-white relations is put in perspective by contemporary Flathead Indian people. From the perspective of the tribes, three historical events played the key roles in fashioning relations between Indians and whites at the reservation: (1) the arrival of Jesuit missionaries in 1840; (2) the creation of the reservation in 1855 and the forced relocation of one reticent band onto reservation lands; and (3) the opening of reservation lands to homesteaders in 1910.[9] The implicit backdrop of precontact life in the telling of these early events of Flathead history imparts a tremendous rhetorical strength to the message of betrayal and disrespect that constitutes the essence of early Indian-white interactions from the Flathead perspective.

THE COMING OF THE BLACKROBES

Catholicism has been integral to Flathead Indian life since the appearance of the Jesuits one hundred fifty years ago. From the early days of the mission through the mid-1970s, Catholic missionaries had been involved in the provision of medical care to the Flathead people. Until

1972, most tribal members received at least part of their education from one of the series of Catholic schools that have operated at the reservation for a period of over one hundred years. The vast majority of contemporary Flathead Indians were baptized as infants, and most will be buried in one of the Catholic cemeteries. Most Flathead people observe important holy days, and many individuals cite parish priests as important sources of spiritual guidance, especially during the terrible time of grief after the death of a loved one. At community gatherings, leaders lecture the group about the importance of faith, and the recitation of Catholic prayers and the singing of Catholic hymns are integral to these communal get-togethers. Elders speak both publicly and privately about the importance of prayer.

From the Flathead perspective, the story of the coming of the Blackrobes begins with the vision of Shining Shirt, an early Flathead prophet who foretold the arrival of Jesuit missionaries. Pierre Adams, an elder of the tribes who is now deceased, told the following version of the story of Shining Shirt in 1947 at a discussion organized by the University of Montana. The translation from the original Salish account was done by another tribal member, Pierre Pishette.

> Before the Iroquois arrive and before anything was told about Christ to the Selish, there was a married couple—just forgot name of the man—his wife fell ill, suffered quite a bit and passed away. This man had quite a sorrow; and strayed away mourning about his wife, didn't want to be among the tribe; left the tribe and wandered away. Days and days passed on. He was away on the high mountains on the Rockies somewheres and during that time such things as animals, beasts, insects, reptiles, tried to offer him medicine power for sickness and this and that but he did not accept. Finally a day came, he met one he said had the form of a human being and he was the one that told him he had better go back to the tribe because there would be a time that will come that there will arrive one. He is a man but he is dressed like a woman, has a mantle on, but has a black robe, which means a priest, and he is the one that will teach you. That is where you will learn and find out that there is a God in Heaven in the high sky somewhere. (Hansen 1947: Appendix 3)

According to the written history compiled by the tribes, their search for the spiritual revelations prophesied by Shining Shirt drove the Flathead people to dispatch four different delegations to Jesuit headquarters in St. Louis over a nine-year period, from 1831 to 1839, each with the request that a mission be established among the Flathead people. The long and dangerous trips, which claimed the lives of a number of the sojourners, were also motivated by the teachings of Big Ignace, an

Iroquois traveler who reached the land of the Flathead tribes around 1820 and stayed to share his knowledge of the ways of the "Black-robes" (Flathead Culture Committee 1988: 6–7). The arduous efforts of Big Ignace and the Flathead people bore fruit when, in 1840, Father DeSmet traveled to Flathead country and promised to return the following year. With the establishment of the St. Mary's Mission in 1841, the Flathead Indians seemed to have achieved what they had sought for so long. The honeymoon was short-lived.

An often-told story provides the tragic denouement of the Flathead pursuit of the spiritual power of the Jesuits. Set in nonchronological time, it does not appear in the written history compiled by the tribes; however, I heard it told by elders and others in any number of settings across the reservation. Sitting in the midst of a bustling household of children, grandchildren, and great-grandchildren, Sam Dumont, of seat belt fame, told the following version to me at his home in 1988. Shaking his head with disbelief, he said, "It was at the mission, long time ago. It was on Sunday. Priest had hole dug out there on side of church. He wanted all the Indians to throw their medicine bundles in. Quite a few of them done that. And they all died. I told priest about it. [The priest said,] 'That's still God's will.' I don't know. . . . Yeah, that's what happened."

Pete Beaverhead, an elder of the tribes who is now deceased, told this version to members of the Flathead Culture Committee in 1975.

> Before there were any priests, these Indians did not have any whiteman's religion or beliefs because there was no whiteman here at the time. I myself, also Pete Woodcock and others our age group, seen the days when there wasn't any whiteman around. It was all just Indian land. The beliefs and the religion of the Indians were all from the earth. It is said, "The Indians have medicine power. The animals are powerful. If a person is poor or pitiful an animal will come and talk to you. The animals will give you medicine to get well." These are the ways and beliefs of our ancestors. It was this way until the whiteman came and he had news that there was a chief up above. We didn't know. We didn't know him. Then a lot of Indians turned to the whiteman's religion and there were a lot of medicine men that died.
>
> The priests told the Indians that it was bad to have a medicine man and to believe in the Indian religion, because it was the devil's work. The Indians were told to bring their medicine bundles and put them in the hole the priest dug near the church and placed a cross on top. The priests told them, "You are to throw away your medicine bundles and you are always to be praying. Quit what you are doing." The medicine men believed them, so they did what they were told to do. They put their medicine bundles in the hole. Not long after that some of these medicine men started to die off.

Some died from different kinds of illnesses; some died from injury. Almost all the medicine men died this way. The Indians' way of belief, their livelihood were considered very priceless. Their children's lives were precious. The Indians didn't wish for a good life for themselves and their children for nothing. Indians wished for a good life so that they and their children will live until the next year. (Flathead Culture Committee 1975)

Each element of this historical accounting of the coming of the Blackrobes contributes to its messages about the piety and obedience of the Flathead people and the tragic results of their interactions with the Jesuits. Shining Shirt's prophecy of the coming of the Blackrobes establishes the profound spirituality of the Flathead Indians before the arrival of whites. The arduous journeys made by the four sets of delegates seeking the spiritual power of the Jesuits document the lengths to which the ancestors of contemporary Flathead Indians would go to secure the spiritual knowledge that was foretold to them. The ironic tragedy of their quest is revealed in the loss of these medicine men and their special knowledge of traditional sources of spiritual power. The story of the coming of the Blackrobes sketches how Flathead openness to the ways of the Jesuits was met by intolerance; belief, by betrayal; and obedience, by illness and death.

THE FORCED RELOCATION OF THE BITTERROOT SALISH
ONTO THE RESERVATION

In 1855, just fifteen years after the arrival of the first Jesuits, representatives of the U.S. government and the chiefs of the Salish, the Pend d'Oreilles, and the Kootenai tribes convened at the Hellgate Treaty Council to discuss provisions for the establishment of the Flathead Reservation. In return for the cession of over 12 million acres of land in western Montana and Idaho to the United States, the Flathead tribes were guaranteed the exclusive use of an area of about 1.2 million acres in the area of the Jocko Valley, the principal valley on the Flathead Reservation. Chief Alexander of the Pend d'Oreilles and Chief Michel of the Kootenai both signed the agreement. The Salish, however, preferred to live in the Bitterroot Valley, both to avoid sharing land with other tribes and because the location was significant in their annual travels. Chief Victor of the Salish refused to sign the Hellgate Treaty as it stood, and conditional provisions were made for a separate reservation for his people in the Bitterroot Valley. Four years later, in 1859, when Congress ratified the Hellgate Treaty *without* plans for a separate reservation in the Bitterroot Valley for the Salish, the U.S. government committed the first act of betrayal in the story of the forced relocation of the Bitterroot Salish onto the reservation.

From the Flathead perspective, the story begins with the failure of the federal government to honor the commitments its representatives made at the Hellgate Treaty Council and spans nearly fifty years before coming to its tragic finale. The story depicts the series of betrayals leading to the forced relocation of the Bitterroot Salish—from the failure of the federal government to establish a reservation in the Bitterroot Valley and the forged signature of the Salish chief on a government document to the mournful migration of the Bitterroot Salish onto the Flathead Reservation and the petty and cruel eviction of the chief's widow from her home. Equally important, however, the story also documents the continued patience and restraint of the Flathead people in the face of those betrayals.

The Salish, under Victor, refused to move to the reservation and endeavored to continue with their traditional ways of life in the face of increasing pressures created by the constantly encroaching white population. When Chief Victor was killed in battle on a hunting trip to the east, his son, Charlo, was chosen as his successor. Charlo, like his father, refused to move to the reservation. In 1871, President Ulysses S. Grant issued an executive order for the removal of Chief Charlo's band from the Bitterroot Valley to the Indian agency at the reservation. In 1872, General James Garfield was sent to induce Charlo and his band to move, setting the scene for the second betrayal in the story of the forced relocation of the Salish. According to the history compiled by the tribes,

> in August the Salish chiefs met James Garfield who was empowered to negotiate a contract with the Flatheads for their removal. After a couple of days of discussion Garfield invited the Chiefs to inspect the Jocko [Valley] with him. Garfield learned after their visit that the Bitterroot Chiefs were divided on the question of removal. Garfield then drew up a contract, had it translated, and Arlee and Joseph signed with their marks. Charlo refused. Garfield thought that Charlo wanted to talk further with his headmen at home.
>
> Arlee and Joseph felt that if preparations were made according to the contract, Charlo would finally consent to go with the tribe.
>
> Garfield then put his understanding in writing for the territorial superintendent which said, "In carrying out the terms of the contract made with the chiefs of the Flatheads . . . I have concluded after full consultation with you to proceed with the work in the same manner as though Charlo had signed. . . ." When the contract was printed in the commissioner's annual report Charlo's mark appeared as if he had signed the original.

When the report was printed it appeared as if Charlo had consented and signed the agreement. This apparent fraud caused the Chieftain to become further embittered against the whiteman who had taken his country and was making a strange life for him. Although all of this was going against Charlo he would not take sides when Chief Joseph asked him to join him in 1877. (Flathead Culture Committee 1988: 9–10)

The intervening years were bitter ones for the tribes. On the reservation and in the Bitterroot Valley, smallpox and tuberculosis ravaged the people, at times destroying entire families (Eneas Conko, cited in Hansen 1947: 5). Hunger was rampant as wild meat became more difficult to obtain with the virtual extinction of the buffalo in the 1870s and the increasing number of fences erected by white homesteaders in traditional hunting areas (Schaeffer 1937: 46). Chief Charlo's sustained attempts to procure a reservation in the Bitterroot Valley, including trips to Washington, D.C., to lobby federal politicians, continued to meet with failure. The nearly 350 Salish who were still living in the Bitterroot in the mid-1880s were being reduced to pitiful conditions (Ronan 1890: 64–75). In 1891, the same year the BIA officially prohibited Indian ceremonies, war dancing, and stick games and thirty-six years after the creation of the reservation, Charlo's band left the Bitterroot Valley. The Flathead Culture Committee history details Charlo's desperate decision and the mournful emigration.

Arlee, who had been appointed Chief of the Salish on the Jocko Reservation died. Charlo's people were getting hungry. Finally on October 10, 1891, Charlo declared that the time had come. He called his people together, they prayed, and announced that they would go. Several days later following an all-night feast, the Salish assembled at dawn, loaded horses and wagons and started for the Jocko reservation.

Mary Ann Combs remembers when they had to move. She said it was the government who made them move out, not the neighbors. When Charlo refused to give up his lands, he was told the soldiers would bring him if necessary. At first they had not believed they would have to go, and it was about two years before they were forced to leave. . . .

She also remembers all the people crying about having to leave. They drug their teepee poles but not everyone used a travois to carry their things. All the farmer's fences along the way were old, wooden type fences. She remembers the spots where they camped. The first place was on the other side of Missoula.

Charlo held prayer in the evening at camp. This helped relieve the agonized gloom that hung over the camp. They camped again on this side of Missoula near Schley. They stayed there for two more days at a place known as Two Creeks in Salish.

Two people were hurt during their journey. Louise Lumpry, wife of Joe, fell when her horse spooked. Her hip was broken and she was left crippled. Another man fell near Schley and suffered a broken shoulder blade. He came out better.[10]

Those people at the Jocko church saw shirtless braves in red warpaint and best tribal dress galloping up on swift horses. They were firing their rifles in the air and singing. The women came behind crying. The Reverend Phillip Canestrelli got all excited thinking they were under attack.

Mary Ann's future husband, Louis Combs, was there among the crowd awaiting Charlo's arrival. Being young he panicked and tried to run and hide, but he was stopped and calmed by a woman who was sister to the chief of the reservation band.

Mary Ann felt they were well received by the people on the reservation. The government, however, failed to come through with the promised house for those making the move. Five buildings were built near the Jocko Church for the leaders, but Mary Ann's father was among those left without help. One of her biggest complaints about the way the government handled things here on the reservation was the . . . [way] they evicted Charlo's widow from her home after he died. (Flathead Culture Committee 1988: 12–13)

The story of the forced relocation of the Bitterroot Salish onto the reservation is told with both pride and sorrow.[11] The story conveys pride in the exemplary restraint of Chief Charlo and the Flathead Indians in the face of adversity caused by the U.S. government. Tragedy lies in the loss of a past way of life, in the loss of the use of the Bitterroot Valley, in the injuries and grief that plagued those who were forced to move from their homeland, and in the inability of the Flatheads to be able to fully trust whites.

THE OPENING OF THE RESERVATION TO HOMESTEADERS

Chief Charlo, champion of the Salish, died in 1910—two weeks before the U.S. government once again violated the terms of the Hellgate Treaty and announced that the Flathead Reservation would be opened to white homesteaders. Two years earlier, four members of the Flathead tribes, an old man, two men, and a boy of fourteen, were killed without provocation by a Montana game warden and his assistant. A white version of the incident, quoted earlier, appeared in a Missoula newspaper under the heading "Game warden killed by Flathead Indians." A Flathead version of the event was published in 1956 as the "Story of the Shooting of Four Flathead Indians in Swan River Area,

Western Montana, 1908" (Finley 1956). Mary Stousee Finley, the youngest survivor of the shooting, told the story in Salish to Louis Tellier, another tribal member, who inscribed and translated her account.

According to Mary Finley, the Swan River Area Massacre, as the incident came to be known locally, was precipitated by the aggressive and unprovoked actions of the game warden, who on two previous visits to the campsite had threatened the group of eight Flathead Indians. The three married couples, along with the young daughter and teenage son of one of the couples, were on a fall hunting trip. On the third visit, the game warden and his assistant entered camp as the group was making preparations to leave, shot, and killed the three men and the boy, as the women fled. The Flathead version traces the roots of this tragedy to the continued undermining by the state of Montana of hunting rights guaranteed by the Hellgate Treaty. One of the provisions of the treaty was that Flathead Indians would retain the right to hunt and fish in their usual places without interference. Jurisdictional disagreements with the state of Montana over the regulation of hunting and fishing by Indians were implicated in the killings, in part, because the old man in the hunting party did not have a permit to accompany the hunters as required by the state, even though he was too old to hunt. This stipulation was not understood by the man and was used by the game warden as the basis for his threats of incarceration and violence.[12]

For many Flathead Indian people, the opening of the reservation to white homesteaders epitomizes the losses and devastation of the early years of the new century. The telling of the story of the opening of the reservation evokes Chief Charlo's death, the Swan River Area Massacre, and the demise of the self-sufficiency of the Flathead tribes. The story of the opening of the reservation is one of loss and the morally informed Flathead response to that loss. In 1947, at nearly eighty years of age, Sophie Moiese talked about the losses at a discussion organized by the University of Montana: "Forty years ago before the reservation was opened it was easy for the people to get rich. It was not fenced and they had lots of cattle and lots of horses. But since they closed up they cannot do that" (Hansen 1947: 19). At the same meeting, Paul Charlot, Chief Charlo's grandson, echoed Sophie Moiese's words: "Ever since they threw the reservation open we all went broke and the stock disappeared. There wasn't an Indian among the tribe that was poor like they are today. They had too much stock and they could not take care of it on the allotments that they got, so the Indian just gave up his ambition and sold their stock and got poor. That is what I have seen and witnessed" (Hansen 1947: 19).

Later in the meetings, Eneas Conko, another tribal member, continued the story with his recollection of a meeting between government officials and the headmen of the tribes.

> I was young and not interested in the thing but I just happened to be there. Three commissioners were present. The first question was, one of these men spoke to Paul's grandfather [Chief Charlo] asking him for a little piece of land—he did not mention how big a piece. This is what the man said to Paul's grandfather. If he consented to give a piece of land to him he would repay it in some way. Charlot said no, he did not want to have anything to do with it. Then he turned around to another chief—the chief of the Mission and asked him a question. He told him the same thing—now would you give me a piece of land and he also said he would not. Then he turned to another chief by the name of Isaac. And that is the way he objected to it. He stamped his foot and said even if you would cover me up with gold I would not accept it. Then these men said—all right we will go home. But we will come back and the law says so that they are coming to throw it open anyhow. A year after that some Indian from here with Joe Dixon had it out in the papers that they had thrown the reservation open, and a year after that they came and told us it was all passed. (Hansen 1947: 45)

Paul Charlot remarked, "When they opened the reservation I do not believe the Indians were in favor of it. I was not in favor of it. In the first place, they were not asked about it—it was sort of stolen from them" (Hansen 1947: 44).

From the perspective of the tribes, the story is only brought to closure with the detailing of the Flathead response to the repeated violations of legal and moral responsibilities by the government. When another descendant of Chief Charlo, Mike Charlot, expressed disapproval for the actions of the whites—"I really believe they made a mistake by opening the reservation for outsiders"—he received a mild rebuke from another tribal member (Hansen 1947: 38). Pete Pierre admonished him, "We should not find fault with what the white people do, in order to get along with them and be friends. We should try to make an understanding between the Indian and white man so they will get along" (Hansen 1947: 38). Pete Pierre's admonition repeats the theme that characterizes the Flathead accounts of early Indian-white relations: despite the continued treachery of the whites, the Flathead Indians will remain true to their moral code.

The betrayal in the story of the opening of the Flathead Reservation

to whites lies at an even more fundamental level than the failure of the
federal government to fulfill certain legal obligations, egregious as that
failure was. In the ethos of the Flathead world, those who are powerful
are morally obligated to help those who are needy. Pity and compassion for the less fortunate is one of the hallmark values of the Flathead
world. Representatives of the federal government, and other representatives of white men, betrayed this important canon of morality in the
opening of the reservation to homesteaders and have consistently betrayed it since the first days of their contact with the Flathead people.
As in the other stories of early Indian-white history, the trust and obedience of the Flathead people were met by loss of livelihood and land.
The respectful treatment of whites by Indians was met by greed and
betrayal, and the pitiful condition of the Flathead people was met by a
lack of caring rather than compassion.

The Salish and Pend d'Oreilles people have been at the receiving end of
a history of brute oppression that involved legislated confinement and
relocation, bureaucratic delay and fraud, and the systematic and
planned eradication of the economic, social, and religious practices of
precontact life.[13] The three key events of Flathead ethnohistory establish the historical context for understanding the apprehension and
wariness that most contemporary Flathead Indians bring to their con-
templation of the actions of whites. The stories of the coming of the
Blackrobes, the forced relocation of the Bitterroot Salish, and the
opening of the reservation to homesteaders reveal the sense of suffering
and victimization that characterizes contemporary assessments of early
Flathead history. Conversely, that early history has led to the fear and
expectation of continued victimization that characterize contemporary
Indian-white relations.

Flathead accounts of the early history of Indian-white relations capture more than the stark facts. To use the words of Marshall Sahlins,
Flathead ethnohistory reveals both the intransigence of the world and
the intelligence of the subject (1985: 156). The events of early history
are told as moral dramas that invest the virtues of compassion, tolerance, trust, and restraint in Flathead identity through contrast with the
uncaring, unscrupulous, and dangerous ways of whites. This history of
Indian-white relations reveals the contours of the moral landscape
against which the historical actions of the Jesuits, federal and state
government officials, and other whites are judged, against which the

behaviors of Indian ancestors and contemporary kinsmen are evaluated, and against which the reprehensible acts of whites are positioned in storytelling about encounters with whites.

STORYTELLING ABOUT CONTEMPORARY ENCOUNTERS WITH WHITES

In general, storytelling about contemporary encounters with whites resembles storytelling about other subjects, including historical encounters with whites. Delivered slowly, in soft tones, storytelling tends to be stylistically simple; there are no elaborate formulas to set storytelling off from other genres of talk. Still, while prayer is marked with the phrase "qeqs čawm" (let's pray) and teasing is followed with "Heh" or "I jokes," storytelling is marked more sparingly—preceded only by a pause.

Pauses are not unusual in Indian interactions and can signify a great deal. In storytelling, pauses help to set the emotional tone of the story to follow: slightly shorter pauses suggest that a humorous story is on the way; slightly longer pauses indicate a more serious topic is at hand. The tenor of the story is also indicated by narrators with subtle changes in facial expression.

It is these minimal signs that listeners pick up on and amplify in their responses. In storytelling about encounters with whites, the more seriously the encounter is assessed, the more muted the responses to the story about it tend to be. For the most grievous cases, a period of silence follows the ending of the story and someone, perhaps, will intone a quiet "Hmm" to mark the gravity of the situation.

Storytellers recounting the events of early Indian-white history uniformly adopted a serious attitude toward their stories, and their stories uniformly elicited expressions of demoralization and sorrow from Indian listeners. In contrast, storytelling about contemporary encounters with whites were told with a far greater range of affect and generated a wide variety of affective responses among the listeners. To be more precise, while these stories as a group were met with a wide range of responses, a given story elicited a given response. Indeed, the uniformity of response to the narration of a specific story resembled at times a disciplined, almost ritual, rehearsal of proper sentiments. Some stories evoked shaking heads and muted murmurs of condemnation. Others evoked astonished, incredulous glances. Still others, perhaps the majority, evoked laughter, joking, and appreciation for a story well told.

When I first heard such stories, I invariably responded with harsh criticism for the perpetrators of what I saw as acts of racism, and I was confused by the range of responses of my friends and acquaintances. Amusement, in particular, was difficult for me to comprehend at first, especially given that the stories seemed to strain with the weight of the message that whites found Indians unworthy of respectful treatment. Yet after I incorporated the emotional tenor of the stories into my understanding of their meaning, I was left without a doubt that storytelling about encounters with whites was an active structuring by tellers and listeners of Flathead identity and the significance of white domination in their lives. Moreover, in examining the ways in which stories were structured, I could more easily discern the specific moral and ethnopsychological terms within which this structuring took place.

In the previous section on the history of Indian-white relations, we have seen how Flathead identity is constructed in moral terms as tolerant, respectful, compassionate, and restrained in contrast to a picture of whites as the opposite. As in storytelling about historical events, storytelling about contemporary encounters with whites cannot be understood apart from Flathead morality. By framing the profaning acts of whites in moral terms, storytelling about encounters with whites is an attempt to undermine the negative messages of these encounters by discrediting the moral authority of the source of the messages, that is, by discrediting the moral authority of racist whites. Implicitly, the moral authority of Indians is credited or enhanced through contrast with the scorned behaviors of immoral whites. As in the Flathead recounting of early Indian-white relations, storytelling about contemporary encounters with whites constructs Indian and white as opposite moral categories.

AMUSING ENCOUNTERS

Stories about amusing encounters with whites are typical fare for conversation. The source of their humor lies in the depiction of the weird ways in which white people think and act. Whites are weird when they are unable to trust Indians or to treat them as fully human—a situation that is usually attributable to the ignorance of those whites about Indians and the Flathead way of life. In one story, Dennis, a mentor for many in the community about traditional ways, told about the time a white man on a motorcycle happened to pass by a place in the woods where he and a small group of other Indian people had gathered. The

men and women were preparing to bake camas root, a traditional food
of the tribes. Individuals were engaged in different tasks: trees of a certain type were being cut by some for firewood, a deep pit to bake the
roots was being dug by others, special broad leaves to line the baking
pit were being gathered, and the bulbous camas roots were being sewn
into a canvas bag. Without stopping to talk to the workers, the white
man hurried into town and looked up the sheriff. Dennis deadpanned
the clincher of the story: the white man had reported to the sheriff that
there was "a bunch of Indians doing something suspicious out in the
woods." The humor of this story lies in the ridiculousness of the white
man being suspicious of an activity that reenacts and recalls the valued
ways of precontact life, ways that could not be more harmless.

In the story that opened this chapter, Sam Dumont expertly casts
the patrolman as a silly figure with nothing better to do than pull over
elderly Indians on their way to buy fried chicken for their great-grand-
daughters. The guarantee that this story is humorous resides in its
being told as such by Sam Dumont, an elder and a man who knows
from experience when the racism of whites is funny and when it is not.
Sam, born a few months after his father was killed in the Swan River
Area Massacre, carries the moral authority of being the last "surviving victim" of that tragic encounter with whites. If Sam can laugh
about the suspiciousness and ignorance of a highway patrolman, it is
funny.

The comments of a local school official were singled out as the basis
of an amusing story told by various members of a well-known Flathead family. In the story, a white woman who was applying for a job
as a teacher overheard the school administrator in conversation on the
telephone. The official, not realizing that the applicant was married to
a tribal member, replied to a question that had been put to him over
the telephone with, "Yes, about 60 percent of the school population is
Indian; they are our largest minority group."

Laughable anecdotes of blatantly racist encounters are sometimes
followed by amusing examples of the ignorance of whites about Indian
life. These encounters are told and received as amusing stories of white
ignorance that underscore their essentially harmless nature. For example, in one instance, a story about a white person who asked whether
Indians chew the hide of an animal during the tanning process, a question often considered offensive and racist, was followed by a story
about a white person who asked whether contemporary Indians still
live in tepees, a question considered pretty dumb. In another story that

was repeated several times in my presence by different people, white cameramen who were covering Jesse Jackson's presidential campaign stop at the reservation took a number of shots of one member of a drum group that had come to perform for the Reverend Jackson. What the cameramen did not know was that the young man they had singled out as classically Indian-looking was in fact a long-haired Japanese exchange student who was attending the local college.

SERIOUS ENCOUNTERS

In contrast, stories that relate encounters with whites that involved a direct cost to Indians and seemed to stem not from ignorance but from deliberate disrespect are delivered in more serious tones and elicit condemnation. An example of a serious story concerns the yearly hassle of obtaining license plates. I first heard it from a young woman who recounted with some exasperation to me and to several of her younger relatives that enrolled tribal members are required to bring a letter to the state license bureau every year attesting to their exemption from paying state taxes, despite the fact that this regulation has been in effect for years and years. In this story the devaluation of the Indian self inheres in the blatant betrayal of an Indian mode of trusting others until some event proves that it is necessary to be more suspicious. Indians who are asked to bring "proof" of their exempt status often feel singled out and questioned. The lack of trust portrayed in the need for yearly proof is attributed not to bureaucracy per se but to the suspiciousness and discourtesy of whites. That the suspiciousness and rudeness of whites is focused more sharply on Indians than on other whites is highlighted by the particular ending the young woman gave to this story. She finished her narrative by noting that a white patron standing in line at the license bureau was overheard making a derogatory comment about all of the "rich" Indians on the dole from the federal government.

The next story evokes negative responses as well, not just because the incident of racism has a direct cost for individual tribal members but because it also involves children, the most needy and vulnerable persons in the tribe aside from the elders. In the story, a family from the reservation was traveling and stopped to eat at a small restaurant in Idaho. The waitress studiously avoided their table despite the fact that there were few, if any, other customers. Finally, the husband called out, asking for menus. At this point, the waitress approached the wife, who looked white because of her blondish hair, and said, "We'll serve you but not them," indicating the husband and children. This story presents a clear example of the conspicuous absence, from an outsider's perspective, of what the family *did* in response. It is simply assumed that the family members adjusted themselves to the situation instead of attempting to manipulate it through confrontation. The typical response of listeners is one of disbelief that such rudeness could really happen in the face of the transparent needs of the family members. The compassion and assistance for the "pitiful" condition of the travelers that would be expected from other Indians was not forthcoming from whites. This story gains meaning against other stories told in other settings in which old Indians are revealed as offering food, lodging, money, and other forms of support to visitors and strangers needing their pity and help.

A story told by an elder and repeated by others in other contexts provides a final example of stories about racism that evoke more serious responses from listeners. Mary, the old woman who told this story, was one of the more respected elders of the Flathead tribes. She usually refrained from passing judgment on whites, but in telling this story she shook her head and mused about "crazy" whites. Mary called attention to the Medicine Tree, a site of annual pilgrimage for the tribes for generations, admonishing her younger and older listeners alike to visit and care for the tree. In a monologue that had the complete attention of all her listeners, she lamented that the tree was becoming discolored and was apparently dying. She told how arrows had been found shot into the tree, and even though tribal members had removed them, they reappeared regularly. In a final statement met with solemn looks, she assigned blame for the malicious shooting of the arrows to "some crazy white people."

DANGEROUS ENCOUNTERS

A more negative response is evoked by certain institutionalized forms of racism, but usually only among personnel whose work is in an associated field. Workers in various fields see the tremendous costs of institutionalized discrimination for the tribes and report and respond to this kind of racism with disapproval and anger. For example, those involved in attempts to teach the native languages will criticize the school system for language programs that may include French and Spanish but not the traditional languages of the Salish, Pend d'Oreilles, or Kootenai peoples. Similarly, attorneys and legal workers will condemn the local judicial systems for the systematically harsher sentences that are handed down to Indian offenders, and tribal politicians will react strongly to biased news accounts or letters to the editor about recent political decisions.

Most instances of institutionalized discrimination, however, such as higher rates of unemployment and incarceration, tend to remain unnoted in general conversation. In fact, when I asked several people if they or anyone they knew had received harsher or biased treatment in various institutional settings, the answer was usually "No." The exception to this pattern was when I queried respondents about the treatment of Indians in foster care settings. Very often, friends and acquaintances would relate stories about the poor treatment of Indian children who had been placed in foster care with whites. This relates to the one type of institutionalized racism that is acknowledged and elaborated in stories by many Flathead Indians: racism that affects children.

This is the most dangerous racism. And storytelling about encounters with whites that affect children differs in tenor from other storytelling. For one thing, such stories are usually told in a more abstract, less detailed manner. They seem less like stories, in a formal sense, than the more serious and amusing ones. Most striking, however, stories about encounters that affect children evoke the strongest negative sentiments; they are *never* considered humorous. Outrage, bitterness, and sometimes hopelessness are the routine responses to these generalized stories of white racism affecting children.

Talk about these kinds of encounters is often in general terms that state simply that racism affecting children exists. Someone will briefly mention how the racism of parents filters down to affect schoolchildren. It is generally held that the racist tensions of adults are manifested in name-calling and fistfights in the schools at about the fifth- or sixth-grade level. The numbers of Indian children who fail to achieve in an academic setting or who show disinterest in their Indian heritage are cited as additional evidence of how pervasively racism affects children.

The following two stories each evoked strong negative responses the one time I heard each told. The first example details a self-reported childhood experience of a man who is currently in his thirties. He remembered playing on a Sunday and happening to see some of his non-Indian school buddies dressed up and on their way to church with their parents. He told the group that as his friends neared him, he overheard the parents admonish their sons to stay away from "that dirty

Indian boy." In a more recent example, the mother of a high school student told about how her son was injured at a sporting event held off the reservation after responding to the fighting taunts of "wagon burner" hurled by a white boy.

A typical turn in storytelling about encounters affecting children confirms and helps to clarify its seriousness. Stories about the effects of racism on Indian children are often followed by stories about the only kind of racism considered more damaging: Indian against Indian. Stories about Indians who disparaged their relatives, friends, or Indian ways are also told with disapproval and anger. Just as with racism affecting children, this kind of racism is never considered amusing. In one such story, a young school-aged girl would hide every day when her mother would come to the school to drop off her lunch. The girl wanted to avoid being seen with her mother, who, by dressing in traditional clothing such as a wing dress, moccasins, and scarf, was undeniably Indian. In another story, a girl would deny to her schoolmates, Indian and white both, that she was related to her uncle, a man who was considered by others to be "Indian from his head to his toes."

Stories are regularly told of tribal members who denied their Indian heritage: some by leaving the reservation, others by claiming an alternate heritage such as French or Irish. Individuals about whom such stories are told are held responsible for their actions and are scorned for them. They often become the recipients of the stinging and powerful criticism of "becoming" Indian only recently and only because it served some selfish purpose. Similar contempt is leveled at individuals who condemn powwows, the sweatlodge, eagle feathers, or other Indian ways in public settings.

TELLING ABOUT WHITES, TALKING ABOUT INDIANS

Storytelling about the early history of Indian-white relations and about contemporary encounters with whites shows the Flathead Indians to be far from the passive victims of omnipotent whites. Flathead storytelling reveals an active construction of the meaning of white racism as *variably* important, the meaning of their history with whites as tragic but also inspirational, and the meanings of Indian and white as moral categories in the contemporary world.[14]

Flathead morality is more than a mere matter of manners; it expresses the Flathead understanding of human nature and the larger world. A cultural logic of the self, in which the boundaries between self and other are permeable and fluid, underpins Flathead morality. The self is understood as dependent on others, that is, on family, friends, tribe, spiritual beings, and occasionally strangers, for meeting its basic needs. In a complementary way, each individual is also responsible for the fulfillment of the needs of others. A mature person carries a profound awareness of his or her dependence on others and the dependence of others on him or her. The awareness of interdependence fosters a depth of feeling in mature individuals that shows itself in loneliness and grief for one's own losses and in respect and compassion for others and what they have suffered.[15]

"Pity" is the salient local term that encapsulates the Flathead stance toward the interdependent self. Out of pity for those who are hungry, ill, grieving, or simply lacking in something, mature persons are moved to generosity. A man will move into a friend's home for several weeks or months to take care of him because the friend is pitiful since the death of his son. A niece will offer an extra pair of shoes to an aunt who is poor and ashamed that she lacks the resources to buy shoes of her own. Pity is the guiding principle of relations between the human and spirit world as well. Pierre Adams's story of the prophecy of the coming of the Blackrobes begins with the pitiful wandering of a grief-stricken Shining Shirt and the numerous animals and insects who come to offer him help. Similarly, Pete Beaverhead recalls a world before the appearance of the Jesuits in which "if a person's poor or pitiful an animal will come and talk to you." Being pitiful, as all selves are at some time, means to inspire the pity of others, human and nonhuman, who try to help by virtue of their compassion.

Flathead canons of morality and maturity contribute an important element to a framework for understanding not only the content of stories about encounters with whites, the "who we are and who they are" of these stories, but also the variable significance of white oppression in an American Indian world. Despite the fact that all acts of racism are rude and violate canons of respectful behavior, not all such encounters with whites are uniformly dangerous for Flathead life. Stories about amusing encounters paint a picture of whites as ridiculous in their ignorance about Indians. Ultimately, amusing stories dismiss potentially racist acts as funny signs of stupidity or peculiarity. Serious stories describe whites as choosing to be disrespectful and hence as morally responsible for the results of their actions. In the words of an Indian man from western Canada, "I sometimes think about it, think that maybe the White man treats us like he does 'cause he don't understand us, and that's too bad. Some other times I think he does understand us, and that's worse" (Braroe 1975: photo following p. 110). While illuminating racism as reprehensible, serious stories also dismiss racist acts by casting them as reflections of the immaturity, the craziness, or just plain meanness of some whites. What separates stories about serious encounters from those about dangerous encounters is the degree to which the perpetuation of the Indian community and Indian values are threatened by the specific acts of whites. Acts of racism that affect children and acts of racism that are perpetrated by Flathead Indians against other members of the Indian community are too threatening to be dismissed and receive the strongest censure.

In the telling of stories about contemporary encounters with whites, just as in storytelling about early Indian-white history, the dynamics of power and coercion between Indians and whites are shown to be shaped as much by Indian values and interpersonal practices as by the "brute facts" of that relationship. But does this mean that Indians can go about their own business, basically ignoring the dehumanizing messages of whites? Is the implication of storytelling about encounters with whites that the history of oppressive treatment that tribal people have endured is negligible for Flathead identity?

Elsewhere, I have argued that one could look to the value structure of storytelling itself to determine whether the Flathead people have been able to resist without significant deformity a century and a half of domination and oppression (O'Nell 1994). There, I concluded that the evidence was not clear. But one could also follow the direction of storytelling about whites into the cultural practices that explicitly construct the Indian identities of Flathead people, the topic of chapter 2. There, in an analysis of formal and informal mechanisms of Indian identity, the evidence is less equivocal: the Indian identity of contemporary Flathead people shows clear signs of distortion, traceable to defensive posturing against the threat of white domination.

CHAPTER TWO

The Making and the Unmaking of the "Real Indians"

Power relations at the Flathead Reservation favor whites over Indians. The history of force, violence, and the violation of legal obligations makes any stance other than wariness vis-à-vis whites foolhardy for the Flathead people. For Indian identity, however, there is another important consequence to the lengthy history of oppression of the Flathead Indians. By virtue of the defensive posture that Indians have been compelled to take against the dehumanizing processes of oppression, the world has been divided, rigidly and untenably, into Indian and white, a division that ultimately fragments Flathead life.

The division of Indians and whites into two separate categories obscures an important reality of community life at the Flathead Reservation: whites and Indians are not always easily separable categories. Rates of intermarriage between the Flathead Indians and whites are fairly high. In a 1970 set of statistics reflecting data from twenty-five reservations, the Flathead Reservation ranked first in rates of "out-marriage" for both men and women, at 37.5 percent and 39.1 percent, respectively (Eschback 1990).[1] And the results of Flathead out-marriage are easy to spot. It is not unusual, for example, to see more than a few individuals with light skin and blondish hair at one of the local powwows, dancing, drumming, or simply watching and visiting. These individuals may be Indians whose coloring indicates their dual Indian and white heritage, or they may be whites who have become part of the Indian community through friendship or marriage. In either case, their presence discloses the intermingling of Indian and white cultures as clearly as does the predominance of French surnames among the Flathead.

The rigidity of the categories of Indian and white that emerges in storytelling about whites belies the "untidiness" of Indian and white as lived realities on the Flathead Reservation. Everyone in the Indian community has family members who are white, whether spouses, in-laws, cousins, children, or grandchildren. Moreover, few persons can claim to have no white ancestors. Thus not only do some Indian families become fragmented with the critical bifurcation of the world into Indian and white, good and bad, but ultimately *selves* are fragmented for some as well.

As they are forced to make rigid distinctions between themselves and whites at the ideological level, what it means to be Indian has become increasingly problematic for individual Flathead Indians. One might think that it would be a simple matter to turn to the tribal rolls to determine Indian identity.[2] However, neither formal regulations nor informal definitions capture the fragmented and negotiated reality of contemporary Flathead Indian identity. The following sketches illustrate how the Indian identities of individuals at the reservation unfold within a charged setting in which not everyone who is formally enrolled in the tribes is Indian; in which there are Indians who are not enrolled; in which people can be "more Indian" or "less Indian" than others; and in which stinging accusations of the self-serving nature of some people's claims to being Indian sometimes surface out of the underground currents of social relations.

Cathy, a thirty-year-old mother of four children, all of whom were enrolled in another tribe, who tanned hides and who as an enrolled member lived in one of the homesites for tribal members but none of whose siblings were enrolled members of the tribes.

Fred, a man in his fifties married to a white woman, recently returned to the reservation after a lifetime in the military service, who was active in tribal politics and very knowledgeable about tribal history and who wore his long hair pulled back into a ponytail, but who was sometimes accused behind his back of only recently "becoming Indian."

Louise, a thirty-five-year-old woman raised by her very traditional grandmother and an expert in beadwork, who was so apprehensive about the shameful possibility of revealing her ignorance of certain traditional practices that she would not attend community cultural or spiritual gatherings.

Renee, a young woman married to a white man to whom she had taught beadwork and powwow dancing but who suspected that others thought of her as only a "powwow Indian."

Pat, an adult man married to another tribal member who had grown up in the community and who had maintained extensive kinship ties within the community despite an absence of many years for schooling but who when faced with a question of "Indian culture" on a matter of concern in his job with the tribes would turn to the Culture Committee for the answer.

Susan, a full-blood elder who in unguarded moments would criticize "half-breeds" for their various shortcomings but who actively sought the enrollment of her less than one-fourth-blood great-grandchildren.

Marshall, an older enrolled man whose son worked for the tribes and who proclaimed himself "part-Indian" but who was never considered Indian by anyone in the community.

Paul, a young father who puzzles at the fact that his daughter has a higher blood quantum measurement than he does.

Dennis, an adult man from one of the more traditional families on the reservation who was acknowledged by most members of the community as "really Indian" but who at times would talk about how his ancestors would not consider him a "real Indian."

For each of the people in the sketches—from Cathy, whose siblings were not enrolled in the tribes, to Pat, who felt he had to turn to the Culture Committee to answer questions about his culture, to Dennis, who claimed his ancestors would not consider him a real Indian— being Indian is a complicated and high-stakes venture. Indian identity at the Flathead Reservation is not simply given—by formal enrollment, by birth, by degree of blood, by language, or by cultural practice. Nor is it consistent for individuals across all contexts. No set of core characteristics defines an essence of Indianness that remains valid at all times, for all people, in all places. In the following pages, the untidy and weighty reality of Indian identity is captured through a portrayal of what is at stake for individuals, families, and the tribes when claims of an "authentic" Indian identity are constructed, destroyed, and rebuilt within two primary contexts of Flathead Indian identity: enrollment and talk about the "real Indians."[3]

ENROLLMENT: FORMAL INCLUSION AND EXCLUSION

Some enrolled members of the Flathead tribes make little claim to being Indian; some make claims that are ignored or ridiculed by others; still others are considered fully Indian but feel a sense of personal uneasiness about their own identities as Indians. Yet by virtue of their inclusion on the roll books, all of these tribal members are legally Indian. Formal enrollment thus forms one of the primary contexts of Indian identity, and an examination of its history offers a convenient entry into some of the complex forces shaping contemporary Flathead identity.

Formal enrollment in the confederated tribes in this day and age confers a number of benefits, including basic health care, preferred status in hiring decisions for positions within the tribal government, twice-yearly per capita payments,[4] assistance with funeral expenses, exemption from paying state taxes, and some kinds of educational assistance. Access to restricted areas of the reservation and certain uses of reservation land, including logging, hunting, and the harvesting of Christmas trees, are also advantages available only to tribal members. Enrolled members who meet low-income requirements are also eligible to receive general welfare assistance, housing assistance, fuel subsidies, and surplus commodity foods. A number of services are also provided for the elderly, including semiweekly meals at various centers around the reservation and home visits by Community Health Representatives (to monitor health concerns) and Homemakers (to help with housecleaning).

The first formal enrollment of Flathead individuals was directly linked to the congressional extension of the Allotment Act of 1887 to the Flathead tribes in 1904. Although purportedly designed for the benefit and advancement of Indian people, the act was in fact a barely disguised authorization by Congress of the enforced assimilation of Indian people and the coercive taking of Indian lands. Under the terms of the act, individuals would typically receive either 80 acres of prime farmland or 160 acres of nonprime farmland. By tilling the land, Indians were to become self-sufficient and lose their dependence on "primitive" tribalism. Moreover, "excess" reservation lands would then be available for white homesteaders. It was in the context of opening the reservation to whites that the Register of Indian Families, also known as the Downs Roll, was compiled and completed at the Flathead Reservation in 1905.

Housed at the National Archives in Seattle, Washington, the Downs Roll is an impressive document. Researchers must make written application to view the record and then wait for an archives assistant to roll it out of storage on a metal cart. When its hard leather covers are opened, the Register of Indian Families fills the larger part of one of the tables available to researchers. Its musty smell, its thick, browning pages, and its fading entries handwritten in a dated script attest to its historical age. For each of the 2,133 individuals enrolled in 1905, the register records enrollment number, name, age, blood quantum, tribe, family relationship (i.e., single, widow, husband, wife, son, or daughter), date of marriage, "type" of marriage (i.e., priest, clergyman, or "Indian custom"), father's name, father's enrollment number (unless deceased, in which case the death is noted), mother's name, and mother's enrollment number (again, unless deceased, in which case the death is noted).

According to figures published by the Flathead Culture Committee, of the total number of individuals who were enrolled in 1905, 557 were classified as Flathead, 640 as Pend d'Oreilles, 197 as Lower Pend d'Oreilles, 556 as Kootenai, 135 as Spokane, and 48 as coming from other tribes (Flathead Culture Committee 1988). The Downs Roll also initiated a new way of indexing Indian identity—by blood quantum, a numerical figure, expressed in a fraction, that indicates degree of "biological" relatedness to other Flathead Indians. The 1905 enrollment figure can be partitioned according to this alternate criterion as follows: 915 full-bloods; 1,183 mixed-bloods (of varying degrees of blood quantum); 25 adopted Indians from other tribes; and 10 adopted whites (Trosper 1976: 265).

The advent of formal enrollment signals a significant shift from an informal and inclusive system of group membership to a system with strains of exclusivity. Before the Downs Roll, group membership was defined by kinship, marriage, a shared way of life, and behavioral mores. The adoption of individuals from other tribes was common, intermarriage with people from other tribes occurred frequently, and non-Flathead spouses and children were easily incorporated into the tribal structure (Fahey 1974; Trosper 1976). Early interactions with white traders and settlers followed the same patterns of intermarriage, adoption, and inclusion (Downs Roll 1905; Schaeffer 1935).

Including, as it does, individuals with a variety of tribal origins,

individuals with mixed Indian and white heritage, and even a few
whites, the Downs Roll is an eloquent and convincing testimonial to
the inclusiveness of the Flathead tribes at the turn of the century. It is
unlikely that "blood," and less likely that "blood quantum," was
being used by Indians themselves at the time to talk about Indian identity. Louise McDermott, an ethnographer of Flathead life at the turn of
the century, used the terms "full-blood" and "mixed-blood," but her
use of the terminology probably reflects the discourse of whites at the
time rather than that of the Flathead Indians (McDermott 1904). She
also used the terms "Irish-Indian" and "French-Indian," which by
virtue of their specificity seem more reflective of the social divisions of
white society. Other authors writing about reservation life in the early
decades of the twentieth century tend to ignore the "mixed" nature of
Flathead Indian society and therefore are uninformative regarding the
relevance of formal enrollment and "blood" in Indian identity (Teit
1928; Turney-High 1937; Ray 1939).

By the 1940s, however, "full-blood" was a salient local category
among members of the Flathead tribes for talking about Indian identity and divisions within the Indian community (Hansen 1947). Yet,
despite the apparent divisiveness between full-bloods and mixed-
bloods from the 1940s through the 1980s, patterns of openness and inclusiveness continue to predominate among contemporary Flathead
Indian people. This can be seen in the persistently high rates of out-
marriage and in the efforts of individuals to enroll their supposedly in-
eligible descendants as members of the tribes. Like Susan, the elder
whose attempts to enroll her great-grandchildren are mentioned in one
of the sketches at the beginning of this chapter, tribal members sometimes conduct extensive genealogical searches in the hope of finding
additional sources of Indian ancestry to bolster their claims.

If the apparent inclusiveness of individual Flathead Indians were to
dictate formal enrollment policy, enrolled membership would exceed
its present number. Factors that keep the enrollment figure down are
evidently also at work. In "Native American Boundary Maintenance:
The Flathead Indian Reservation, Montana, 1860–1970," Ron L. Trosper argues that in an effort to "protect tribal wealth," the confederated
tribes adopted a "racial" and "exclusive" mode of defining group
membership in 1935 and maintained that mode over the next thirty-
five years (1976: 259). However, as Trosper himself notes at a later
point (267–268), the enrollment procedures of the tribes have not been

static since 1935. Policies oscillate between poles of exclusivity and inclusivity that reflect the waxing and waning of the threat of legal annihilation of the tribes posed by the federal government. When the threat of legal annihilation is greatest, formal enrollment policies become more exclusive. Formal practices of enrollment can respond to the inclusiveness of Flathead Indian people only when federal Indian policy appears to be more benign.

Since 1960, a minimum of one-fourth blood quantum has had to be demonstrated for all new applicants before enrollment is granted. Various regulations had existed before this. From 1905 to 1935, demonstrating descent from any enrolled member was sufficient for someone to be enrolled. In 1935, however, a more restrictive approach to enrollment based on descent *and* residence on the reservation was instituted. The 1935 regulations, which stipulated that enrollment was limited to the offspring of enrolled members resident on the reservation, was part and parcel of the Flathead adoption of the terms of the Indian Reorganization Act of 1934 (also known as the Howard-Wheeler Act). Under the act, which the Confederated Salish and Kootenai Tribes were the first in the nation to adopt, tribes were encouraged to abandon "traditional" patterns of leadership and to assume a form of government based on a constitution approved by the secretary of the interior and the periodic election of representatives to a tribal council. At the suggestion of John Collier, then head of the BIA, the residence requirement became part of the constitution adopted by the tribes.

The addition of the residence requirement to the descent requirement engendered discontent at the reservation because it excluded the children born to Indians who were living off the reservation, even if only on a seasonal basis. In 1946, the tribal council responded to local dissatisfaction and changed the requirement, stipulating a minimum of one-sixteenth blood quantum regardless of residence. Thus the first concrete use of blood quantum in enrollment can be traced to the tribes themselves, who used it as a device to mitigate the *exclusivity* of the previous regulation.

Five years later, however, blood quantum was used by the tribes to mitigate the *inclusivity* of the 1946 regulation. The reversal occurred within the context of a major shift in federal Indian policy during the late 1940s and early 1950s, when Utah Senator Arthur Watkins led a national movement to "terminate" the tribal status of certain Indian tribes. The movement culminated in 1953 in a congressional resolution stating Congress's intent that certain Indian tribes and individuals "be freed from Federal supervision and control and from all disabilities and limitations specifically applicable to Indians" (U.S. Congress 1953). Unlike other tribes in many respects, the Flathead Indians appeared more "assimilated": they were more intermarried with whites, and they lived on a reservation checkerboarded with white-owned property. Leaders of the termination movement saw the Flathead Indians as a logical and legitimate choice for their experiment in the ultimate in enforced assimilation: "termination."

It was a dangerous and anxious time for members of the Flathead tribes, the first of several tribes slated for termination under the resolution. In 1947, at the first meeting of the Full Blood Flathead Montana Study Group, one of the first questions addressed by Paul Charlo, son of Chief Charlo, to the white organizers of the meeting was whether the meeting had anything to do with the rumors they had heard about "turning the Indians loose" (Hansen 1947). For the Indians, termination carried real economic and political threats. Not only would the political authority of the tribes over Indian individuals be turned over to the potentially hostile Montana state government, but certain federal services in the areas of health and welfare would be lost. Many Flathead Indians, especially the more full-blooded Indians, were already living marginal economic lives in comparison to their white neighbors, and the loss of federal benefits and protection against paying state taxes was a frightening prospect. Equally, if not more, menacing was the potential for the eventual loss of the Indian community.

Under the threat of termination, the council again revised enrollment requirements in 1951, setting a more restrictive level of a minimum of one-fourth blood quantum for off-reservation members. A formal amendment to the constitution extending this rule to residents on the reservation was passed by the tribal council nine years later, in 1960. By creating a more purely "Indian" membership in the terms set by whites in 1905, these more exclusive regulations functioned to construct a community that could more readily be defended against the threat of federally instigated termination, whose proponents often argued that the Flathead Indians were already "white."

Historically, the exclusivity of formal enrollment policies can be traced to various moves on the part of the federal government to control and limit tribal membership either directly or indirectly, starting with enrollment itself in 1905 and culminating in termination. Today, despite the current climate of self-determination and the apparent eclipse of the threat of termination, enrollment policies maintain an exclusivity that continues to be at odds with Flathead values. Even though the era of overtly terminationist policy may have come to an end, the historical weight of treaty violations, betrayal, and racism is never far from consciousness, suggesting one reason for the continuation of exclusive enrollment regulations.[5]

Table 1 summarizes the temporal relations among the actions of the federal government, tribal enrollment policies, and Indian identity. An examination of the forces maintaining the exclusivity of tribal membership reveals some of the penalties associated with inclusivity. Exclusivity, however, is not without its own costs. Restrictive enrollment requirements are often charged with separating one family member from another. It is not clear why this should be so, given the inclusive tendencies of Flathead group membership. The fact that one family member receives benefits from the tribe, even if others do not, would seem to be a benefit to the whole family. Money that might have been spent, for example, on the medical bills of the enrolled member would then be freed up for other expenses. And, in reality, this is often the case. Nonetheless, there is a shared sense that the current situation, in which some family members may be enrolled and others not, is harmful. It is this sentiment that is expressed in the periodic proposals before the tribal council that non-Flathead Indian blood be included in the assessment of blood quantum for the purpose of tribal enrollment and in private conversations, in which people will say how unfair it is that certain Indian children cannot be enrolled simply because they do not have one-fourth Flathead blood.

Statements such as these express more than simple economic concerns and stem from an uneasy relationship among enrollment, blood quantum, and Indian identity. What that relationship is, however, is not straightforward. Historically, judging from the inclusion of both full-bloods and mixed-bloods on the Downs Roll, blood quantum did not constitute an important aspect of Indian identities. Today, for the most part, the blood quantum levels of individuals are not discussed, even though they may be generally known. Still, to recall a few of the sketches from the opening pages of this chapter, there is a sense that blood quantum is, somehow, important. Paul felt confused about the fact that his daughter had a higher blood quantum level than he did, sensing that she might be "more Indian" than he was. In Cathy's case,

TABLE 1   CHRONOLOGY OF FORMAL ENROLLMENT POLICIES

Year	Federal Policies and Practices	Tribal Enrollment Requirements	Flathead Indian Identity
1905	Allotment Act of 1887 extended to Flathead Reservation; Downs Roll—start of formal enrollment and introduction of blood quantum (b.q.)	Descent (inclusive)	Downs Roll includes mixed-bloods and full-bloods, a few whites, and individuals with various tribal affiliations; McDermott (1904) uses terms "full-blood" and "mixed-blood" in ethnography but also uses "Irish-Indians," "French-Indians"
1935	Indian Reorganization Act; tribes urged to reorganize political structure and to adopt more exclusive enrollment requirements	Descent and residence on the reservation (exclusive, in response to BIA suggestion)	
1946–1947		1/16 b.q. (inclusive, in response to local discontent with exclusivity of previous requirements)	Full-blood and mixed-blood are local categories that signify, among other things, haves and have-nots (Hansen 1947)
late 1940s–early 1950s	Watkins organizes efforts to "terminate" tribes; Congress passes resolution in 1953	1/4 b.q. for nonresidents, 1/16 for residents (exclusive, passed in 1951 in response to threat of termination)	
1960		1/4 b.q. for residents and nonresidents (exclusive, in response to threat of termination)	
1987–1988 (fieldwork)	One decade after the Self-Determination Act of 1975	1/4 b.q. maintained (exclusive, in response to history of threat and budget constraints)	Enrollment and b.q. insinuated into talk about Indian identities of individuals

she was the only one of her siblings who was enrolled, because she was born just prior to the 1960 changes in enrollment requirements. Cathy was the only one of the children in the family to "do Indian activities," that is, beading and hide tanning. She had also had four children by an Indian man. Again, in some vague way, Cathy was "more Indian" than her brothers and sisters. Finally, there was Susan, who was active in trying to enroll some of her great-grandchildren with less than one-fourth blood quantum but who at the same time would criticize "half-breeds" for not having the proper attitudes in certain matters.

Having a recognized Indian ancestor virtually guarantees membership of some sort in the Indian community, if one chooses to participate, even if that ancestor was distant and the resulting blood quantum is minimal. Although even here the matter is not straightforward, as the sketch of Marshall illustrated. Marshall proclaimed himself to be "part-Indian," but this self-perception was not legitimized in the community, despite his status as an enrolled member of the tribes and the facticity of his claim to Indian ancestry. A number of factors probably entered into his case, including the fact that he was involved in local white and state politics, ran a large and prosperous ranch, and had the look and bearing of a white man.

For the most part, the use of blood quantum appears to be relegated to limited aspects of everyday life, that is, to legal decisions stipulating eligibility for certain benefits. Despite its apparently minimal role, however, enrollment and blood quantum have become insinuated into daily life and talk about the Indian identities of individuals. A full-blood friend of mine keeps a list of the remaining full-bloods, referring to it jokingly as "The Endangered Species List." At the core of this "joke" is a lament about the loss of the "real Indians" and a reflection on the detrimental effects of intermarriage and assimilation. This elaborate lament, which I call the rhetoric of the "empty center," argues that there are no more "real Indians." As in storytelling about whites, the rhetoric of the empty center is a conscious construction about what it means to be Indian.

However, unlike storytelling about whites, which focuses on collective Indian identity, the rhetoric of the empty center is used primarily to frame the identities of individuals. Like enrollment, the empty center emphasizes degrees of being Indian. But, unlike either storytelling about whites or formal enrollment requirements, the rhetoric of the empty center culminates in a message that contemporary Flathead Indian identity is, in essence, inauthentic.

THE EMPTY CENTER: INFORMAL
INCLUSION AND EXCLUSION

The Indian identities of individuals at the Flathead Reservation are shaped and constructed within a context of a conscious detailing of what it means to be Indian. A useful way to bring this rhetoric of Indian identity into focus is to imagine a set of concentric circles, with the center circle representing the "really Indians," the outer circle representing enrolled members of the tribes who make little claim to being Indian, and the intervening circles representing successive gradations of being Indian (see fig. 2).

The image of concentric circles communicates four integral aspects of an elaborated and conscious response to what it means to be Indian at the reservation today. First, there is a generally shared sense that there is *no one* alive today who can unambiguously be assigned to the center circle, hence the designation "empty center." Second, there is also a generally agreed upon sense in the community that there are people who are "more" Indian and others who are "less" Indian, as well as a generally agreed upon sense of who belongs at the extremes. The image of concentric circles helps to clarify the structuring logic of gradation and authority that infuses negotiations of Indian identity in this context. Third, the heuristic also graphically displays the oppositional nature of Indian identity in the positioning of Indian identities in the spaces between two ideal types, real Indians and non-Indians (whites). The idealized characteristics of those in the inner circle and those outside the outermost circle are used to assess and negotiate the relative positions of individuals within the intervening circles. It is, in fact, in these intervening circles that the weightiest negotiations about Indian identity transpire. Finally, the solid lines between the circles help to communicate how assessments about the relative positions of individuals tend to set up divisions between individuals and within the community between those who are "more Indian" and those who are "less Indian."

The rhetoric of the empty center is both an elaborate lament of loss of the past and a system of authority in which certain individuals are invested with the power to decide what constitutes "genuine" Indian identity. Both aspects are evident in the widespread expression of the rhetoric in both public and private settings and across age categories. I heard the refrain of the empty center in interviews with people of all ages, many of whom cited the loss of the real Indians as one of the causes of their depressive experiences. I heard it in the lecturing words

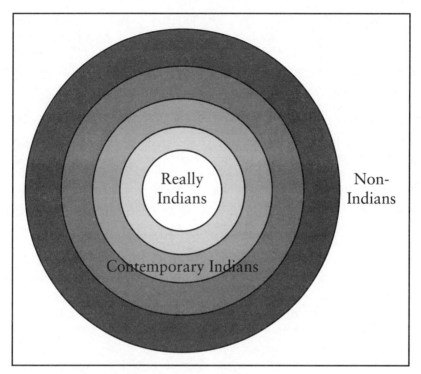

Figure 2.   The empty center: A rhetoric of identity

of prayer leaders at masses and at wakes where they would repeatedly harangue the participants to be like their elders, to offer condolence and assistance without being asked, to rely on God. I heard it in the mournful stories of elders about how life used to be, how the Indians used to visit each other regularly, and how, unlike the medicine men of today who are only "mocking" the real ways, medicine men of the past used to have real power to bring game, cure illness, and change the weather. I heard it in the widespread lament about the loss of the traditional language, both by those who could still speak Salish and by those who knew only a few words. I heard it in the private doubts of whether the traditional winter stories were "true" anymore. I heard it in the public debate about whether the sweatlodge should be made available at a local healing center to members of the community who may not know how to use it. I heard it in the private revelations of individuals who suffered with the feeling that they did not know how to be really Indian. I also heard it in the divisive aspersions of "not being really Indian" cast on others.

These expressions of the empty center hint at some of the relevant dimensions of how real Indians are conceptualized by members of the Flathead community. However, a closer look is warranted because it is against this backdrop of what constitutes a "really Indian" Indian that contemporary Indians assess themselves and each other. As we saw in chapter 1, in the context of storytelling about whites, Indian is primarily a moral category that relies on ethnopsychological propositions about the self and its relation to others. The following discussion reveals additional semantic links between the moral dimension of being Indian and particular "Indian" practices. The primary source for understanding who the "really Indians" are is in the abundant anecdotes and stories that are told about them in everyday settings. Narrators often begin their stories by making reference to concrete signs of dress or hairstyle to signal that the story is about a "really Indian." For example, "She wore a shawl, she wore a handkerchief [on her head], she wore moccasins." Or, "His mother was Indian. She wore little moccasins." Or, "He was Indian from head to toe. He wore long braids."

These concrete visual cues substantiate that the protagonist valued Indian ways, that he or she refused to succumb to the ways of whites even in dress or hairstyle. They also mark the fact that the story takes place in a different time from the present day, with an implicit preference given to that preceding era. Other criteria in this vein include the protagonist's preference for living in a tepee or for eating real Indian food (i.e., wild meat, berries, camas root, and bitterroot). Sometimes this concrete documentation of the real Indian's preferences for Indian ways is a device for setting the scene for a story that follows. Very often, however, the documentation of how the real Indians *were* real Indians is the whole point of the story and is a powerful moral lesson in itself.

The stories of "really Indians" often enumerate the multiple rewards that result from the practice of real Indian ways and highlight the losses for the present generation that stem directly from not practicing them. The real Indians knew things that current generations do not. They knew when death or sickness was approaching and could often ward off these disasters. They knew and spoke Salish, a language that connected to the realities of the world in a way that English cannot. Many of them could speak with certain animals. Some of them had the knowledge and power to control the weather, to influence the workings of love, and to cure disease. The old-timers were healthier, they lived to very old ages while suffering few infirmities, few of them went bald or gray. The men were excellent hunters, the women were modest and hardworking. The really Indians knew who all their relatives were. They made frequent visits to each other and always came together to help with the disruption and pain of illness and death. Wakes and memorial feasts for the dead were fully attended.

Especially important, stories about the really Indians link a specific history of losses with a specific system of authority. What is most often stressed in the enumeration of the characteristics and ways of the really Indians is a practice of discipline and obedience. The really Indians believed in their elders and in God. They disciplined their children and in turn were disciplined by the chief of the band or tribe. The world was a more orderly and safer place, its hazards more firmly under control.

Although the fact that there are no more really Indians is sometimes explained by contemporary Flathead Indians as a result of assimilation and intermarriage between Indians and whites, there is a second, more covert and powerful, explanation that emerges in the rhetoric as well: there are no more really Indians because the younger generations are disobedient. The rhetoric unfolds by telling how the real Indians, that is, the Indians of the past, tried to keep the subsequent generations on the straight and narrow path of being Indian, by teaching them the right ways to do things and by admonishing them not to be ashamed of their ways. The fault for the loss of Indian ways, and therefore of the real Indians, lies with the younger generations' rejection of the teachings of their elders.

Although the rhetoric of the empty center is primarily a rhetoric of loss at the surface level, its expression is charged with this undercurrent of blame. This aspect is evident in the following quotation from a transcript of a meeting of the Indian Studies group, a changing coterie of treatment providers and clients, who had gathered one day to discuss the problems of depression, suicide, and anger. The words were spoken by an elder who, while not telling a story of a specific "really Indian," clearly used reference to the empty center to exemplify and authorize a moral lesson. When asked about the problem of suicide, this elder responded with the following words.

> To me, what I thought, it's because nobody believes anymore, they don't even go to church. Just one day, not even one day, they go to church about one hour, half an hour. That's something you're supposed to listen to, priest, but there's no way you can go over there, just for that one hour, half an hour. You just, Sunday comes, that's where you're supposed to be going.

That's when I growed up, that's where we always go. Even we're way up in the mountains, how many people's there, how many people there, we'd go to church. Priest telling us what's right and what's wrong. So we always listen to our folks.

Now, [in] this time, [people] listen to TV. That's what's making everybody bad. They listen to TV. That's why everything is going wrong. [Back] then, we go to church. Just them few words what priest says, keep it in your mind. Find out it's something good for your whole life. Not just one person, everybody. When I used to go to church, there used to be a lot of Indians at the church. It's for one day. They got one day, sign [in sign language] for that. And then the rest of them [the rest of the week], they can go wherever they want to go. But now, I listen to that [TV]. That's not the way it's supposed to be. That's why everything is, not doing right anymore. Cause you don't listen to somebody's preaching. You just follow. . . . I watch TV, so that's where they're learning all these bad things—from TV. They won't listen to the priest. Just one day, they could go over there. They don't got to spend no money to go to church. It's just, just that one place to go on Sunday. That's where you pick up your, where you'll be on the right track, that you don't go to the wrong. If you stay home and watch TV on Sunday, that's where you learn all these bad things.

. . . A long time ago, they had their folks. Long as their family, kids, their folks, would stand, say, "Sit down. I want to talk to you." Just listen to them. And they talk about something. They never talk about something bad, they always talk about something good for you. And that's why a long time ago, everything was going good. Because, we have to listen, no matter where. Sometimes in the morning, sometimes in the evening, late in the evening, they make you sit down and listen. So there was no trouble then. They tell you what, what you're, do, you kill yourself. They tell you where you're gonna go after you're dead. [Hell.] How do they know? But they always come out and say that. They always say there's one day for you in your life and it's Sunday. Don't kill yourself, go to church.

Like at my place, I had mass over there. I was glad there was a lot of people there. We just had half an hour, hour there. Pretty good. So that's where you pick up your words, from your folks, from the priest. And that's, that helps you. No matter who you're mad at, go to church, come out, you'll be different.

In this example, the elder locates the source for the ills of modern Indian life at the reservation, including the problem of suicide, in the loss of "belief" among Indians of younger generations. The elder documents a replacement of the words and authority of the priest and the elders with those of television. The argument is that Indians of today no longer believe in their elders: not only are they not doing what the elders of the past would have them do, they are fundamentally different *because* they do not listen to and obey their elders. In other words, it is not simply that the problems of contemporary life are traceable to changes in a range of practices but that a fundamental practice, a practice of belief and obedience, is no longer part of daily life. Within the rhetoric, loss of obedience underlies the loss of Indianness.

In some ways, the actuality of historical losses may obscure the way in which the rhetoric of the empty center also functions as a system of authority. To counteract this tendency, it is useful to speculate that the rhetoric of the empty center is not new but is instead a cultural form that extends backward into precontact times. Given the valuation of tradition and the characterization of the present as a corrupted version of an idyllic past, the ways that elders talk about each other, and the few indicators in the sparse historical record of the Flathead practice of elders and chiefs lecturing to their people, it is not unreasonable to hypothesize that the elders of the Flathead tribes have been haranguing the younger generations and admonishing them to be more like their ancestors from time immemorial. It is not unlikely that the ancestors have always been touted as more pious, more powerful, more knowledgeable, more moral, and so on, than the current generation, for it is against this idealization of former generations that current generations are disciplined. Although important differences in these discourses will become apparent as we proceed, the similarities in the form are most relevant at this point.

It is the possibility of the cultural continuity of this discourse that informs my understanding of the rhetoric of the empty center as a system of authority. It is at this point in the discussion, though, that the limitations of the empty center, as a heuristic, begin to become apparent. The empty center is not really empty at all. It is, in fact, replete with no longer living people from generations past. Thus the first problem with the heuristic is that, as a static image, it obscures the fact that contemporary Indian identities are positioned in ever-moving history. To capture the flux of time, it is more useful to imagine a moving picture made up of a series of telescoping images, in which the individuals closest to the empty center in earlier generations are continually moving into the empty center as new individuals in succeeding generations are moving into the circle immediately surrounding the empty center.

A second problem with the heuristic is that it fails to capture that Indian identities are positioned not only in social time but also in social space. In other words, the composition of the empty center changes according to the position of the individual. In general, the empty center is more empty of living people the closer the observer is to the center. Thus for individuals who find themselves positioned in the outer circles, there are a dozen or so living individuals, typically full-blood elders, in the center. But for those dozen or so at the center (according to the previous individuals), there *are* no living individuals at the center. It is those persons who are considered to be in the center or nearest to the center by many, if not most, in the community who are the strongest advocates of the position that the center is empty, that there are no more "really Indians" left.

Although the empty center oversimplifies some of the important dimensions of contemporary Flathead identities, it nonetheless captures a significant sense of inauthenticity that permeates personal and public narratives about Indian identity. In a real way, the rhetoric creates a sort of double bind for members of the younger generations of Flathead Indians living at the reservation. On the one hand, to be really Indian, one must listen to and obey the words of the elders. On the other hand, to believe in the words of the elders means to accept and affirm that there are no more real Indians. There are two choices for the individual, either of which undercuts the possibility of being a real Indian. If one chooses to characterize oneself as a real Indian, one has to disregard the words of the elders, something a real Indian is incapable of doing. If one believes the elders, as a real Indian must, one has to believe that there are no more real Indians, a statement that then applies to oneself and others.

Daily life among the Flathead Indians bears the imprint of this double bind. The climate engendered by the empty center for many Flathead Indians is one of despair about loss of the real Indians but also of covert manipulation of the rhetoric. So while there is rhetorical consensus that the Indians of today cannot be "real Indians," there are continual attempts by individuals to have their claims of being "more Indian" authorized or legitimized by others. It is by demonstrating that they have direct links to the real Indians that individuals make claims to being more Indian. The most powerful links are those of kinship or friendship, and the most tenuous links are those of indirectly acquired knowledge about the ways of the real Indians, that is, learning how to speak Salish or how to bead in a classroom setting instead of from relatives during childhood. But it is a risky business to make claims too boldly, for to do so opens up the individual to rejection of his or her claims, not only on the basis of the specific claims but also because to be bold is, in itself, "not very Indian."

It is now possible to return to the sketches at the beginning of the chapter with a better understanding of some of the dynamics of Indian identity at the Flathead Reservation. The sketches describe the "problematics" of Indian identity for nine individuals. The problematics are neither "typical" nor "atypical." They are simply the stuff that those particular Flathead Indian identities are made of contextually and not essential characteristics of "Indianness." It is fruitless to talk about what it means to be Indian for all members of the Flathead community and equally fruitless to talk about the Indian identity of an individual apart from the situations in which he or she is, or is not, Indian. There is no such thing as Indian identity divorced from individuals in contexts of meaning and authority, and, furthermore, the Indian identities of individuals are not separable from those contexts.

To take the first sketch, Cathy's identity as Indian is constituted in various settings involving non-Indian relatives, Indian relatives, non-Indian friends, and "really Indian" teachers and elders, each of whom has a certain, albeit shifting, degree of authority vis-à-vis Cathy and her "Indianness." In some of these settings, especially in the presence of really Indians, Cathy mutes her claims for an Indian identity, often by positioning herself as a "student" of Flathead ways, expressing, for example, a desire to correct her shameful ignorance of the Salish language but confessing a complete inability to learn it. At the same time, however, Cathy enthusiastically offers to teach the Indian skills she has learned at the local junior college and from really Indians to her Indian and non-Indian relatives and friends. In settings such as these, she is, additionally, a robust storyteller of racist incidents that she has experienced as an Indian. Nor are these claims made exclusively by Cathy for herself. Very often claims are made for Cathy's Indian identity by others: a teacher might extol her abilities in Indian crafts, while a fellow student might note how Cathy learned these skills only recently.

Cathy's attempts, and the attempts of others, to use the powerful rhetoric of Indian identity gain and lose persuasive force as other elements of her life as an Indian are brought into play. Thus her enrollment may become meaningful in some contexts, whereas the nonenrollment of her siblings may be the more meaningful fact in others. Or the fact that she has four "Indian" children may appear important at times, when at other times it is the fact that her children are enrolled in another tribe that is salient. Cathy's full participation in local Indian life—searching the reservation for her enrolled cousin's runaway daughter, sharing her per capitas, bearing children fathered by Indian men, helping to cook at the wakes, and attending the local Indian-run meetings of Alcoholics Anonymous—often reduces the possibility of critical gossip or teasing about her claims to being Indian. At the same time, her participation embroils her in relationships of jealousy and disagreement, which then increases the possibility of opposition.

Cathy's identity as a Flathead Indian is a seemingly paradoxical combination of several contexts. I suggest, however, that her Indian identity is only *seemingly* paradoxical, for if the supposition of a single essence of Indianness is suspended, as I am arguing, the paradox disappears. Indian identity for Cathy is a shifting, negotiated process that cannot be captured by a simple checklist of Indian characteristics. And because Indian identity is contextually constituted, it is more appropriate to talk about Cathy's Indianness in terms of her Indian identities, in the plural. Cathy is both "more" Indian and "less" Indian, depending on the context. And this is equally the case for every other individual described in the opening pages, the differences residing in the degree of control each has over definitions of self and others.

It is now easier to see how Dennis, whose Indianness is rarely at issue in the general community, is unable, as one of the strongest advocates of the loss of the really Indians, to fully claim the position of really Indian for himself. The same mechanism is at work in the case of Pat, who although quite knowledgeable about tribal culture and tribal values, as an expression of obedience, turns to the Culture Committee and the elders whenever he is questioned on these matters in his work. Similarly, we can better understand the anxiety of Renee, who worries whether her participation in powwows may be judged as an "illegitimate" claim to Indian identity, and Louise, who refuses to participate in traditional gatherings, such as the annual Jump Dance or the Bitterroot Feast, because she fears some shameful revelation of ignorance about Flathead ways that casts doubt on her own Indian identity as well as the Indianness of her relatives. In each of these cases, we can see the contours of obedient acquiescence to a system of authority but an acquiescence that while affirming the system places individuals in tenuous positions vis-à-vis their own identities as "authentic" Indians.

So far, I have bracketed the important implications of this system for the community in order to explicate its meanings for the individual. But the signature of the "empty center" is also written in social divisiveness across the Indian community. Within the community, one sees a continually shifting set of social groups that unify and then fragment over the issues of the legitimacy of particular claims to being more Indian. For example, a cohort of the same age, whose members grew up together and often have extensive kinship ties, might agree in general as to the relative ranking of Indianness of each of their members but differ acrimoniously over the recent strategies of a member to become "more" Indian. Some will refute his statements that he did not know any English until he went to school; others will note how he found a non-Indian girlfriend who does not know, and will never find out, just how recent his long hair is and how new his interest in sweatlodges is; and others, perhaps relatives, will reinforce his claim by calling up memories of his parents as really Indians. In addition to these shifting alliances, one also sees more stable divisions within the community between those who advocate opposing positions on issues of Indian identity, that is, whether it is more Indian to shun Catholicism, whether blood quantum should include only Flathead "blood" or "blood" from other tribes as well, or whether modern powwows reflect true Indianness.

While some claims are negotiated entirely within the existing framework of the empty center, there is often embedded within others an effort to *redefine* what it means to be Indian, either by redefining the essence of Indianness or by redefining who is entitled to arbitrate and legitimate claims. Some of these attempts straddle the line between acquiescence and redefinition, such as in the case of Nan, a middle-aged woman who as a recovering alcoholic and drug addict is a leader in local efforts to address the problems of substance abuse. Nan argues that while others may have rejected the teachings of their elders, she has not. The reason that she does not know the right way to be Indian, as she narrates it, is because her elders failed to teach her. The system of authority is in essence valid; it is just that her own elders did not live up to their end of the bargain, because of their alcohol addiction and their attempts to deal with the racism of whites.[6]

Some attempts, however, are more blatantly resistant, such as when Charlie, a man in his fifties who has worked in various capacities for the BIA and the tribal government, loudly proclaims that none of the elders today is in the position to teach the younger generations about how to be Indian. He argues that the elders of today are part of a "lost generation" that was sent off to boarding schools and taught to be ashamed of their Indian language and customs and that has been decimated by problem drinking. Even here, however, the rhetoric of the empty center remains in full view, for it is the ways of the past that dictate what it means to be a real Indian. What Charlie calls into question is not the authority of the past but the authority of *this* generation of elders to arbitrate claims of Indianness.

A final example shows the subtlety with which these redefinitions can be played out. A young woman, Liz, had applied for housing assistance and a house had been built for her on a plot of land adjoining a site that had been used for generations for a sweatlodge. Through a series of miscommunications or noncommunication, the house had been built too close to the site of the sweatlodge in the opinion of some of the elders and their spokespersons at the Culture Committee. The latter, as a group, wanted the house to remain unused or moved to the other side of the tract of land. The agency in charge of building the home wanted to avoid additional expense, and Liz herself wanted to move into the house as soon as possible.

What followed over the next weeks was a series of strategic posturings in which the interested parties cast the dilemma in terms of Liz's Indian identity. The elders and members of the Culture Committee sought to impose a definition of "more" Indian on Liz, citing her nearly full-blood parentage. By doing so, the implication was that Liz would then have to acquiesce, as a "real" Indian, to the wishes and dictates of her elders. Liz countered by saying that although nearly full-blood, she had been placed in foster care very early in life and therefore did not understand such things as the workings of the sweatlodge. By claiming to be "less" Indian, Liz implied that she should not and could not be held accountable for upholding Indian traditions. Members of the Culture Committee continued to press for an Indian identity, saying that while it is true that Liz was "fostered out," she nonetheless grew up in the area and had maintained contact with her family throughout her childhood and adult life. Still, while Liz maintained her stance that she was not enough Indian to know about the sweatlodge and therefore could not hurt it or be hurt by it, she never denied being Indian. This was due primarily to the necessity of being Indian in order to qualify for housing assistance in the first place. Her position was that being Indian did not inhere in either knowledge (knowing about the sweatlodge) or behavior (obeying the elders). Her position was that being Indian was a legal definition: as an enrolled member of the tribes, she had certain rights.

Ultimately, this dilemma was arbitrated by the Tribal Council, and, for the first time in recent memory, the council voted against the wishes of the elders and the Culture Committee. The striking result of this negotiation points to the current, perhaps inherent, fragility of the empty center as a system of meaning and authority. Other signs of this fragility include the numbers of Flathead individuals who turn to whites or to Indians from other tribes for confirmation of their Indianness. This is evident not only in patterns of intermarriage but also in the teaching of Indian skills and practices of spirituality to visiting and local whites. This pattern may also be reflected in the numbers of enrolled members who, in a sense, opt out of the system, those who move away from the reservation and those who no longer participate in the Indian community in any way.

Another sign of the fragility of the system is in the apparently increasing rigidity of what it means to be Indian. When asked about "traditional" Flathead ways, many young and middle-aged adults on the reservation became apprehensive and reticent in a manner that seemed to be part of an effort to maintain the appearance of tribal unity. It was as if by talking about what they know or do not know they might reveal variations in practices that would belie the constancy, and therefore the validity, of traditional practices. Among many people at the reservation there was an inflexible valuation of Indian ways; both younger and older Indians seemed to lack a differentiating sense that some ways of being Indian might be more important than others, that being able to identify certain plants, for example, might be less important than, say, practices of gift exchange. Thus, for example, individuals who have only recently begun to use the sweatlodge talk about and use the lodge fearfully, whispering about the proper ways to conduct a sweat, unsure of which elements of the ritual constitute its essence and whether certain practices are supposed to be secret. In contrast, those individuals who grew up using the sweatlodge tended to be relaxed about its use, for example, telling stories of how as children they would lie halfway in the doorway, leaving their heads out because of the heat, or of how they would talk to their elders through the wall of the lodge.[7]

The fragility of the system is a different issue from its continual creation and re-creation in the maneuvering of individuals and groups to raise their own statuses within its confines. It should not be inferred from this discussion that this constant negotiation about how to be Indian, about who is Indian, and about who is entitled to judge the legitimacy of claims is a sign of this fragility. In fact, it is the increasing rigidity of this process that seems to portend its possible decay. It is more the fact that this judgmental rhetoric is a rhetoric of Indian identity, not simply of morality, that seems to indicate its fragility. Earlier, I argued that it was plausible to hypothesize that the empty center constituted a cultural form that has marked Flathead society for a long time. At that point in the discussion, though, I omitted to call attention to an important distinction between contemporary rhetoric and "traditional" rhetoric; that is, contemporary rhetoric is framed primarily in terms of Indian identity, while traditional rhetoric was framed in terms of simple morality. Thus the rhetorical strategy of the past would be to strip individuals of their standing as morally exemplary persons, whereas the rhetorical strategy of the current age is to strip individuals of their standing as *Indians*.

There is a world of meaningful difference for individuals and for the community in the two versions of the empty center rhetoric. Vestiges of the morality version, as opposed to the identity version, of the rhetoric can be found in the ways that elders applaud and condemn each other: "None of them speak the language the way they were taught"; "She tells too much about our Indian ways to white people"; "He was just waiting for the year after her death to be over so he could dance again"; or "He's really lost because of the deaths in his family." Statements such as these are attempts to indicate some moral failing or some positive moral trait on the part of one of the elders, yet nowhere in these statements is there the implication of not being Indian. In contrast, statements about how half-breeds should not hold wakes, or how most of the younger generation should not be taught the use of the sweatlodge, or how the younger medicine men are only mocking the ways of the real medicine men do indicate a loss of Indianness.

OPPRESSION AND IDENTITY

Writing about French colonialism in Algeria in the 1950s and 1960s, Frantz Fanon raised the important question of the link between identity and oppression. He wrote, "Because it is a systematic negation of the other person and a furious determination to deny the other person all attributes of humanity, colonialism forces the people it dominates to ask themselves the question constantly: 'In reality, who am I?' " (1963: 250). For Fanon, the negation of one's humanity is the key feature of the experience of oppression.

It is tempting to imagine that we can empathetically know the dehumanizing experiences of oppression. Yet Fanon's treatise makes clear that we must investigate each particular manifestation of domination, and its history, if we are to understand the experiences of the dominated. One of the most eloquent and powerful aspects of Fanon's writing is his concrete description of how particular forms of oppression mold the answers that individuals give to the important question, "Who am I?": the victims of nonviolent colonial oppression (or previolent in Fanon's view), the victims of revolutionary violence, and the victims of political occupation during war, for example, are forced to ask, and to answer, the challenge to their identities in different ways.[8]

The historical subjugation of the Flathead people manifests itself differently from the colonial domination of the Algerian people by the French.[9] While the occasionally violent history of Indian-white relations has created a context for contemporary Indians within which the threat of violence hangs palpably, the overt violence of revolution that Fanon documents for the Algerians does not define oppression in the same way for contemporary tribal residents at the Flathead Reservation. And while the subjugation of the Flathead people resembles the colonial domination of the Algerians by the French in its constant challenge to personal and group identity, we must look beyond Fanon's insights to come to terms with the relationship between oppression and identity among the Flathead.

Most important, repressive and monolithic notions of power appear inadequate for understanding many contemporary situations of inequality, especially those in which one group seems to control the material and symbolic resources in a society but in which the use of overt violence to maintain that control is rarely evident. Along these lines, Michel Foucault argues that power cannot be understood as residing in "a massive and primary condition of domination, a binary structure of 'dominators' on one side and 'dominated' on the other" (1980: 142).[10] He argues, instead, for a creative and diffuse, or nonessentialist, notion of power in which the relations of power within a given society are induced by a culture-specific "regime of truth" that determines how the "effects of truth are created within discourses which in themselves are neither true nor false" (1980: 118). To adopt this alternative notion of power and resistance moves us from a predetermined analysis, in this case, of whether Flathead people "believe" what whites imply about them to an investigation of the ways that Flathead people establish an effect of truth, or untruth, about themselves and whites. It shifts focus from the point at which a subject acquiesces to a repressive power, either because of the threat of violence or by ideological control, to the concrete specifics of the epistemological and praxeological grounds on which the struggle for veracity takes place.

In a way, this seems to be the project of Ashis Nandy who, when speculating about British colonialism in India in *The Intimate Enemy,* defined colonialism as "a culture in which the ruled are constantly tempted to fight their rulers within the psychological limits set by the latter" (1988: 3). For Nandy, what is telling is not whether Indians believed or disbelieved, consented to or argued against, agreed with or disagreed with British definitions of them, but the rationality within which the "fight" took place.[11] Another student of India, Bernard S. Cohn, takes on a similar task. From the personal statements of European-educated intellectuals of India, Cohn deduces a shift in how Indians in India think about their history, their traditions, and themselves. He writes,

> Not only have the colonial peoples begun to think of themselves in different terms, not only are they changing the content of their culture, but the way that they think about their culture has changed as well. The Indian intellectuals of Bengal in the 19th century and then the whole Western educated class of Indians in the 20th century have objectified their culture. They in some sense have made it into a "thing"; they can stand back and look at themselves, their ideas, their symbols and culture and see it as an entity. What had previously been embedded in a whole matrix of custom, ritual, religious symbol, a textually transmitted tradition, has now become something different. What had been unconscious now to some extent becomes conscious. (1984: 28–29)

Cohn traces the impetus for the "objectification" of culture in India to the need of the indigenous people to explain themselves to their colonizers. Accordingly, Cohn analyzes the processes of objectification through a case study of what is, perhaps, the clearest example of enforced explanation, the Indian Census. Based on the use of caste, as given in the census, for the validation of claims for benefits and status in political battles starting in the late nineteenth century, Cohn concludes that the census played a significant role in the objectification of Indian culture, especially in creating a consciousness of caste.

Cohn nicely details the history of the Indian Census from the fledgling efforts to simply estimate population figures for tax purposes in the late 1700s through to the "modern" operations of the late 1800s. As thorough as his historical investigation is, however, Cohn's formulation of the apparent shift in how Indians think about themselves and their culture misses its target in important ways. If there has been a shift in India, it is not simply in response to the need of Indians to "explain themselves" to the British. The contact between the Indians of

India and the British, just like the contact between the Flathead Indians and whites, was not some generic contact between two mutually curious groups. In the case of the Flathead people, questions about Indian identity as formulated in the Downs Roll were not the result of some academic's or traveler's interest to which the Flathead Indians might or might not respond. Rather, they were the result of the efforts of a numerically and technologically more powerful group who sought to control, if not to annihilate, the Flathead tribes. Similarly, the questions and answers that constitute the basis of the new "objectivity" that Indians in India bring to themselves and their culture were formulated as part of a system of specific benefits and penalties controlled to a large extent by the British. It is necessary to determine what, in fact, was at stake in the adoption of caste as an element of formal identity in India.

Furthermore, if there has been a shift among Indians in India in their use of formal categories of caste to achieve certain publicly defined benefits, we cannot assume a corresponding shift in the use of caste in other, perhaps less formal, contexts. As this chapter shows, certain elements of the requirements for formal enrollment in the Flathead tribes do appear in more informal contexts in which Indian identity is being negotiated, but there is no one-to-one correspondence between the two realms. In fact, formal enrollment in the Flathead tribes by itself cannot predict whether someone will be considered Indian by others or whether someone will consider him- or herself Indian. The isomorphism that Cohn assumes between the formal use of caste in India and a "consciousness of caste" must instead be investigated directly.

Finally, if there has been a shift in how Indians in India think about their history, their traditions, and themselves, it has not been one that has moved from "unconsciousness" to "consciousness." It is inconceivable for any people, especially in the case of India with its long history of literacy and contact with others, that there existed some pristine, precontact life of unconsciousness for their past, their unique ways, who they are. If we are to understand the effects of the institutionalization of formal definitions of identity that have been put into place by external powers, we cannot simply compare the "objectified" discourses of postcontact life to an assumed "lack" of those discourses during precontact life. We must instead look for the specific relationships among discourses of identity that predated and antedated those historical events.

CONTEMPORARY FLATHEAD INDIAN IDENTITY

In this chapter, I have suggested that there has been a shift in discourses and practices of Indian identity that has been influenced, at least in part, by the advent of federally mandated formal enrollment in 1905. The periodic adoption of exclusive rules of formal group membership by the Flathead Indians is tied to the very real threats of annihilation posed at different times by the U.S. government. Moreover, within forty years of the creation of the Downs Roll, formal group membership began to take place in terms of blood quantum.

Enforced exclusivity and the use of blood quantum in formal enrollment affect the lives of contemporary Flathead people in significant ways. While the correspondence between formal enrollment and "Indianness" is not direct, a shift, much like that described by Cohn in India, is evident. The precontact identities of Flathead individuals seem to have been constructed in moral terms against the nature of the ancestors. Postcontact discourses of individual identity also frame identity in terms of morality vis-à-vis the ways of the ancestors. The difference lies in the fusion of morality with "Indianness" in the latter. "Blood quantum" and the "empty center" are elements of this postcontact discourse that reflect the post–Downs Roll concern with authenticity among the Flathead people.

In "Identity in Mashpee," James Clifford depicts the proceedings of a trial in which the jury was charged with the task of determining "whether the group calling itself the Mashpee Tribe of Massachusetts was in fact an Indian tribe" (1988: 277). Recalling testimonies and histories that seem to alternately reveal and conceal the authenticity of Indian lives in Mashpee, Clifford probes some of the assumptions underlying the legal negotiations of Mashpee identity. Two-thirds of the way into the piece, in a section entitled "Courtroom Notes," Clifford writes,

> Remember not to take what happens here as normal. Notice the abstractness of the rules and rituals, the way life in Mashpee appears in court through an odd refracting and enlarging lens. Mashpee on the stand: nervous, tight, secretive, eager. In the audience: car pools of the faithful, selectmen in three-piece suits and stylish haircuts, young Indians in jewelry, headbands. Mashpee scattered on the courtroom benches, nodding to or looking coolly past one another, sharing private jokes. None of this is admissible evidence.
>
> Earl Mills [a Mashpee witness] pulls his [Indian] necklaces out from under his tie, but too eagerly. The act uncomfortably expresses what the

trial is about: *proving*, making visible and theatrical something subtle, near the skin. (1988: 327)

Clifford's description powerfully captures the charged atmosphere of the federal trial. But his conclusion that it is the legal setting that distorts the picture of Indian lives in Mashpee, that what is happening in the courtroom is not "normal," contrasts sharply with the conclusion that must be drawn from this study of Indian identity at the Flathead Reservation. "Proving, making visible and theatrical something subtle, near the skin" is what Flathead Indian identity in the context of contemporary reservation life is about, in part. The sketches in the opening pages of this chapter bear witness to the profound complexity and personal importance of being Indian at the Flathead Reservation today. To be Indian at the Flathead Reservation is to be on the stand, answering questions posed by outsiders and insiders alike about one's Indian identity in a language that fuses authentic Indian identity, moral worth, and proper affect.

Part I has explored contemporary Flathead Indian identity from a variety of perspectives that have converged to illustrate the emotionally charged context of Indian identity at the Flathead Reservation and some of the historical, political, social, and cultural factors that have produced that context. This illustration is important for understanding depressive experience and depressive disorder among the Flathead for several reasons. Not only does it help to clarify the specifics of "acculturative stress" as a possible cause or predisposing factor for depressive disorder, it also introduces the culture-specific "regime of truth" that links authentic Indian identity to proper sentiment. The Flathead regime of truth, in which moral judgments provide the ultimate basis for positing the truth or falsity of claims, is rooted deeply within a complex of ideas that relate directly to Flathead accounts of depression, including loneliness, pity, compassion, generosity, and responsibility. These terms, and the cultural practices that form and inform them, are the subject of Part II.

Loneliness and Pity

Moving from the charged context of Indian identity to the equally charged context of social responsibility, Part II continues to explore some of the practical and poetic contexts that imbue the Flathead language of depressive-like experience with its specific meanings. The following two chapters pursue via several pathways the continuing translation of loneliness and pity—two related concepts central to the emotional lives of Flathead people. First, the chapters detail the ways that Flathead loneliness and pity are linked in moral discourse and ritual practice to an ideology of belonging through reciprocity and social responsibility. Second, they describe the everyday practices of reciprocity that derive their significance from the morally based ideology of social responsibility underlying Flathead loneliness and pity. Third, they elucidate the meanings of loneliness as disruptions of belonging within that world of meaningful social action.

Chapter 3, "Speaking to the Heart," probes the ideology of Flathead emotions, noting the powerful ties between the language of emotion and culture-specific ideals of the self and social relations. An analysis of a set of Flathead death rituals shows how grief, as the paradigmatic form of loneliness, is ritually transformed into the socially responsible affect of pity. Chapter 3 also explores those relations of compassion and exchange that provide the day-to-day contexts within which the actions of family members, friends, and others are evaluated, and how these contexts are shaped by the economic marginality of the Flathead people on the reservation. Everyday practices of gift giving, visiting, and good manners provide the material with which Flathead individuals display, or fail to display, their pity for others. Chapter 3 shows that loneliness and pity are more than empty symbols; they are key elements structuring interpersonal interactions at the Flathead Reservation.

As the primary idiom of distress in Flathead narratives of depression, loneliness expresses the anguish of finding oneself outside usual or expected relations of compassion and exchange. Chapter 4, "Feeling Bereaved, Feeling Aggrieved, and Feeling Worthless," depicts three qualitatively distinct experiences of being left out of relations of reciprocity. *Feeling bereaved* is loneliness attributable to the death of an important friend or relative. *Feeling aggrieved* is loneliness attributable to undeserved slights by one's family and friends. And *feeling worthless* is loneliness that feels absolute and is attributable to being abandoned by everyone because of one's fundamental unworthiness.

Much as in Part I, Part II documents a dialectical structuring of Flathead lives, by a moral patterning of self and social relations, on the one hand, and by a continuing history of oppression and scarcity, on the other. Without question, the same moral discourse of belonging and social responsibility that undergirds the construction of Flathead Indian identity in narratives of being Indian configures the construction of Flathead emotion in narratives of feeling loneliness. By the same token, however, the moral discourse within which Flathead identity and emotion are both negotiated is shaped by the same set of political and economic forces that seem to threaten the basic moral worth of the Flathead people. Together, chapters 3 and 4 illustrate the cultural embeddedness of loneliness, the key idiom in individual narratives of depressive-like experience and disorder at the Flathead Reservation. Along with Part I, Part II unpacks the rich semantic field of loneliness. In narratives of collective identity, loneliness solidifies a history of loss and betrayal into a rhetoric of Indian identity throughout which rings the lament of the loss of the "real Indians"; in narratives of individual experience, loneliness is a plaintive cry for compassion, for incorporation into networks of caring and exchange, throughout which resounds a lament for the loss of important others. Together, Parts I and II reveal the moral and relational underpinnings of this important idiom of distress and show the sources of its performative force in the construction of Flathead identity and emotion.

CHAPTER THREE

Speaking to the Heart

Sitting in the front office of the Longhouse, Annie and I heard the weeping begin in the back room and knew that Ron's body had been delivered by the mortician. Ron's wife, his mother, and his brothers and sisters had gathered in the community room not long before. As the hearse was seen approaching, one of Ron's sisters had left and returned with her father, whose house was only a few blocks away. After twenty or thirty minutes, the knot of weeping, embracing relatives huddled by the coffin slowly disentangled as individuals moved to sit on the couches facing the casket.

Earlier that day, after we had heard the news of Ron's sudden death from his father-in-law, Annie and I swept and mopped the floor of the large back room and then moved the three well-worn, but ample, couches to the front of the room. Knowing that this wake would call out many supporters, we used all of the folding metal chairs, arranging them in rows with aisles down the middle and sides of the room. The painted portraits of Flathead elders absorbed some of the echo and seemed to ease the loneliness of the empty room as we set out boxes of tissues, bowls of cigarettes, and ashtrays on and around the couches for the grieving family, as well as bowls of cigarettes and ashtrays on chairs around the room for other visitors.

After we had set up the large coffee urns, along with cups, spoons, creamer, and sugar, at the back of the room, our work was done for the time being. Soon, the first shift of volunteer cooks would arrive to take stock of the kitchen equipment and supplies, to estimate numbers of visitors, and to tally lists of needed items for the meals they, and other volunteers, would be preparing four times a day over the period of the wake. Over the next days, most community members would gather at some time or another with Ron's grieving family and with the prayer leaders to sing and pray for the deceased. With prayer and song, family members and community members would protect and ease Ron's passage to the next world. With gifts of food, money, and other kinds of assistance, community members would try to help Ron's family through their grief. With carefully chosen words, the prayer leaders would try to weave the experience of grief and separation into a tapestry of comfort, reconnection, and social responsibility. Together, they would attempt to transform the chaotic spectacle of death into a charter for life.

RON'S WAKE AND BURIAL

By evening a dozen or so visitors were seated randomly around the room. A few sprays of flowers had been delivered and placed on stands on either side of the casket. Three days hence, on the morning of the funeral, Ron's casket would be flanked on both sides by forty or fifty floral arrangements and there would be more visitors than the chairs could accommodate. For now, however, the gathering was small, comprised mainly of family members, close friends of the family, a few others, and two or three prayer leaders. On arrival, most visitors stood and chatted informally with the cooks or with other visitors who were not yet seated and drank a cup of coffee before proceeding to the front of the room. After standing or kneeling in silent prayer before the casket for a time, visitors turned to shake hands with each member of the family, taking care to exclude no one. Visitors with older children soundlessly instructed them to follow suit. Elderly and more traditional visitors also shook hands with each of the other visitors.

Shaking hands with everyone present is an important sign of a traditional gathering in contemporary Flathead life. Like the communal meals and the repetitive prayers and songs of the wakes, it is a powerful convention that marks a shift from the everyday world to ritual time. For most participants, the sight of elders and more traditional members of the community shaking hands with each of the visitors resonates with the authenticity of tradition, and the feel of hands softly clasping evokes visceral memories of other wakes and Indian gatherings. Repetitive acts of shaking hands slows social interactions to a ritual pace. It also ritually enacts the unity of the group, a particularly important element of Flathead death rituals given the threat that death poses to the cohesion of families and the community.

The slow rhythm of the first night of Ron's wake was marked by short periods of murmured prayers and mournful hymns separated by longer periods of informal visiting. The quiet tenor of the gathering was occasionally punctuated by heart-rending expressions of grief. Silent sobs and muffled moans crescendoed when relatives and friends arrived to pay their respects. Every so often, someone, overcome with grief, would cry more loudly. Ron's mother sang a traditional song of grief and loss that resonated with sounds of unbearable pain and evoked tears from most of those who were present. Sung on both the out-breath and the in-breath, the dirge resembled an intense, melodic weeping.

The dangers of death for the group reside, in part, in the loss of a member of the community to death. However, perhaps because of the firm knowledge that there is an afterlife in which loved ones will eventually be reunited, the dangers of death for the community also lie to a great extent in the potential loss of the living to their grief. Grief is known to pull people out of daily life. Witness, for example, the story of the prophet Shining Shirt who received his vision of the coming of the Blackrobes when grieving the loss of his wife. It was told that Shining Shirt "had quite a sorrow; and strayed away mourning about his wife, didn't want to be among the tribe; left the tribe and wandered away. Days and days passed on. He was away on the high mountains on the Rockies somewhere" (Hansen 1947: Appendix 3). Grief is dangerous because it can produce a mournful sense of abandonment, and the resulting tendency to isolation requires the vigilant efforts of others to redress. At the collective level, wakes represent such efforts.

When I left Ron's wake sometime after the midnight meal on the first night, most of the visitors and some members of the family had also left to get some sleep. One prayer leader remained with the family through the night. Disheveled and bleary-eyed, he left around ten the next morning, after conducting prayers at dawn and eating breakfast with those gathered. After a few hours sleep, he would return in the afternoon to resume his vigil with the family. Around the same time, several members of the family had also left to shower and to rest. It would be a short respite. For the prayer leader and for most of the adult members of the family, there would be no more sleep until Ron was buried and the large crowd that would attend the funeral the next day had been fed. By the end of the wake and funeral, many of those present would be ashen with grief compounded by exhaustion.

Until burial, the soul of the deceased is at large and prey to evil spirits. Flathead wakes and funeral practices are designed to protect the soul of the deceased during this dangerous time, but the around-the-clock recitation of prayers and songs is a hardship that requires endurance on the part of family members, prayer leaders, and close friends. Endurance, like shaking hands, is another convention that resonates with tradition by calling forth images of vision quests and the hard work of grandmothers and grandfathers striving to care for their families. Endurance embodies the ability of the ideal self to adjust to circumstances, no matter how difficult. Endurance is a culturally grounded form of discipline whose purpose is not to harden the self so much as to foster an acute awareness of the needs of others, from which springs a sense of pity that motivates caring, "helping" behaviors.

Endurance embodies more, however, than an attribute of an individual, for it also embodies the mutuality of ideal relations. To endure hardship inspires the compassion of others who, like prayer leaders, cooks, or grave diggers, are motivated to help. To give is to put oneself in the position to receive. Endurance on the part of an individual is predicated on relations of reciprocity, on the knowledge that others will come to one's aid. To perform the arduous tasks of the wake is to demonstrate disciplined compassion; it is a ritual rehearsal of "right attitudes." But it is a rehearsal of right attitudes not only on the part of family members and friends who endure for the sake of their loved one but also on the part of prayer leaders and community members who labor to show their compassion and pity for those who are grieving.

Throughout most of the second day of Ron's wake, the pace continued much as it had the night before. Between the more formal periods of prayer and song, visitors refilled coffee cups, went to the rest room, and smoked cigarettes. Visitors often used this informal time to deliver cash or groceries to the cooks, who carefully recorded each gift in a notebook to be given later to the family. Small groups would gather to converse: "Has Ron's father eaten?" "Has his mother slept?" "Who is watching the children?" "Did Joe, Ron's cousin, arrive from Wyoming yet?" And, as at any other time, stories would be told. Out-of-town visitors would be welcomed warmly and the details of their trips eagerly sought. Moving to the front of the room to sit on the couch with Ron's relatives, some visitors attempted to dispense comfort with conversation, commenting, perhaps, on the size of the turnout, who had yet to arrive from out of town, the good quality of the meals, or the beauty and number of flower arrangements that flanked the casket. As additional flower arrangements arrived, family members would get up from their couches to read the attached cards. The periods of visiting would draw to a close, either with the arrival of a new prayer leader or when one or more of the seated visitors began a hymn or set of prayers. Visitors standing at the back of the room would then put out their cigarettes, move back to their seats, and join in the prayers, or step outside the room to continue quiet conversations begun during the break.

Grief is not the only dangerous emotion associated with death. It is not uncommon for family members, and sometimes others, to suspect that death has been "sent" by the ill will of others.[1] Others may interpret the death as evidence that the deceased or a member of the family had been abusing their medicine power, their *sumeš*. In the case of a suicide or a suspected suicide, many will speculate that the action was "justifiable" in response to ill treatment by another family member. Explicable as the result of jealousy, resentment, or corruption, death threatens to expose the dark underside of social relations and to rip the veil of respect that usually conceals the fissures and cleavages of community life. To work this underlying tension into a creative force to heal the looming possibility of permanent rifts between families in the community is one of the main purposes of the wake. Both the informal talk of the visitors and the persuasive preaching of the prayer leaders are directed toward this unstated task.

"*Qeqs čawm*. Let's pray." So spoke Dave, one of the more respected prayer leaders in the community. It was late afternoon and the

chairs were beginning to fill up. Dave had entered quietly not long before and had sat down in one of the chairs in the back of the room to
pray for the right words to speak to the grieving family. Having received inspiration, he moved to the front of the room, stood facing the
casket briefly, turned to face the family, and called for prayers to
begin. He began praying aloud in Salish, intoning the first half of the
Our Father. Many of those present ruffled through their hymn books
to the back pages to find a phonetic rendering of the prayer in Salish,
in order to respond with the second half. After ten Hail Marys in Salish, Dave repeated the set of prayers in English, again intoning the first
half of each prayer and receiving the second half in response from
those congregated. After announcing a page number in the hymn
book, Dave led the group through a long, sad funeral hymn in Salish.
Pockets of bilingual speakers sang with more confidence while some
sections of the audience stood in embarrassed silence, unable to follow
the printed phonetic cues. Most, however, sang along with a modicum
of facility that derived not from a thorough understanding of the
words but from having heard the songs so often.

    Repetitive prayer and song lend an aura of sacredness and tradi-
tion to the wake as powerful conventional instruments of passage to
ritual and Indian time.[2] Songs, in particular, evoke recollections of
uncles leading hymns at other wakes, grandmothers singing to com-
bat their loneliness or fatigue as they worked, elders and middle-
aged men at the yearly Jump Dance singing songs to keep everyone healthy throughout the new year, the Indian Choir singing at
Christmas mass, drum groups accompanying the dancers at powwows, and medicine men in the sweatlodge helping to relieve someone's suffering.[3]
    Ritual songs draw on the power of the phonic, the locus of sen-
sory authority in Flathead life. It is the ears, not the eyes, that receive the highest truths. The songs of the wakes, traditional peti-
tions for compassionate treatment of the deceased, possess an efficacy
much like the words of the prayer leaders.[4]

Breaking the silence that followed the ending of the hymn, Dave
spoke to the family and to the people convened behind them. Empha-
sizing the importance of prayer and faith, he encouraged the family to
rely on God. For the others, his message was to extend themselves to
help relatives and friends in these and other hard times. Elaborating on

his own efforts to help others, he exhorted his listeners to transcend their selfishness and their preoccupations with their own busy lives. He reminded the audience of the loss of old ways and lamented the fact that they had not listened better to their elders. The teachings of their elders were good and right. The elders had known the importance of prayer and the importance of helping one another. The elders had always found time to help one another and to visit. A wake, Dave continued, is the time to remember the elders and others who have passed on before this and to grieve their absence anew. Dave admonished the visitors to show their respect to the grieving family by getting up to pray and saying a few words. He reminded those present that prayer leaders ought not to talk about any topic that will increase the pain of the grieving family.[5]

Speaking to the hearts of those who have gathered, prayer leaders at the wakes discipline members of the congregation with powerful words, linking personal affect to public morality. The authority of the words of the prayer leaders at the wakes derives, in part, from the power of speaking/listening as a culturally grounded form of discipline. Among the Flathead, there are many kinds of talk—everyday conversation, teasing, storytelling, self-castigation, prayer, and preaching—each of which possesses a certain force. As the quintessential form of discipline, the preaching of prayer leaders reinforces a set of binary opposites that unite meaning and authority, informing images of the ideal self and its relations to others. Salish is privileged over English; Indian over white; the past over the present; the spiritual over the mundane; elders over youth; male over female; discipline over disorder; life over death; the community over the individual; pity over grief and anger; and connection over separation. Speaking to the hearts of those who have gathered, prayer leaders attempt through a persuasive set of metonymic equations to transform the grief, anger, and fear of the members of the congregations into pity, compassion, and social responsibility.

During the last part of Dave's talk, the scent of hot food spread through the room and the sound of tables being set up and of dishes being laid out grew more difficult to ignore. Looking to the back of the room, Dave caught a signal from one of the cooks that the evening meal was ready to be served. Praising the efforts of the cooks and asking for special blessings for the bereaved and for travelers still en route,

Dave finished his speech with grace and invited everyone to join in the meal. Throughout the wake, meals were served four times a day: at dawn, at noon, at dinnertime, and at midnight. At previous meals, tables had been set with paper plates, plastic silverware, napkins, and bowls of food. Now, however, the crowd had become too large, and the meal was being served buffet style. As at any gathering, elders were served first. Members of Ron's immediate family tended to eat last, out of respect for their visitors; and some, whose appetites had been stolen by grief, did not eat at all.

The Rosary had been scheduled for that night, and from after dinner until Father Reinhard arrived a few hours later, the crowd grew in size to almost the dimensions it would reach the next morning for the funeral mass and burial. While arriving community members looked for a place to sit or stand, the prayer leaders led the congregation in nearly continual prayer and song, breaking for only five or ten minutes at a time. By the time Father Reinhard appeared at the front of the room to begin the recitation of the Rosary, the large room was filled. In contrast to other parts of the wake, a noticeable number of white friends, neighbors, and co-workers of the family attended the Rosary, to add their voices to the praying that evening.[6]

After the Rosary, the gathering broke up. Many left and would not return until the next morning. Others simply left to arrange things at home before returning later. And some just left briefly to walk outdoors to clear their heads of the heat and smoke of the community room. After an hour or so, the prayer leaders resumed their duties. As before the Rosary, prayer and song were nearly incessant. Younger prayer leaders also spoke to the crowd this evening. Although they repeated the same themes, their talks were less directive and more confessional than those of the older preachers. Their talks were like lugubrious mea culpa laments that proclaimed the speakers' grief over the pain they had caused their elders by being disobedient and the tragic results of an entire generation's inattentiveness.

In the culturally grounded disciplinary form of speaking/listening, speakers are entitled to address the gathering for extended periods and to expect that their listeners will quietly attend to their words. For the most part, it is not proper for those who are generally in the role of listener to take the role of speaker. An exception is when potential preachers of the future, men in their late thirties and early forties, are not only allowed but encouraged to speak in public settings. In contrast to the preaching of full-fledged prayer leaders, when younger prayer leaders speak publicly, it is to proclaim their own unworthiness and to reveal their pain at the memory of their disobedience. The self-excoriation and self-castigation of these mea culpa laments represent another side of the authority of speaking. Not quite powerful enough to actually preach to the congregation, younger prayer leaders use this other form of public speaking to reassert the teachings of their elders and to enact their increasing status as community leaders.

Individual expressions of grief were infrequent now, as the evening hours of the final night of Ron's wake wore on and as the tempo of the periods of prayer and song increased. Most members of the family seemed less wracked by grief than exhausted. Yet none left after the midnight meal, even though most of the visitors had left once again. Throughout the final night, Ron's family stood vigil over his body. Thirty or forty friends and several prayer leaders kept watch with them, as the prayer leader who had been asked by the family to say Morning Prayers slept for a few hours in his car. At dawn, during Morning Prayers, members of the family said their final good-byes to Ron. At perhaps the most intensely desolate time of the entire wake, the prayer leader urged the family, and everyone present, to express their grief, to spill their tears not only for Ron but for all who have passed away.

In a booklet on wakes, funerals, and feast days prepared by the Culture Committee, the vital importance of expressing one's grief, especially at Morning Prayers, is highlighted. The text states,

> The tears that are shed are a gift from God, a gift which is set aside for times such as this. If you hold back your tears, this may cause a sickness. By releasing your tears, this relieves your heart. An example of this: a young lady lost her baby during the month of October, so she became very depressed as each October came about. Several years later, during October, this young lady, in her depressing times, died in a car accident. During her funeral, her mother was rushed to the hospital with a heart attack. She said that she was trying to be strong for the rest of the family. Later that day she had another heart attack and went into a coma and died the next day.

After the care of the dead, the facilitation of the expression of grief is the most important of the explicit tasks of the wakes. The undisputed reality that death begets death through unexpressed grief energizes the ritual messages of the wake with a vitality born of the urgency to preserve lives.

After breakfast, the final morning of Ron's wake was filled with continual prayer and song of a quickening pace that heralded the fast-approaching culmination of the wake—Ron's burial. The size of the gathering grew until the time of the final Rosary, conducted this time not by the priest but by a prayer leader. After the Rosary, a choir gathered to sing mournful Salish hymns as the nearly two hundred visitors lined up to say a final word to the deceased and to shake hands with the immediate family. Close friends hugged the weeping family members. With the exception of children and a few others, everyone was in tears. When everyone had gone through the line, the pallbearers gathered together, carried the casket to the waiting hearse, and started the procession of cars to the church for the funeral mass.

After mass, the members of the congregation returned to their cars to start the procession to the cemetery. Tribal and town police blocked off the route from the church to the cemetery and directed the long line of traffic. At the cemetery, visitors walked slowly around headstones bearing the names of their ancestors to where Ron's family had gathered around Ron's grave site.[7] When the crowd assembled, the prayer leader and the priest blessed the site, and the casket was lowered into the ground. In a special tribute to Ron, a local drum group sang a final song in farewell. All present, starting with the priest, the prayer leader, and the family, then filed past the grave and threw a handful of dirt from the accumulated piles onto the casket. When all the visitors had gone through the line, young men picked up shovels and two at a time took turns filling the grave. When Ron's grave was completely filled, the mood lightened and the crowd moved to reconvene for a final meal at the Longhouse.

RON'S MEMORIAL FEAST AND GIVE-AWAY

Wakes mark the first link in a chain of activities designed to help both the deceased and the bereaved. The chain culminates for more traditional families like Ron's in a memorial feast and give-away. The length of time between the wake and the memorial feast varies tremendously. In some instances, the memorial feast and associated give-away are combined with the final meal after the burial. Some families hold the give-away within days after the burial and then sponsor a feast at a later date. In other cases, the memorial feast and give-away take place together up to eighteen months later, although generally within a year, after the family has had time to collect the necessary resources. For still others, the memorial feast becomes an annual event in memory of the deceased.

Preparations for a combined give-away and memorial feast for Ron began shortly after his burial. His possessions were cleared out of his house and stored at the home of one of his wife's relatives, many bundled with tags indicating to whom they should be given on the day of the give-away. His relatives also began saving money to sponsor the memorial feast that would be held nearly fourteen months after his death. In the spring, a few months before the feast, efforts began to gather the foods that play such an important part in any traditional gathering. Male relatives of Ron's hunted for wild meat—deer and elk but sometimes moose—that the women would boil for the feast. As the date drew closer, a member of the community donated a deer he had recently shot, and an officer of the Tribal Fish and Game Department delivered a confiscated elk that had been shot illegally. Women cut up the meat and took day trips to gather other traditional foods: bitterroot, tree moss, and huckleberries. In the days preceding the feast, volunteers were enlisted to cook the essential fry bread. Other volunteers baked pies or offered to bring salads and soups. Relatives began bringing cartons of apples and oranges and cans of vegetables.

Both traditionally and during my stay at the reservation, memorial feasts and give-aways were held at the home of the deceased. The primary purpose of the memorial feast was to erase the traces of the material life of the deceased from the earth so that the deceased would not keep returning to the site of his or her daily life. Until this was done, the deceased would be prevented from resting easily in the afterlife and members of his family would continue to be bothered by his or her ghostly presence. Children attending the feast are instructed to walk around the area to cover the tracks of the deceased, and his or her possessions are given away. In addition to discouraging the deceased from returning to earth, his or her possessions are also dispersed so that the bereaved do not have to endure the constant daily reminders of loss and loneliness that these material objects evoke. This explains, in part, why the possessions of the deceased are given away to friends and distant relatives and only rarely to family members themselves.[8]

On the day of Ron's memorial feast, visitors started arriving in the morning. Some helped with the preparations, but most visited among themselves after greeting everyone. Around midday, the meal that had been prepared by Ron's female relatives was served by Ron's male relatives, but not until a prayer giving thanks for the food had been offered.[9] As visitors sat on the ground and ate their meals, the servers continued to fill visitors' plates until they were overflowing. Fresh fruit, canned goods, and additional plates of food were placed in front of the visitors. It is incumbent on those present to take all the food that has been prepared. Far from being thought of as greedy, visitors would be considered socially remiss if they were to refuse the food.

Customs and an ideology of reciprocity undergird Flathead practices of the give-away and memorial feast. As March Mauss (1967) so eloquently expressed, reciprocity entails not only the obligation to give but also the obligation to receive. By receiving food and material reminders of the deceased, visitors at the feast and give-away sanction the efforts of the family of the deceased to reassert its normal place in the community by resuming its role as "giver," an ideal status that carries at once moral, economic, political, religious, and aesthetic meanings.

The meal came to an end after two or three hours when Ron's belongings were brought to the center of the group by family members and laid on a blanket. Prayers were said and various prayer leaders and speakers stood to deliver a talk. As at the wake, some of the talks were lengthy. Some delivered their talks in Salish and others in English. Most often, if the speaker spoke in Salish, he repeated his or her words later in English. After the speeches, one of the prayer leaders, chosen by the family, started the give-away portion of the memorial. The prayer leader exhibited the last outfit of clothing worn by the deceased and gave it to Ron's mother. It was a time of quiet grief, and many of those assembled cried as the articles of clothing were being shown.

According to local wisdom, grief must be expressed in order to avoid sickness and possibly death. Grief cannot be allowed to continue indefinitely, however. Not only will excessive grief detain the deceased from resting easily in the next world but it will also separate the mourners from their community.[10]

The memorial feast and give-away mark the formal end to the

period of mourning. In their practice, grief is contained and brought to closure.

Before distributing the remaining possessions, the prayer leader chosen by Ron's family said a few words about the meaning of receiving one or more of the possessions of the deceased, stressing that receivers are to keep Ron and his family in their hearts and prayers as the object is used. The prayer leader then lifted each object (a bundle of clothes, a suitcase, a piece of beadwork, some pots and pans, a framed picture), described it, and announced the name of the person Ron's family had selected to receive it. Members of the family then took each object to its new owner. Visitors facilitated the process by raising their hands or discreetly nodding toward where the recipient was sitting.

The gathering broke up slowly. Visitors gathered their containers of food and whatever they may have received at the give-away and packed everything in their cars. Those visitors who did not have cars searched for a ride home. After shaking hands with each member of Ron's family, visitors took their leave, bringing the feast and give-away to a close with the same ritual hand-shaking that demonstrated the unity of the group at the start of the wake.

THE RITUAL CONSTRUCTION OF BELONGING

Death rituals are, arguably, the most important communal ceremonies of contemporary Flathead Indian life. While the annual Bitterroot Feast, the New Year's Jump Dance, the yearly pilgrimage to the St. Mary's Mission in the Bitterroot Valley, and even the semiannual visits to the Medicine Tree reflect and organize important cultural values, none consistently attracts sizable numbers of participants. Indeed, there are many Flathead people, especially among the younger generations, who have never been to any of them. It is, instead, death's descent that enlivens the energies and emotions of the community. And it is, in part, through the ritual performances of the wakes, funerals, and memorial feasts that the Flathead Indians learn to discipline their hearts.

In what is perhaps the most ethnographically compelling chapter of her book on discourses of identity in Japan, Dorinne K. Kondo describes the rigors of an "ethics retreat" that she attended as an employee/anthropologist of a bakery in Japan (1990). Set apart from the everyday world, the retreat "articulated a powerful, vivid doctrine of

selfhood" that elaborated culture-specific ideals of the self, relations
between self and other, and methods for creating better selves (1990:
77). Through a set of activities that combined rigid, at times almost coercive, discipline and doctrinal instruction that drew on wider cultural
meanings and authorities, the ethics retreat asserted and sought to reinforce in the participants a particular view of social relations in which
individuals were willingly and cheerfully sensitive to the needs of others and in which work relations were modeled after filial relations.

Like the Japanese ethics retreat, Flathead death rituals can be understood and analyzed as a site for the disciplined production of ideal
selves. At first sight, the comparison may seem strained. After all, the
ethics retreat attended by Kondo was "in the business" of rationally
transforming selves, whereas Flathead death rituals seem to be an
arena for the unfettered expression of grief, a space for the communication of "natural" emotions. Without denying the true pathos of Flathead wakes, funerals, and memorial feasts, it is important to recall
Stanley J. Tambiah's insightful analysis of formalism in ritual, in which
he asserts that formalism and convention enable a process of distanc-
ing, that is, a separation of "the private emotions of the actors from
their commitment to a public morality" (1985b: 133). In Tambiah's
terms, ritual, including death ritual, "is not a 'free expression of emotions' but a disciplined rehearsal of 'right attitudes'" (1985b: 133–
134).

If Flathead death rituals are imagined as the disciplined rehearsal of
right attitudes, Kondo's analysis of a Japanese ethics retreat becomes
relevant.[11] As in the retreat, the proceedings of Flathead death rituals
draw on culturally grounded practices of discipline and transformation
to articulate powerful images of the ideal self and its relations to others
in the attempt to produce better selves. As at the ethics retreat, a particular vision of the individual in the world is asserted at the wakes, funerals, and memorial feasts of the Flathead people. Most striking, Flathead death rituals assert a vision of the individual in the world in
which the painful emotions of grief, loneliness, and pity are constructed as natural motivators for social responsibility.

Flathead death rituals draw on culturally grounded conventions and
disciplines to transform the dangerous emotions of grief, fear, and
anger—emotions that threaten to take individuals from the living community through self-imposed isolation, sickness, or death—into proper
emotions of compassion and gratitude—emotions that bind individuals
to the group. Repetitive prayer and song wreathe tradition and sacred-

ness around the ritually communicated messages of ideal selves and ideal social relations. The unifying rituals of hand-shaking and commensality enact a sense of community. Ritual endurance softens the hearts of those who have gathered, making them sensitive to the needs of others and making them feel pity for each other. The preaching of the prayer leaders shapes pity into social responsibility, into an obligation for each member of the community to assist and support the others. Ritual acts of exchange, including the structural reciprocity of prayer recitation, the give-and-take of foods throughout the set of rituals, and the give-away, construct images of ideal social relations as based in reciprocal exchange. Together, the elements of the wake construct painful emotions of grief and fear of loneliness as the natural motivators for mature affect and responsible behavior. Flathead wakes, funerals, and feasts ritually rehearse a sentient awareness of human interconnectedness, obedience to traditional ways, compassion and pity for others, generosity, uncomplaining endurance, and gratitude. They help the participants to discipline their hearts, by transforming their sadness into compassion and by converting their fear of loneliness into pity.

By describing the ideal self as embedded within relations of reciprocal exchange that are fostered in part by a fear of loneliness and feelings of pity, death rituals assert the paramount importance of belonging for the Flathead people. As the opposite of belonging, the meaning of loneliness/depression cannot be understood apart from an understanding of what it means to be embedded in relations of compassion and exchange. Moreover, the embeddedness of the individual in relations of reciprocity implies that the most important dimensions of loneliness/depression are constructed in the realm of social interaction. Only through an examination of the behavioral dimensions of pity, the everyday enactments of what it means to belong among family and friends, can we begin to grasp the experiential realities of loneliness in the lives of contemporary Indian residents of the Flathead Reservation.

FRIENDS AND FAMILY

The ideology of loneliness and pity in Flathead wakes and feasts constitutes all community members as deserving of pity and the fruits of social responsibility. Although the community does gather periodically to support one another, in day-to-day practice persons engage in relations of compassion and exchange within a far more circumscribed social network. For the most part, these networks are defined first by family relations and then by friends.

Although the importance of the family in the Flathead way of life cannot be overestimated, friendship also holds considerable cachet. People generally have networks of friendship that extend beyond the boundaries of the reservation into the Indian communities of other reservations. Flathead people frequently take advantage of the summer weather to visit friends, or "partners" as they are often known, at other reservations. Visits with partners often coincide with powwow celebrations.[12] These long-distance friendships can extend over generations, with individuals continuing to visit their parents' or grandparents' partners and their descendants. Individuals and families look forward to visits from these distant friends and plan for the kinds of gifts they want to give to their visitors, clothing and cash being preferred.[13]

People also regularly visit local friends, usually for a few hours in the evening or on the weekend but sometimes spending the night or camping together. Gift giving is evident in these local friendships, too. A young man will buy a pack or two of cigarettes on his way over to visit his friend; two middle-aged women who have been friends throughout their childbearing years will take turns buying the beers on their night out together; a young woman will buy a box of disposable diapers for her friend's baby when she is shopping for groceries; an older man will give twenty dollars to his friend who is leaving on a trip.

In some ways, the distinction between family and friends is an artificial one. On the one hand, one's friends are very often one's relatives. On the other hand, as it is commonly reported, one can easily find some evidence of being related, either by blood or by marriage, to almost anyone else at the reservation. In other words, friends and family are not easily separable categories in the lived experience of Flathead life, nor does there seem to be much interest in doing so. Thus, for example, when people tell stories about their childhood escapades they will often use the words "cousins," "friends," or "buddies" interchangeably. Similarly, when a woman was telling me about her son-in-law, she reported how he had been a friend of a man known for his occasionally obnoxious ways. Another woman then chimed in, saying that you couldn't hold anything against the son-in-law because he had no choice in the friendship since "they were cousins."

The values and practices of friendship reinforce the importance of family in the Flathead way of life. Not only are one's friends usually one's relatives and the friends of one's relatives treated as one's own friends, but the entire practice of friendship is modeled after an ideal of family relations, both in terms of gift exchange and affection. Moreover, friendship is understood as secondary to family, and its primary importance is seen as confined to those who, through misfortune, do not have a large family. Pity is extended to those unfortunates who must rely on friendships for what a family usually provides because there is a sense that friendship can never fully compensate for the lack of family.

Affectively, what is meant by family is a much wider range of relatives than the simple nuclear family. Ideally, family encompasses all those people to whom one can trace relatedness, whether by descent or marriage. Again ideally, one should be able to recognize and name all of one's relatives. At the level of practice, family usually includes any living great-grandparents and their siblings and spouses, grandparents and their siblings and spouses, parents and their siblings and spouses, and one's own siblings and their spouses. Family also includes the children of any of these people, the family members of one's spouse, and the spouses and children of one's own children, grandchildren, and great-grandchildren.[14]

Obviously, this kind of kinship reckoning can result in very large families, and indeed this was often the case. One woman I knew was able to claim nearly seventy grandchildren and great-grandchildren. In contrast, another woman I knew had had no children and had come from a small family to start with. As a consequence, she was in a very pitiful situation, being able to count only one distant relative, a grandchild of one of her deceased siblings. Various people also expressed pity for my son because he had no siblings and very few cousins. They also marveled that my parents, even though they had had six children, only had three grandchildren. In my experiences at the reservation, children were uniformly welcomed additions to the family, and special compassion was reserved for those who were barren.

At the level of affect and idealization, family consists of this network of grandparents, aunties, uncles, parents, siblings, cousins, spouses, children, nieces and nephews, and grandchildren. At the level of daily instrumental action, family tends to be a slightly smaller group and is often as much a function of close residence as of close relatedness. Ideally, family members live together or in close proximity to one another. In reality, however, there were very few extended families that were able to live in the kind of close proximity that is desirable, and even in those few cases some family members were living elsewhere. In most of these cases, the familial complex of households was located on original allotments that had been retained since the early part of this century. Given the history of landownership at the reservation, in which most Indians lost their original allotments through economic need, the aggregation of households remains an unrealizable goal for most extended families. Nonetheless, many families have been able to secure households within walking distance from one another. More important, however, many Flathead families have managed to maintain close ties, despite the inaccessibility of closely aggregated housing, through a set of residence practices that are both fluid and multigenerational. The following sketches illustrate the fluidity of household composition.

Mel is a young woman in her early thirties who was raised for the first years of her life with her parents but who then spent the remaining years of her childhood alternating between the residences of her maternal and paternal grandparents. For the last six years or so, she has lived in a three-bedroom house that used to belong to her older sister. Before that she had lived in two different trailers with her husband and child. Her husband is absent for most of the spring, summer, and fall months in conjunction with his job as a firefighter but is around during short breaks and through the winter. Mel lives with her eight-year-old daughter, who has been with Mel since birth. A fourteen-year-old niece, Mel's older sister's child from her first marriage, also resides there. This niece has lived with Mel off and on through childhood but has also lived with the mother, the father, and a grandparent at different times. A ten-year-old nephew, the son of Mel's husband's sister, has also lived in the household for the past year. Mel is surrounded by the rural residences of two paternal uncles, a paternal aunt, her paternal grandmother, and a maternal great-uncle.

Dennis is a single man who lives in a large two-bedroom trailer that is located in a complex that also contains three other households belonging to family members of his generation. Although he has no children of his own, his house is nearly always enlivened with the excited voices and tumbling bodies of his grandnephews and nieces, some of whom live with him full time over the summer months.

Jean is a married woman in her sixties who began her adult life in the home of her first husband's parents but who now lives in a two-bedroom house with her second husband and their ten-year-old grandson. The grandson has lived with them since he was a few years old. Jean's mother and several of her siblings and their families live within a few blocks of each other only a few streets away from Jean's home.

Paul is an older man, in his eighties, who lives with his elderly wife and their six-year-old granddaughter, whom they have raised since she was born. His sons' residences abut his property, and his house is usually filled with the families of his children and grandchildren.

Rachel is an older woman who lives with a young woman and her infant son. Rachel refers to the young woman, who is in fact the daughter of one of her sons, as her youngest daughter. Rachel raised the woman from childhood and has raised several other grandchildren as well, at one point simultaneously breast-feeding both a son and a grandson. Many of her children live in other towns, but a daughter lives close by and other grandchildren often visit after school.

As these cases illustrate, household composition varies over time, with young people moving in and out of the households of middle-aged and older adults. Young people of marrying age are especially mobile, living, for example, for a few months in a trailer, then moving back to one parent's household for half a year, then maybe over to an aunt's or grandmother's house for a month, and then back into an apartment of their own. Younger children are often shifted from household to household as well. Nieces, nephews, and grandchildren are often raised by their aunts, uncles, or grandparents for periods extending from a few months to all of their childhood. This is a practice that has been in existence for generations and is reinforced in contemporary Indian life by the explicitly preferred practice of placing children in need of foster care in the home of a relative.

The importance of the family in Flathead life is couched primarily in terms of affection. It is the affection of family members that provides the safeguard against the worst fate that can befall a person—being alone. Children are welcomed because they are a guarantee against loneliness, because they ensure that the parent(s) will never be truly lonely again. Parents are typically loath to let their children be away from them for long periods, at camp, for example, because they say that both the child and they, themselves, will get too lonely. Still, if the child will be accompanied by a family member, someone who can prevent the child from feeling lonesome, he or she will be allowed to go. I knew of parents who would sometimes let a child stay home from school if the child complained of being lonely there.

The tenor of parent-child relations is gentle and permissive for the first decade of the child's life. One elder suggested to me in an interview that if children are not treated well, they can develop a feeling of not being "cared for" that can continue through their lives, with tragic results. As in the example of allowing a child to be absent from school because of loneliness, parents try to minimize those situations in which the child might feel lonely or as if no one cared for him or her. Other examples include not forcing a child to eat food that he or she does not want or, conversely, letting a child eat a bag of chips for dinner instead of a bona fide meal. Similarly, bedtimes are loosely enforced and the entire household may end up falling asleep in the living room in front of the television set. In fact, children often share their parents' bed through age ten or so, gradually sleeping more and more in their own beds. Sleeping together is not instigated only by the child, however, for it is often the parent who brings the child into his or her bed when he or she is feeling especially lonely.[15]

Parent-child interactions in later childhood continue to be characterized by a gentle and permissive style but begin to be infused with elements of discipline as well. Younger children are treated in accordance with their inherent inability to understand the sentiments and needs of others. They are seen as selfish but blameless in this selfishness because of the lack of understanding that is part and parcel of childhood. Older children are expected to begin to enter into the world of "caring for others," the world of reciprocal obligations that characterizes the adult lives of the Flathead Indians. Preadolescents enter into this world and show that they can care for others primarily through obedience to their elders.

The parent-child bond, ideally, persists as a strong and important bond throughout the life span and continues to be characterized by relations of affection and obedience, with adults obeying their parents just as they did in late childhood.[16] The mother-son relationship appears to be particularly close. Traditionally, sons brought their wives to live in the homes of their parents. Today, this is no longer a common practice, but unmarried sons often continue to reside with and take care of their elderly parents. At communal gatherings in which the past is recalled and lamented, it is usually the men who express their grief in brief and tearful recollections of their mothers or grand-mothers.

Profound grief, like that which accompanies the death of a parent, is expressed at the passing of one's grandparents as well, especially by the substantial number of Flathead people who were raised by their grandparents. A large subgroup of the Indian population, if not the majority, seem to have spent a significant part of their childhoods in their grandparents' home(s). Even if one was not raised by one's grandparents, the loss of grandparents is felt sharply because of the special closeness between grandparents and their grandchildren.

The loss of one's parents and grandparents is terrible and pitiable. I have heard adult men and women talk about being orphaned in a way that made it clear that they were talking about losing their parents or grandparents after they were adults. The loss of one's parents or grand-parents in adulthood is felt as keenly, if not more keenly, than in one's childhood. In a not too diluted way, though, the deaths of any of one's circle of kin are seen similarly. The loss of a family member is almost always difficult, no matter how distant the relationship. This emphasis on depth of grief for all family members is merely another facet of the importance of family in the Flathead way of life. To lose a family member is to come face-to-face with the possibility of being alone, the possibility of having no one to care for you.

PITY IN PRACTICE

Family relations are characterized by a reciprocal relationship of "car-ing for" and "being cared for," a concept that communicates both af-fective and instrumental interaction. So far, I have concentrated on the strictly affective meanings of family relationships. To leave the discus-sion at this level, however, would be to violate the lived reality of the Flathead way of life, since family also means a group that shares mate-rial resources and skills. "Pitiful" is a term that is often used to de-scribe those individuals who because of misfortune are left with little or no family. It can also carry the connotation that someone is materi-ally poor. For the most part, the two conditions, material poverty and lack of family, are seen as inextricably related.

While in the field, I noted many examples of family members shar-ing material wealth and skills under the rubric of gift giving: an uncle who regularly paid his niece's electric bill; a man who came over to change the tires on his cousin's car; a niece who regularly brought cigarettes to her aunt; a daughter who gave rides to her elderly mother or who spent the afternoon cleaning her father's house; a son-in-law who regularly doled out cash to his mother-in-law; an adult son who brought over to his mother's home a large share of the meat from his latest hunting trip; a mother who sent "emergency" funds, on a regular basis, to a daughter living off the reservation; and the multiple end points of the "underground" distribution of the free commodity foods received by some low-income families.

The ubiquity of such incidents gave me a concrete understanding of the reality of familial sharing and helped me to grasp that relations of reciprocity fit into a constellation of other practices. For example, many Flathead people appear, and at times profess themselves to be, uninterested in saving for the future. For the most part, members of the Indian community trust the future, and their family group, to provide in the event of need. In fact, saving is often seen in a negative light and can be characterized as hoarding. In a story told by an elder of the tribes, a woman, long deceased now, is held up as an example to mock the tendency to hoard. The woman is painted in a ludicrous light for routinely packing her belongings on her horse to take with her whenever she left home, even for short visits. In storytelling about whites, some younger Indians will ridicule whites for being so attached to material goods that they jeopardize family bonds.

The ideology and practices of pity/generosity are buttressed by their functionality within an economic system that promises security to very few. When I first arrived at the reservation, I was often given informal estimates of the unemployment rate that went as high as 80 percent. More conservative estimates placed unemployment at around 50 percent. While the precision of such estimates is open to question, it was evident to me that the rates of unemployment and underemployment were extraordinarily high. Yet by the same token, homelessness and hunger were unknown in the Indian community while I was there.

In part, the direst consequences of poverty were erased because of the existence of federal, state, and tribal programs supplying basic necessities for those individuals and families who are unable to find work, through lack of opportunity or training. Housing is made available through several programs. A rent subsidy program, funded by the federal government and administered by the tribes, requires recipients to pay a certain percentage of their income for rent, in some cases merely a token amount, with the remainder paid by the government. A homesite program provides actual homes, located either in congregated areas or on individual tribally owned land tracts in the country-side.[17] Some Flathead tribal members have secured subsidized loans to build homes on their own property. Finally, there are clustered one-bedroom units that are allocated for elderly Indians. Waiting lists for these various forms of housing aid tend to be long, but relatives usually pick up the slack, providing living space either in their own homes or in a trailer or an old house to which they have access.

Similar kinds of programs exist for the provision of food. Like all residents of Montana, low-income residents of the Flathead Reservation are eligible for food stamps. They can opt, instead, to receive a monthly distribution of surplus commodity foods. Commodities generally include canned meats and fish, canned fruits and vegetables, flour, honey, sugar, lard, cheese, and powdered milk. Individuals and families are allowed a certain number of items in the various categories of foods and "shop" once a month in the commodity storehouse. Although commodity foods are sometimes of lesser quality than store-bought foods, they remain an attractive option for reservation residents because they are easy to distribute among relatives and friends. Infants and expectant mothers are also eligible for Women, Infants, and Children (WIC) assistance.

Poorer Indians can also be eligible for various other kinds of aid, including fuel assistance for the winter months, tribally administered General Assistance (GA) for cash during times of unemployment, and the state-administered Aid to Families with Dependent Children (AFDC). Elderly Indians might also receive assistance with meals and house-cleaning or for a unique situation, for example, having a storage shed built. Finally, although not a routine procedure, tribal members in need of emergency aid can petition the tribal council for funds.

While these programs are not unimportant in providing an economic safety net for those who are without resources, there can be no doubt that the pooling of resources within the family is primary for most Flathead people. While nearly every family I knew included at least one person who was eligible for and receiving some sort of assistance, and that assistance contributed to the economic functioning of the family in significant ways, I also encountered very few families in which there was no one who received income from some form of wage labor, whether year-round or seasonal.[18]

Year-round full-time employment opportunities for Indians at the reservation are limited. Most of the available positions are offered by the tribal government and the federal government, most often with the

BIA or the IHS. Employment opportunities for Indians have improved in recent years, since these agencies now have preferential hiring policies for tribal members. An assortment of jobs are available, ranging from secretary, file clerk, post and pole worker, and circuit board assembler to alcohol counselor, Community Health Representative (CHR), language instructor, game warden, and tribal court judge. Jobs with the tribal government are considered "good jobs" that offer decent salaries and benefits and, frequently, opportunities for training and travel. Jobs with the BIA and other federal agencies also offer reasonable benefits and opportunities but also often require relocation, an unpalatable prospect for many residents of the reservation. There are probably only about four hundred such positions, of which approximately three-fourths are held by tribal members.

Outside of these agency jobs, year-round positions for Flathead people are scarce. Rural areas in the United States, in general, tend to offer fewer employment opportunities than industrial and urban areas, and Indian residents are less likely to secure positions than the non-Indian residents of the reservation. In some cases, the hiring practices of white employers have been overtly racist. Of greater significance, however, is the institutionalized racism inherent in the separation of Indians and whites in the community. The concentration of wealth and income-producing resources in the hands of the latter creates a hiring bias in favor of white job-seekers who find employment more readily as the kin, friends, and neighbors of white employers. The few job opportunities that exist in this rural area, such as linemen for the power company, workers in lumber mills, and clerks and waitresses in local stores and restaurants, are difficult for Indians to secure.

Outside of the relatively few positions offered by the tribal and federal governments, Indian employment is characterized first by its marginality and then by its seasonality. The seasonality of Indian employment might be seen as an adaptive response to lack of opportunities, or perhaps as a modern manifestation of the traditional annual cycle of work. Regardless of its source, it leaves its mark on reservation life in perceptible ways. The reservation seems almost deserted during the summer and fall months, in part because people take advantage of the good weather for camping, hunting, visiting, and berry picking, but mainly because most families have one or more members who are gone for extended periods in connection with seasonal employment. In contrast, individuals are least busy with wage labor in the winter months and, as a consequence, are most visible and available.

Although some Indian women secure seasonal employment, the pattern is most evident among Indian men, who can be quite adept at finding work during the summer and fall months. Important types of summer work include jobs in forestry as lookouts for fires or as park guides, in fire fighting as firefighters or support staff, on ranches as all-purpose ranch hands, or on road crews operating heavy machinery. Although these jobs can be dangerous, they tend to pay very well in comparison to other positions. Furthermore, for some people, the element of danger and proving oneself in the face of physically arduous tasks can be attractive. Some people complement the strenuous work and significant economic gains of summer and fall with unemployment during the winter. Others use the winter months to pursue subsidized study at the Salish and Kootenai College. Still others find alternate kinds of work to supplement their incomes and to fill the winter and spring months.

A variety of small-scale enterprises are often used to supplement family incomes. These seasonal activities range in scope and organization from raising a small herd of cattle, cutting Christmas trees, and cutting firewood to tanning hides, doing beadwork, making moccasins, picking berries, and dancing and drumming at celebrations. The few individuals who own cattle tend to have small herds that are pastured on tribal lands for most of the year. Roundup takes place in the spring and fall, at which time cattle will be counted and branded and a few or all may be sold to local butchers.[19] Fall is also the time for cutting firewood. A good number of people will cut firewood for their own use, but some will also cut firewood to sell. However, as with raising cattle, the numbers are small. Those who sell firewood often do so primarily to other Indians and only rarely to members of the white community.

Another fall activity, one that even more people pursue, is cutting Christmas trees. Individuals will sometimes go alone, but often a few family members or even a whole family group will travel by car or truck up the winding dirt roads to tribal forestlands to cut and gather Christmas trees for sale at a later date. Most often, trees are sold to non-Indian distributors who travel to the area to purchase trees and then transport them to metropolitan areas. Occasionally, however, individuals will drive a load of trees to cities on the West Coast or in the Southwest to sell the trees themselves.

On a smaller scale, there is hide tanning, beading, and berry picking. These tend to be, although they are not exclusively, women's activities and are also seasonally marked. Midsummer is the time for berry picking, and although most is done only for family consumption, some people will gather enough for sale to friends and more distant relatives. The primary cash crop is the huckleberry, a sweet purplish berry slightly larger than a blueberry that grows on low bushes at a relatively high altitude. Huckleberries can fetch a good price, up to $20 to $30 a gallon, but gathering them is labor-intensive. Huckleberry picking is often an all-day affair, sometimes stretching into a several-day affair, and is a time for friends and family to visit. Picking time is enlivened by the teasing of children about their purple fingers and mouths and shared stories about encounters with bears, the size of berries at a certain locale, and ankles twisted in the excited pursuit of a plentiful patch.

Hide tanning is also done in summer, although there are a couple of women who are specialists and have built facilities that enable them to tan hides year-round. Most contemporary Flathead Indians claim to be unable to tan hides, a skill common among Flathead women only one or two generations back. Nonetheless, there are a number of people who continue to tan and sell hides, and there is a fairly constant demand for their work. Tanned hides are often made into moccasins and war-dancing outfits by the people who tan them, but they are also sold to others who use them for similar projects. Whites rarely, if ever, buy hides directly but may purchase finished goods made out of hides. The primary consumers of hides and products made from hides continue to be Indians. The same holds for beadwork, an activity that is less seasonally marked. Beaded belt buckles, hairpieces, earrings, moccasins, and dancing outfits are often commissioned from expert beaders, who spend long hours engaged in their work. Others who are less expert also supplement their incomes by producing similar items for sale at some of the tourist stops.

Competition dancing and drumming at the summer powwows also generate cash. Although few Flathead Indians "go on the circuit," some compete in local and not-too-distant powwows. Powwows are often judged by the amount of prize money awarded to dancers and the amount of money paid to the drum groups. Prize money is usually offered to the winners of a set number of categories, such as Men's Traditional Dancing, Women's Traditional Dancing, Boy's Fancy Dancing, Girl's Fancy Dancing, and Best Elder's Performance. Payments to "drums," as the drum groups are called, are usually not competitively based but are rather distributed on a first-come basis.

Finally, all tribal members, regardless of income, receive biannual per capita payments. Per capitas contribute to household economies in substantial ways. For example, during my stay at the reservation, a family of four could count on an income of $4,000 a year from per capitas alone. Together with the medical coverage provided through federal, state, and county programs, these programs ensure that basic economic needs are met for poor residents of the reservation and provide a cushion against unexpected expenses and unforeseen circumstances for families and individuals who can usually count on slightly higher incomes.

The preceding pages describe an economic system that enhances collective economies. Within this system, familial sharing is essential to economic survival, and to be alone is to flirt with not surviving. Yet while the family is the economic unit of significance, money and resources remain the individual's to do with as he or she chooses. Purchases for others are seen as "gifts" and incontrovertible evidence of generosity and compassion. Those gifts reflect in a concrete way how much someone cares for someone else. Conversely, the absence of gifts is equally strong evidence of selfishness, stinginess, or meanness.

Visiting is another type of gift that borders on obligation. Flathead people visit each other regularly, and persons who are not being visited often feel quite resentful. I learned quite early that this visiting is done informally. People just show up at someone's house and are inevitably greeted with happiness and thankfulness. During the first weeks of my stay at the reservation, I remember trying to get telephone numbers for people I had met so that I could give them a call before I came over for a visit. My requests were met politely but not with much understanding. Finally, a woman told me directly that there was no need to call beforehand, that anyone I visited would be happy to see me. I proceeded to tell the small group there about how, among my circle of friends back in Boston, no one just dropped by and that plans for getting together were often made weeks in advance. This description was met with incredulity, laughter, and the reassurance that things did not work that way at the reservation.[20]

Like visiting, the aesthetics of interpersonal interaction emphasizes social connection and harmony. Disagreements are avoided, and public bickering, such as between friends, spouses, or a parent and a child, is regarded as scandalous. When it occasionally happens, the event can become a topic of conversation for years to come. I recorded several of these stories of public bickering while in the field and noted that their telling was often met with laughter. One story, which retells an event

that must be nearly half a century old now, concerns two women who
were close friends and frequent partners in their work of tanning hides.
One day, while the two women were twisting a soaked hide that had
been draped over a tree branch to remove the excess moisture before
beginning to scrape the prepared skin, one of the women accidently let
go of her end of the stick that the two were using to twist the hide. The
stick swung around and hit the other woman on the side of the head.
As the story goes, the "wounded" woman was so angry that she plot-
ted revenge and several months later was able to repay the injury in the
same way; this time by purposely letting go of her end of the stick.
This kind of public display was recognized as immature and petty and
was found quite humorous.

In another story, a man who is widely extolled for his calmness re-
acted to a visit from his wife at his office with irritation, muttering
under his breath when he saw her approaching, "What does that bitch
want now!" Resonating with the morals undergirding storytelling
about racist whites, the telling of this incident was used to reflect the
rarity of this kind of response from the man, underscoring his usually
reserved and patient nature. In a final example, a story about a mother
who was overheard in the middle of the night loudly chastising her
grown daughter for coming home drunk underscored the impatience
that was known to characterize the mother. The scandalous nature of
her behavior was reinforced with the disclosure that she had locked all
the doors and windows of her daughter's house earlier that evening.
This story was told in half-whispered tones, as if a very shameful fact
were being disclosed, and was met with uncomfortable laughter.

Together, these stories imply that the public display of discord is not
only disliked but rare, a perception corroborated by direct observation
of interpersonal interactions. On the few occasions when disagreement
was brought into the open by someone, others in the group were made
uneasy by the display and, if they felt themselves to be watched, would
make no response at all other than to try to slip away unobtrusively. If,
however, they felt they were not being watched, they would often establish eye contact with a trusted friend and widen their eyes or raise
their eyebrows to indicate disbelief of this transgression against the
value of social harmony and their own discomfort with witnessing it.

While personal discomfort and strong emotion are not often displayed, they may be included in the retelling of an event after the fact. I
recall one incident in which I was riding in a car driven by a friend
when another driver pulled onto the highway in front of us causing us

to slow down. My friend gave no indication of irritation, and yet a few days later in conversation reported being "so mad" when the incident occurred. Similarly, when I used to go outside to smoke with a friend of mine before an evening class in the Salish language that she was teaching, it was often very cold, and although I frequently observed that she was chilled, she never once complained of the fact. The only way I knew she actually felt the cold was by direct questioning or by complaining of it myself, at which point she would mildly concur.

This reserved style was also evident in the sweatlodge. Obviously, it was usually quite hot in the lodge from the steam produced by the water that was poured over the heated rocks. Sometimes, however, for whatever reason, it would be hotter than usual, to the extent that participants would emerge with red splotches on their skin. No one ever commented on their discomfort at the time, but I knew that the heat was uncomfortable to them because later they would say so. A story that was told to a group of participants by the leader of a sweat highlights the norm of reserve by reporting its violation. In that story, which detailed an incident that occurred several years back and at a different reservation, a man who was sweating suddenly found the heat unbearable and stood up and began to run. The funny part of the story is that he uprooted the frame of the sweatlodge when he stood up and thus ran off into the distance with the lodge bouncing on top of him, leaving the other participants unprotected on the ground where the sweatlodge used to be.

Social harmony and ease are also the purpose of the frequent joking that goes on whenever a group of Flathead people gets together. Conversations are frequently punctuated by tall tales concluded with the statement "I jokes" or "I doubt it," followed by laughter. Individuals often tell embarrassing stories about themselves or are the butts of someone else's story, in which case it is inappropriate to respond with resentment. Good storytellers are held in high regard, and good stories are repeated often and received with the same interest on each telling. Even though conversations are lively, people tend to speak very quietly. And this was more prominent in the elders and others who were considered "more" Indian.

Gay, lighthearted conversation is quite typical of gatherings, and yet it is also typical for friends and acquaintances to spend time in complete silence. Participants are generally comfortable with these periods of silence in a way that non-Indians very often are not. In fact, silence can be interpreted quite differently, such as the time a friend of mine came

over for a visit in the evening after my husband and I had had a disagreement. My husband and I were "not speaking" and were more sub-
dued and less talkative with our guest than usual. The next day, when I
met with my friend and began to apologize for our combined "bad
mood," he responded by saying how thankful he was that we were such
good friends that we could be together without having to constantly
talk. Another friend described how when her grandmother had visitors
they would often sit for hours without exchanging a word.[21]

All in all, the aesthetics of social harmony that characterizes Flathead manners produces a very comfortable style of interpersonal relations that is complemented by the relaxed pace and rhythm of life.
Jokes about "Indian time" highlight the more flexible Indian use of
time through contrast with the more rigidly scheduled white use of
time.[22] While those who are employed certainly have to be at the office
or at a work site at a given time, schedules are somewhat flexible. Even
more flexible are the times set for community gatherings, which often
would not actually begin until several hours after the time that had
been established originally. Impatience is rarely expressed by those
who may have shown up at the earlier time, although occasionally
someone might leave and come back later to check on the progress of
the gathering. Instead of impatient looks and craning necks, one observes people visiting and laughing in small groups or sitting quietly.[23]

LONELINESS, PITY, AND BELONGING

To belong among the Flathead means to practice pity through generosity toward family and friends in very specific ways: by regularly attending wakes and funerals; by sharing a paycheck with one's aunt; by re-
fraining from expressing overt disapproval of a sibling's decisions; or
by allowing a child to stay home from school if he or she is lonely
there. These practices of pity are dialectically patterned by cultural
definitions as well as by larger political and economic forces. Within
the Flathead world, where belonging is defined by acts of affective and
economic reciprocity, the scarcity of resources and relative deprivation
deriving from economic marginalization produce a certain fragility in
relation to issues of self-worth—similar in many respects to the effects
of racism and broken promises.

To the outsider, the strength and resilience of the Flathead family—
both affective and instrumental—are striking aspects of contemporary
reservation life. To a large extent, this outsider perspective dominates

my discussion in this chapter of the everyday contexts of Flathead lives. In fact, the preceding pages seem to paint a picture of family cohesion in the face of persistent economic marginalization. To many Flathead people, however, it is the instances in which relations of reciprocity have broken down that occupy the imagination. Thus family and friends are not only the principal source of comfort and joy but also the principal source of pain and discomfort. While friends and family are responsible for one another in principle, the behaviors of individuals do not always match expectations, especially, it would seem, in a context in which economic resources are less than adequate. Jealousies stemming from the perceived nonfulfillment of mutual obligation and resentments arising out of a sense of excessive demands are part of reservation life. Along with accidental injuries and deaths, these jealousies and resentments form a significant source of the psychological distress that is expressed among the Flathead people at the reservation.

Without question, loneliness is the primary complaint of those who for some reason feel themselves to be removed from life-sustaining networks of compassion and exchange. Having explored the nature of belonging as a moral construct built up out of the ideological and practical contexts of daily life, it is now possible to explore with more understanding the meanings of exclusion and separation, that is, loneliness, for the Flathead people.

CHAPTER FOUR

Feeling Bereaved,
Feeling Aggrieved,
and Feeling Worthless

The social implications of the Flathead cultural orientation toward interdependence are many and varied; in fact, for an adequate understanding
of almost any aspect of Flathead social life, whether economics, politics,
or religion, one would have to explicitly incorporate or acknowledge the
cultural structure of belonging. Nowhere is this more evident than in the
case of Flathead depression. The Flathead culture of interdependence
yields not only a prominent social interdependence but also an obvious
psychological interdependence that structures the ways that people perceive, express, and seek help for depressive-like experiences.

At base, this psychology of interdependence constructs the Flathead
self as highly invested in the making and maintaining of relationships,
particularly family relationships. Within this psychology of interdependence, disruptions in or losses of relationships can be tantamount to
disruptions or loss of the self. Nearly sixty years ago, Harry H. Turney-
High, an ethnographer of Flathead life, wrote, "One of the strongest
. . . insults indicates that no one wants you because you are of no more
value than a wornout [sic] article. 'You are abandoned, thrown away!'
is a very grave taunt" (1937: 45). The shared understanding among
Flathead people of their psychological interdependence lends special
force to complaints of loneliness, an emotion that has at its core a sense
of separation or abandonment.

In a recent synopsis of cultural psychology, Richard Shweder delin-
eates a symbolic view of emotion in which feeling states can be viewed
as interpretive schemes "which give shape and meaning to the human

experience of those conditions of the world that have a bearing on the self" (1993: 425). In this view, a given emotion bundles a specific affective, or somatic, experience with its antecedents and its implications. In other words, emotions are meaningful constructs that organize the self vis-à-vis its world. So far, this fits well with the picture that is emerging from this investigation in which loneliness occupies a unique and powerful place within a semantic system that thematizes and valorizes belonging and connection. Within this semantic structure, claims of loneliness are potent emotional expressions about the self and perceived disruptions in important social relationships.

Loneliness means that an individual feels him- or herself outside of the usual or expected relations of compassion and exchange. Yet despite this descriptive unity, loneliness encompasses three very different kinds of personal experience. Loneliness can indicate the feelings of grief that follow the death of a loved one or a significant loss (feeling bereaved); it can demonstrate feelings of being aggrieved because of unfulfilled expectations of compassion or exchange (feeling aggrieved); and it can reveal feelings of abandonment accompanied by an internalized sense of worthlessness (feeling worthless). Each type of loneliness points to a distinct way in which social relations have become disrupted, and each type of loneliness possesses distinct implications for the organization of the self in relation to the world.

Shweder suggests a sequence of specific questions to facilitate the comparison of emotions. The questions explicitly attend not only to affective and bodily experience but also to the distinct social and cultural meanings of that affective or somatic experience. They include the affective phenomenology of the experience; the somatic phenomenology; the environmental antecedents; the implications of these antecedents for the self; the social valuation of the experience; the self-management habits that become activated; and the symbolic means of communicating the experience (1993: 425). I discuss the three main types of loneliness among the Flathead by providing some illustrative case material and by describing each with Shweder's set of questions in mind. In appreciating each of these types of loneliness as an interpretive construction that asserts the specific implications of separation or abandonment for the self, we will be in a better position to understand how and why narratives of "depression" take certain forms among the Flathead. In other words, we will see the specific contours of how culture matters for depressive-like experience and depressive-like disorder at the Flathead Reservation.

FEELING BEREAVED

The following case example describes the grief reaction of Clara, a seventy-five-year-old woman. Once divorced and twice widowed, Clara was a small gray-haired woman who lived alone in her neatly kept home with only her small dog, Rusty, for companionship. I was referred to Clara by several different people who shared the opinion that she had ongoing difficulties with depression.

During the interview, Clara offered and translated a number of different Salish words that were close to depression in meaning, most of which centered around profound feelings of loneliness: *čupé* (lonesome), *ʔosti* (lost), *nixᵂpelsí* (grieving or brokenhearted), *nqᵂnmin* (feeling pity), and *čmšqnmi* (wanting to give up).[1] According to Clara, most of these words apply in bereavement, when you do not know where to turn because you are "thinking about your Indian people that's gone." She said about depression, "That's breaking your heart. That's loneliness—thinking about your people that's gone, the life you had, good things that's happened when your folks were alive, what fun you had. Now you miss it, you lost it, you know, you lost it. So you're lonesome for that."

Clara described seeing her mother go through a period of depression following the death of an infant son in an accident. Clara recalled the radical transformation her mother underwent, citing her mother's continual crying and how she had stopped eating and sleeping. When Clara's mother had lost a significant amount of weight, to the point of looking "thin," Clara remembered that her father brought her mother to a doctor in Missoula where she was given an injection to help her sleep. After sleeping for two days, Clara's mother appeared well again. According to Clara, her mother also took up smoking at this time to relieve her grief. Her mother had resorted to tobacco at the suggestion of an old woman and later heralded smoking as an effective strategy for coping with the loneliness of grief.

Clara also described a grief reaction that she herself experienced after the death of her last husband, after seventeen years of a satisfying marriage. It was Labor Day, and the two of them had planned a camping trip. Clara had stayed at home to prepare for their outing, and her husband, Roy, had gone to gather some wood in the hills. She became worried when he had not returned by the time she had finished her preparations. With painful clarity, Clara related how she found her husband that day.

We had three cars. We had this camper, and then his little pickup, and this brand new little Datsun. It was parked there. We just bought it. So I said, "Well, I better go look. He's not coming." 'Cause he left a note. He said, "I took Rusty. Be gone two hours." And, you know, time flew so, because I was getting ready. So I went up there and my little car, uh, the lights, I didn't know how to adjust them—I had the dims on. And I didn't know how to turn them on 'cause it was a new car to me. But anyway I went, so far, and it was getting dusk and I thought, "I better stop." Roy had a nephew living up there. "I'll stop over there, I'll tell him to switch my brights."

So, I did, which was a good thing for me. I went in there, and I stopped . . . went to the door. His wife's name is Tammy. And she said, "Hello, Auntie Clara. We're just gonna eat." See, it must've been about 6 o'clock, late fall, for Labor Day, you know, September 29th. So I said, "No." I said, "I can't stay." I said, "You know what?" I said, "Roy's been gone. He was supposed to been back couple hours." I said, "He was supposed to be over here where he got that lumber." I said, "He was supposed to be after that lumber, but he didn't come back, didn't come back. Now I'm getting worried. It finally dawned on me after I got all ready for our camp trip."

So, his nephew gets in the car. When I told him my story he said, "I'll take you up there." So he drove my car. And we went so far and I could just see: the car was facing this way, the lumber was on. And I looked, seen Roy laying. I could see from my side, Charlie was driving my car. So he jumps out. He didn't think Roy was dead. He thought he was just taking a rest, laying there. He went to pick him up, he put him back down. And he turned to me, and he said, "We can't do nothing for Uncle Roy."

Choking back tears, Clara described her immediate reaction to her husband's death.

So by that time I . . . I jumped out and I run over there. I think I'd a died right there if I'd a been alone. 'Cause I threw myself on him, you know. I started crying and I wanted to die. I thought, "There's nothing left. Nothing left for me. Why live?" And I started crying, and I kept saying, "I want to die too." It could happen. I found out. 'Cause I went and I choked up, even now I'm choked up. And . . . I . . . I . . . I thought, "Well, what's the use? What's the use, what's the use?" Here Roy had . . . he worked hard putting that lumber on. He must've felt sick. He takes his gloves off, he took his little glasses off and he put them on the seat, on the car seat. And he went and laid down. He laid down, I guess he was exhausted. He must have been. To think after, it's cool, green grass. He was exhausted. He laid like that, that's how we found him. And . . . so that's how he left me, that's sad.

After a pause, Clara continued with her narrative, relating the profound ways in which this shock affected her.

It was a sad case. And then I . . . then I guess I was in a trance.

I seen the people coming, a priest. Father brought me right home, they called for Father then. He come and he blessed Roy right where he was at. Then Father drove my car from over there and he left Rusty at the house. He left him off and took me right to the hospital. Of course he called my daughter in the meantime. As soon as we found him, from Roy's nephew's house they asked me, "Who should we call?" And I said, "Call my daughter." So they called Donna.

So, I was so sick. I wanted to die anyway. So they put me right in the hospital. And, uh, it seemed like my arms got numb and my chest got warm, got numb. I was dying—and I wanted it that way. So they put all that machinery on me.

When asked for more detail about what happened to her in the trance, Clara responded,

Well, from out there when I fell on his body, they had to pick me up away from the body, it's fifteen minutes back to their house. They lived right close there. And they laid me on the bed, tried to give me water. I couldn't drink. I tried to drink but I couldn't drink. So from there on then I kind of was in a trance. I don't remember Father driving for me. I don't remember that. I don't remember stopping here and putting Rusty, my dog, here. Then they brought me right to the hospital. All I know is I was in the bed, and then all this machinery on me, on my feet. I don't know how they were, the connections. And I laid there, I know, see, it must've happened 'bout 7 o'clock when all this happened, maybe an hour to get me to the . . . they had time enough to call Donna. And then, uh, she was right here. Her and Leon came as quick as they got the word.

And I stayed in the hospital. I was laying there, I was alright laying there. The nurses was . . . was looking after me. And I stayed there all night. [Pauses] Gee, it was, I remember the hours, I just kept laying there, I knew it was night and I knew I was resting there with all these machinery. But it was towards morning, it must've been about 4, 'bout 3, 4 o'clock when I started [sighs] feeling like I could, uh, I could feel this arm alright. And this arm would . . . the circulation would come back, and then I'd, last place was on my chest, felt relieved. Then that's the first thing when the nurse came again, I said, "I want to go home." After I . . . I was in that trance, all that while I was, I wasn't all myself.

Expecting Clara to respond with something like "a few more hours," I asked Clara, "How long did that trance last?" I was surprised at her reply.

Oh, it lasted a long time. It seems like I was here and I went about my work, did all what I'm supposed to. Gee, towards the end, when I was coming out of that, I woke up one time, I heard Henry come to the back door and I was already standing here in the middle of my floor. I was gonna open the door for him, and then it dawned on me, "Oh, he has his own

key, he always has his key. Why am I rushing to the door? He'll come in."
And then I finally woke up, and it was just a nightmare. So then I ... I
started getting alright but it must've been two, three months. But I really
didn't actually cry. It was a whole year, I believe, or six months, or so. Because I, uh, carried on like I'm supposed to, I knew I had to do this and I
had to do that. Till it, finally, I started really missing him. "He's never coming home." And then I remembered, "Yeah, he died. He's up there." I remember putting him away up here at the cemetery. I buried him close to my
family. My daughter, you know, she's buried there close. That's where he
is. I remember all that. [Crying softly]

In the interview, Clara recalled going through the funeral but not
grieving. Clara described that it was like she was "crazy" and she "was
going in a dream." She said,

Uh, his body was there. He looked so nice. People came. I was so glad to
see this one and that one come in. And I'd say, "I'm so glad you came." But
I wasn't in sorrow. I wasn't crying. I was stunned. I guess that, uh, it was
shock.

Even after the wake, the funeral, and the burial, she described how
everything "just seemed like it was a dream." Clara reported that she
did not start getting better until after three months and was not fully
herself again until six months to a year after her husband's death.
While Clara managed to continue to function during this time, she
sought help in a number of ways. As her elders before her, Clara found
her solace in spiritual ways—in the rituals of a medicine man, in the
sweatlodge of a friend, in sharing prayers with the parish priest, and in
her private prayers. It was the medicine man who told her that he had
had to call her spirit back from death, reinforcing Clara's sense that
she could have died from grief at any point after finding her husband.
In Clara's opinion, it was only after the help of her medicine man that
she left her trance and began to grieve and miss her husband.

At the time of the interview, several years after her husband's death,
Clara described herself in these terms: "Now I'm alone. But I don't feel
alone. I feel like every day, every day I know he's around. I feel like,
'Oh, well, I'm not alone. Roy's still looking after me.' " Now, rather
than wanting to die when she thought of her husband's death, she assimilated the loss by recognizing her husband's, as well as God's, continued presence in her life.

We all lost somebody. Seems like each year somebody else leaves us, you
know, that you been with. There's a prayer you can use when you're lost.

God is with you. At least He never leaves you. That's the only consola-
tion we have, is to remember that we're not really alone.

Clara's experiences after the death of her husband, from the numbness
in her chest to her use of prayer to resolve her feelings, derive their
meaning from the cultural construction of grief-loneliness among the
Flathead. Clara's grief-loneliness, from its dramatic onset to its continuing significance in her life, is a culturally based interpretive construction that asserts the specific implications of Clara's husband's death for
Clara and that organizes Clara's stance toward others in particular
ways. Using Shweder's scheme, we can explore the phenomenology of
Flathead grief-loneliness, revealing, in its resonance with what I have
already shown of Flathead culture, the deep cultural roots of this
highly elaborated emotion.

Loneliness is the central affect of Clara's grief, and her experience of
her husband's death as having been "left alone" was far from idiosyn-
cratic. This sense of having been left alone was the keystone of every
other description of grief that I collected. In a moving description of
her feelings after the death of her husband, one elder said,

> The way I took it, I was alone. See, no matter my kids was around, it's like
> I was all alone. No matter where I go, I was all alone. There was no "scary"
> 'bout it, just what you call this *nixʷpelsí* [grieving] all the time. Try to eat,
> you just sit there.

Another elder painted the following portrait of grief:

> See, like there was one old lady[2] over here. It's like all her brothers or sisters
> died, her boy, lot of her relations. She used to come here. She would say,
> "I'm staying home. *Čn nixʷpelsí* [I am grieving]." She wants to ride and go
> around. She used to come here. She used to use that word 'cause she was
> lonesome all the time. She must have been crying all the time, the way she
> said it, "*Es nixʷpelsí.*" It's like she's hurt inside—her heart, I guess. She
> didn't say *spʔus* [heart], she just says *nixʷpelsí*, 'cause she was left alone.

Persons feeling grief-loneliness often report feelings of heaviness or
pain in the heart or pressure in the chest. While only a minority of
those feeling bereaved end up in the hospital, as Clara did, the connection between the heart and grief is uniformly acknowledged. Some
people I interviewed pressed their hands over their hearts when asked
to describe either sadness or loneliness. In one interview, when I noticed that the interviewee was pressing her hand to her chest as I asked

her about feeling sad, I asked her if she felt sadness in her chest. She responded, "Yeah. *A spʔus*, your heart, hurts." Another interviewee, responding to my inquiry about additional terms for depression, offered *čalspʔus*, a poignantly descriptive word that can be broken into the two components *čal*, meaning pain or hurt, and *spʔus*, meaning heart.

The essential tie between sad emotions and the heart was most eloquently brought home to me in a conversation I had with an elder. She spoke about some angry words that were said to her by a relative and the sadness that she now carries with her. Pressing her chest above her heart with her right hand, she described her feelings in dramatic terms, "*lxʷpnunm isnpuʔpuʔsenčtn*," which can be translated roughly as "hurt or pierced in my place of feeling," that is, in her heart.

In the interviews and in daily life, the heart attacks and high blood pressure of elders were often attributed to feelings of sadness and loneliness. And, as in Clara's experience, grief can lead to dangerous shock reactions affecting the heart, known to some Salish speakers as *ntʔetče?*. According to one interviewee, "If you're *ntʔetče?*, your heart jumps and then starts beating again. It's like bad news just come to you too quickly. Like, you could say you got shot right in the heart. Sometimes it will make you sick. Maybe you'll pass out there 'cause it stops your heart." In fact, few people were unable to name at least one person who had died from grief within weeks of learning about the death of a loved one. In our interview, Clara named three persons who had died in this way—all mothers who lost adult children in accidents.

The death of a relative is the paradigmatic loss for feelings of grief-loneliness, but other situations of loss are also implicated. One is what I have come to call the "geography of loss," in which reservation lands and surrounding areas are experienced in terms of tragedy and loss.[3] As I traveled over the roadways of the reservation, my friends would help me understand what they saw and felt as they gazed out the windows of the car. Often this would be to tell me about a site as the location of a previous work assignment, where something funny happened or where certain plants grew. Often, however, their gestures and words marked a location as a site of loss. One friend quietly pointed out, for example, the hill where Cathy's parents died in a car accident and the curve where Ed's son lost control of his motorcycle and was paralyzed. Another friend became pensive as we drove past a particular area and later told me that we had passed a field where some of the "old-timers," the "really Indians," used to gather to play stick games through the night. At another time, she nodded toward a house that had been built right in front of where old Mary, an esteemed elder, used to have her shack.[4]

For many people, then, their experience of the reservation is often characterized by a heavy and nearly constant awareness of various places as sites of tragic accidents, as locations of traditional activities that are now only part of memory, or as places of residence of deceased old-timers. The reminders of loss that inhere in the land evoke feelings of grief-loneliness that match bereavement for a long-deceased relative. However, grief-loneliness also stems from having to be away from reservation lands for an extended period of time, whether for military service, schooling, or a job. In other words, the grief-loneliness inspired by homesickness extends to the land itself.[5]

Similar feelings are evoked in various other situations as well, such as missing relatives who are away from the reservation or, conversely, feeling homesick for those left behind. Men, and sometimes women, might feel this way when they are unable to find work to support themselves and contribute to their family exchange networks. Parents and grandparents are likely to feel the same kind of loneliness when faced with the potentially dangerous and socially irresponsible behaviors of their adult children who are drinking excessively. Disruptions in family relations traceable to resentments or animosities can inspire grief-loneliness among older adults as well, much like the one interviewee who reported feeling "hurt or pierced in my place of feeling" as a result of a relative's angry words. Grief-loneliness is also aroused when individuals recall traditional songs that have fallen into disuse or are reminded about the current state of the Salish language.

In each of these situations, whether bereavement for a relative, bereavement for a song, or homesickness, vital elements of a valued world with whom the individual has a relationship are threatened or destroyed. Valued activities have been brought to an end, as Clara reported in her statement about the loneliness of grief, "That's breaking your heart. That's loneliness—thinking about your people that's gone, the life you had, good things that's happened when your folks were alive, what fun you had. Now you miss it, you lost it, you know, you lost it. So you're lonesome for that."

Moreover, the loss represents a threatening diminishment of one's life-sustaining networks of caring and sharing. This is evident in the experience of the death of a close relative, a disruption in good relations between family members, or the inability to garner resources to contribute to relationships of reciprocity and exchange. It is also true, however, in the loss of a traditional song, which has a life force that sustains the singer as it is sung and which the singer has a responsibility to keep alive. Similarly, the loss of the language portends the loss of the Flathead way of life, that is, the close interdependence associated with traditional ways.

The social judgment for someone who feels grief-loneliness is one of pity and compassion. Most often associated with older people who have endured numerous deaths in their lifetimes, grief-loneliness is linked to maturity and Indianness. Thus, for the most part, individuals who experience grief-loneliness can expect others to respond compassionately: they are visited more often, guests bring amusing stories to take their minds off their loss, and visitors listen respectfully as grief-stricken individuals describe their feelings of loneliness or talk about the ones they lost.

After a while, however, the compassion toward grief-stricken individuals shifts in tone. There is a limit to community tolerance of the isolation that those who are feeling bereaved often impose on themselves. Those who feel grief-loneliness for an extended period begin to be the object of increasing intervention, some of which is in the form of ritual care but most of which is in the form of lecturing about the person's responsibilities toward others. For example, grief-stricken persons are frequently admonished, after an appropriate period of grief, to be strong enough to let go of the deceased. They are told that they need to relinquish their grief so that the deceased can go on to the next world unhindered, so that they themselves can rejoin the world of the living, so that relatives and friends do not lose the grief-stricken person to sickness, death, or solitary habits.

In the following quotation, Arlene, a seventy-year-old woman, spoke about her difficulty in letting go of her grief for her seventeen-year-old granddaughter, Vi, and Arlene's companion's efforts to encourage her to let go of her feelings of grief.

> I sure was sad, so many times. It takes a long time to lose the sadness, when you lose somebody close. Like when I lost Vi. Ooo. That was July, and in October I was still grieving. I still wasn't touching anything. Like when I'd go from here to town, I'd start crying. And then, uh, it's worse when I get to the place where she . . . where she got killed [in a car wreck]. I'd go to town, come back and then start crying. Then Mike said, "Hey, you better cut it out. I dreamt that when you would go from here to town, you'd start crying." I didn't say anything, you know, 'cause he was telling the truth. He said, "You better cut it out, you're gonna get sick." I told him, "I just . . . I just feel sad." He used to really get after me for being so sad.

When asked if Mike's efforts helped, Arlene responded, "It didn't help me. It just . . . I just didn't listen to him or anything. I didn't care to do anything anymore." In Arlene's estimation, what helped her to curb her grief was a recurring dream about Vi.

> Vi was seventeen years old when she got killed. And every time I'd dream about her she'd be a baby, just a little baby. And, you know, this was funny, I dreamt that I was this deep in water [motions to midthigh], and I looked down, bottom of the water, bottom of the lake—there was Vi all cut up in little pieces under the water. And you know, when I woke up I thought, "Boy, I guess I'm covering her with my tears." See, that's what that means. She was just covered with water, tears. So that kind of slowed me down. When I start thinking about her I'd just do something or think of something else. So that helped.

In other words, Arlene finally realized that she had to let go of Vi, so that Vi could leave this world and go on to the next. Vi would remain in this world in ghostly form until Arlene could let her go. Arlene said, "They say when you cry too much that they're heavy, too heavy to go to heaven." Although Arlene described how her recognition of her responsibility to Vi helped, Arlene's recovery has taken a long time and was still incomplete seven years after Vi's death. Arlene said, "Oh, it took a long time. And every year, about the time I lost her, I'd get sick. It's still like that."

Isolation, sickness, and death are all too real as possible outcomes of feeling bereaved, and a variety of efforts to help those who have been stricken by grief-loneliness can be mobilized. Like Clara, Arlene had contact with a biomedical practitioner during the immediate throes of acute grief. She described being given pills.

> See, uh, after Vi died, I was crying so much with the hurt, well, they give me pills. It cured me alright, but that was only for so many hours, you know. It just stopped it for a little while. Like my friend, when her mother-in-law died, because she was just like a mother, you know. Her mother-in-law took care of her kids all the time. And then when she died, she was hurt, my friend. So I know they gave her something every little while, then every little bit, she'd start crying and crying and crying. So, it stops it, but it don't cure it for good—like I was saying, just for a little while.

The pragmatism of Flathead help-seeking facilitates a widespread reliance on biomedical practitioners for the acute signs of grief, but greater faith tends to be placed in the traditional Flathead practices for handling both uncomplicated and complicated grief-loneliness: visiting, prayer, and traditional healing. Like Clara, Arlene turned to a medicine man to help her with continued grief. Moreover, Arlene also used rosebushes, placing boughs around the doors and windows of her house. Others reported doing the same. A few people mentioned washing with a brew concocted of rosebush leaf tea, and a few others mentioned drinking the same tea.

While grief-loneliness is felt in the heart and carried internally, it is, nonetheless, clearly visible to others. One elder explicitly stated that if she was feeling depressed, "it would show in my face or the way I act, you know." Another interviewee explained in the case of a man who was known to be grieving especially hard for his mother, "You could tell: people talking to him, he can answer, but still he had his mom right in front of him everywhere he looks." The linguistic construction of emotions in Salish mirrors this understanding in expressions like *i kʷ leč?*, "having the look of being mad," or *qʷnqʷnus*, "having a pitiful look." In the case of grief-loneliness, the external signs are most often tearfulness, disturbance in eating and sleeping (either diminished or excessive), bad dreams and visitations by dead relatives, pressure or pain in the chest, changes in sociability (either increased solitariness or inability to remain alone), the need or the inability to talk about the loss, and increased praying.

FEELING AGGRIEVED

Accounts of loneliness in which narrators were feeling aggrieved were more difficult to elicit. In part, this can be explained by the fact that these emotions are more transient than bereavement. Equally important, however, individuals are less inclined to "confess" to the loneliness of feeling aggrieved because this emotion tends to be associated with youth and immaturity, rather than with maturity and living the Indian way. Additionally, this type of loneliness carries the humiliation of having been mistreated or cast out by one's friend, lover, or relative, despite its injustice. Nonetheless, the loneliness of feeling aggrieved is pervasive in the everyday lives of Flathead people. Rooted deeply in the ideology of belonging and interdependence, feeling aggrieved references the threat of abandonment that inheres in mundane insults of unfulfilled reciprocity or unequal distribution: a wife left at home by a partying husband; a teenage boy denied a new pair of sneakers by his parents; a daughter angrily chastised by her mother; a sister who notes that her brother seems to receive more gifts from their mother than she does; or an elderly invalid uncle left too long without visitors.

Roberta, or Berta as she was more widely known, gave the following account of a three-day period of loneliness/depression that grew out of her frustration over not being able to secure a job and her sense of abandonment about not being supported by her family and friends as she felt she should have been. Now a thirty-five-year-old divorced woman raising her two children without support from their father, Berta reported being about thirty at the time. For the nine months prior to the episode, she had been looking for a job after graduating from school. She recalled that she was very upset about the direction her life was going and that, although she could not remember the reason, she had been "mad." She described a chronic low-grade anger and irritability with friends and relatives, citing an instance of asking for help from her brothers and not getting it and being chastised by a sister for her daughter's misbehavior. On the third day, she took her children over to her parent's house, saying, "Take my kids, or else," and went out "boozing" at the bar with a friend.

When asked to describe what she was feeling, Berta replied,

> Let's see. I went, let me see, somehow I ended up in town. I was driving for my friend. And we were down at the bar. We were boozing it up. It was just, I don't know, it must have been loneliness or something. I felt lonely, I guess. It felt like I had my friends, but my friends were just there. I mean, they were just there, like I was still alone.

Unlike grief-loneliness, however, the loneliness of feeling aggrieved not only incorporates loss but also assigns culpability to others for the loss. While Berta's story specifies a kind of chronic irritability leading up to her sense of loneliness, the following account shows more clearly the focus on the *cause* of loneliness that is part and parcel of feeling aggrieved. The account was told to me in an interview with Sophie, a forty-year-old woman who was married to her second husband and raising four children, two from each of their previous marriages. The story recounts a suicide gesture/attempt Sophie had made when she was twenty years old and married to her first husband.

> My first husband drank a lot. And I didn't know anything about alcoholism and I thought it was my fault. And, so to show him, I guess, that it really was bothering me and hurting me the way he treated me and left me alone all the time [sighs], I tried to slash my wrists.
>
> I was staying with this, uh, friend of mine, who was my best friend. And, she was passed out. I might just as well have been there alone. I just went in

the bathroom and did it. While everybody was sleeping. It was just like that. Just a impulse. I just . . . I wanted to die. I didn't want to be alive anymore. It was like we started drinking to go look for my husband and his friends. And [sighs], we didn't find them. And I . . . I remember it just escalated and escalated.

჻

Feeling aggrieved is marked by feelings of loneliness. However, as these experiences show, it is also usually described in terms of an accompanying anger or irritability. At base, the anger is understood as the direct result of the perception that one has been undeservedly mistreated by friends, relatives, or the world in general. Rather than focusing on the sadness associated with loss, as in feeling bereaved, the emotion of feeling aggrieved attends to the anger provoked by the recognition that someone is to blame for the loss.

Unlike feeling bereaved, the somatic accompaniments of feeling aggrieved are not highly elaborated. However, the Salish word for anger, *ntaxels*, suggests a bodily feeling of bitterness. As one elderly man put it, "*Ntaxels*. I am bitter, within myself. That's the word for anger. *Ntaxels*. When you're angry, you're bitter inside." As he continued, his words implied very different kinds of affective/bodily experiences for depression and anger: "Depression is something that's slow, it's gradual, or it could deplete. . . . Depression is a state that you could in time overcome. Different situations, different events will take place to bring you out of your depression. Anger is now. It's sudden."

Feeling aggrieved is an emotion, as this elder's words show, which tends to be experienced as taking over one's entire mood very quickly. Sophie's story about the rapid escalation of her feelings of loneliness into anger of sufficient intensity to want to commit suicide is one example. In the following case, Bob, a forty-five-year-old single male, describes an equally precipitous slide into overwhelming feelings of aggrievement that occurred when he was in his mid-thirties. During this time in his life, he was drinking heavily for weeks or months on end, resting for only four to five days between bouts. He said,

> I had been drinking around for, I don't know, maybe a couple weeks or so and I was running real low on money. I had just separated from this girl I was with. I just up and left, just took my car and some clothes. So I went back to, uh, try to get a little money. I thought, "Maybe I'll go see if she's got some money, see if I can get some money." But I still had feelings for that woman. And when I went in to talk to her, she just cut me off, wouldn't say anything. I tried two, three times, you know, asked her to

come out and party. Well, I left. Just like that my mood turned black. Guy I
was drinking with, I left him, I didn't want to be around him. I went by myself, got a pint of whiskey. Sat in my car, drinking.

While experienced as sudden, people who report these extreme feelings of aggrievement can usually recount other disruptions in relationships that preceded the specific incident that set off an acute episode of
feeling aggrieved. For example, in Bob's case, he reported, on further
reflection, that he may have been predisposed to feeling aggrieved because of other circumstances as well, including a previous interaction
with his sister that mirrored the rejection he felt with his former girlfriend.

> I had been feeling that for a while, I guess, because of breaking up, not
> doing anything. My money was gone. I didn't have no income. And I was
> drunk a couple days before that and I stopped up at my sister's house. She
> owed me something like $1,000. She had some money, and I asked her for
> some. No, she wouldn't. We got into an argument. It really hurt—she's the
> one I've always been closest to.

As these accounts suggest, the most typical antecedents to feeling
aggrieved are slights and instances of rejection by a friend, a relative,
or—that important in-between category—a lover. These slights, which
can range from being left home alone too often (as with Sophie) to
being chastised (as with Berta) or having a request rejected (as with
Bob), are taken as prima facie evidence of not being cared for, of having been excluded from an important relationship of compassion and
aid. Not surprisingly, divorces or the breakup of romantic relationships typically evoke strong feelings of aggrievement. Similarly, when
people perceive that their relatives have favored others, in terms of
gifts, they very often end up feeling aggrieved. In fact, it is just these
kinds of jealousies that constitute the most important category of perceived "slights" or injustices at the reservation. Another important an-
tecedent to feeling aggrieved, however, is the suspicion that someone
has used witchcraft to foul up your affairs, perhaps causing your girlfriend to leave you or making it hard for you to find work.

The slights that precede feeling aggrieved necessarily imply loss, but
typically loss of a fairly circumscribed nature. These losses, however,
represent not the inevitable losses associated with the death of a loved
one but the shameful, unconscionable losses associated with unjust rejection and exclusion by friends and relatives in one's network of sharing and caring. Behind specific instances of exclusion looms the specter

of permanent abandonment, as well as public humiliation as the rejection becomes known.

Unlike bereavement, where the loss is self-evident and not subject to questioning by others, in feeling aggrieved, claims of loss and blame are subject to judgment by others. In feeling aggrieved, you deserve pity and compassion if your relative, friend, or lover is thought to be negligent or unjust. It could be found, however, that you are simply overreacting, because of your youthfulness or immaturity/selfishness, to an action that was not a bona fide rejection or exclusion. In other words. those who are feeling aggrieved might just as easily end up being judged as immature as they are to be thought of as wrongfully mistreated.

Feeling aggrieved usually involves seeking justice—either by garnering public support for one's feelings and inducing changes in the guilty party or by returning pain for pain. The fact that social judgment in feeling aggrieved extends beyond the individual to his or her family and friends provides a certain amount of leverage to the person who is feeling aggrieved. Few family members or friends care to have their actions within relationships subjected to the judgments of others, and thus they seek to minimize the number of incidents that could be perceived as evidence of unjust exclusion. Moreover, regardless of whether incidents are judged as bona fide rejection, relatives and friends also try to minimize such incidents because the anger/humiliation of the person who feels aggrieved can lead to rash behaviors, including a drinking bout or a suicide attempt.

Feeling aggrieved is thought to precipitate suicide attempts, either as an immature effort to manipulate a relative or lover or as a partly justifiable effort to retaliate against the offending party. According to some of the elders at this reservation, it was not uncommon in the past for individuals to threaten or commit suicide if their worthiness had been called into question through insult, rejection, or exclusion by spouses, family members, or a boyfriend or girlfriend. Yet Sophie's accounts of feeling aggrieved show that this type of reaction is not confined to the past.[6]

In talking about the connection of suicide to anger rather than to depression, one interviewee gave the following description.

> Anger is now. It's sudden. And that's how people commit suicide, suddenly. Like if you were to say something to really hurt me and I wanted to just do something about it, I run out to my car and get my gun and shoot myself—"I'm gonna end it all." See, this is something that's now, that's anger.

Seldom does anybody ever commit suicide while they're in depression. Because, when it's suicide, oftentimes, maybe 90 percent or more of the times,
it's not premeditated. . . . But when you're in a state of anger, that's when it
happens. And it happens now. You go run out of the house and you grab
yourself a rope and go hang yourself. You're doing it in anger. . . .

OK, to be angry enough to kill yourself, it's not self-infliction that you're
looking at—you're looking at hurting somebody. OK, let's say it this way.
This person you want to hurt by killing yourself is somebody that's close to
you, but the person you want to kill, you don't know them. See? Otherwise,
you'd kill this person, rather than yourself. But you want to hurt someone
that's close to you, inflict pain, so you kill yourself.

This just happened. He wasn't trying to destroy himself for himself. You
see, he was striking out at someone. Now, if that person had been a
stranger that made him angry, he would have struck out at that person.
Took that same rifle and shot that person. But it wasn't, it was somebody
very close to him. So, rather than just shoot her, "I'm gonna hurt her,
something that she'll never forget. I'll shoot myself." That kind of reason-
ing is hard to understand but it's there. . . .

If I was premeditating suicide, I would not tell anybody. I would just go
out and do it. But if I was angry, I would tell somebody. "I'm gonna do it."
But I wouldn't tell them why I was gonna do it because they'll know why I
done it. The person that I'm striking at will know why I done it.

Suicide attempts and threats of suicide are the most dramatic evidence of feeling aggrieved. Most instances are less severe and rely on
less life-threatening gestures for communication. Going out drinking,
or threatening to, in the face of the disapproval of a spouse or parent
is a far more common expression. Often, too, the person feeling aggrieved might deliver an argumentative exposition on how the person
responsible for his or her misery has mistreated him or her and,
clearly, "no longer cares." These verbal eruptions, frequently occa-
sioned by drinking, may be delivered to the "responsible party," but
most often they are not.

Perhaps the most common expression of feeling aggrieved is the social behavior known as "pouting around," or sometimes simply "pouting." Pouting is a typically nonlinguistic display of one's humiliation
and anger at having been mistreated that shows in one's face and demeanor. These nonlinguistic signs can be quite subtle, such as avoiding
eye contact with work associates and friends or lagging behind the
group in responding with smiles to the telling of a funny story. Regardless of the subtlety of these signs, however, individuals are generally
considered transparent with regard to feeling aggrieved, and, as noted
in the discussion of feeling bereaved, this is often stated in terms of the

face. During my stay in the community, for example, a teenage boy had shot himself, and for a while popular opinion held that the case was a suicide. That this interpretation was problematic, and was later decided to be untrue, was evident in the statement of a woman who reported that she had seen the boy just prior to the shooting and "he didn't look mad."[7]

Thus while feeling aggrieved also has a sense of loneliness or separation at its core, it organizes the self in a way that is radically distinct from feeling bereaved. While feeling bereaved focuses on loss, feeling aggrieved focuses on blame for loss, entailing a very different phenomenology and stance toward the world. Moreover, because of the different moral valuations of the two emotions, one can expect very different responses from the world. Each of these kinds of differences will be apparent in the following discussion of feeling worthless.

FEELING WORTHLESS

While fear of abandonment underlies both feeling bereaved and feeling aggrieved, it is the sense of *already having been abandoned* that forms the essence of feeling worthless. Moreover, the abandonment is attributable neither to the normal losses of life nor to the selfishness of friends and relatives, but rather is traceable to the unworthiness of the person who has been abandoned. Very often persons experiencing this most debilitating form of loneliness report feeling abandoned not only by family and friends but also by the Creator—thereby expressing the ultimate form of abandonment and casting doubt not only on their worthiness as a child, parent, friend, or spouse but also on their fundamental worth as a sentient human being.

Ethel was a forty-year-old divorced woman whose seventeen-year-old daughter and infant grandson lived with her. While her nineteen-year-old son lived some distance away in an isolated area of the reservation with his girlfriend, many members of her extended family lived nearby. Although Ethel usually participated in the lively banter of everyday conversation, especially when she was in small groups, she often looked sad. Moreover, she was sometimes visibly nervous, with shaking hands, and was frequently ill with headaches and other nonspecific ailments. These signs, as well as others, concerned her friends and family members, most of whom tended to adopt a solicitous stance toward Ethel.

During our two-hour interview, which was punctuated at first with

joking and laughter and later by sighs and tears, Ethel described a depression of nearly six years duration that moved in and out of feeling
bereaved, feeling aggrieved, and feeling worthless. In Ethel's eyes, her
depression was precipitated by the death of her father nearly six years
prior to the interview but then was intensified and prolonged by a series of other difficulties: years of marital discord culminating in divorce
a year after her father's death; problems with her teenage children after
the divorce; and, finally, complications stemming from her drinking.
Of the time of her father's death, Ethel says,

> I guess when Dad died I just felt abandoned. I felt a real deep loss. I felt
> abandoned because I knew I'd never see Dad again. No, I take that back. I
> always believed that I'll see him again. Um, I guess I felt like he was no
> longer going to be with us. The kids weren't gonna get the chance to know
> him like I did. [Pause]
>   And it still hurts. [Begins to cry] Even though it's been six years, in Janu-
> ary. Sometimes it still feels like it's a couple of months ago. Because my
> memories of him are just . . . I wouldn't change any of them for nothing. I
> had a very happy childhood. I wouldn't change any of it, you know.
>   And I guess maybe that's why I felt so [sighs] very hurt and depressed
> when I got divorced, because then I knew the kids weren't going to have
> that father figure like I did. And I blamed myself.

Ethel's feelings of bereavement come through in this passage, as she
laments the loss of her father, but her feelings of worthlessness are also
apparent as she describes her bereavement in terms of abandonment, a
term not typically used to describe grief-loneliness. In her claiming of
the blame for her children's loss of their "father figure," the final passage also reveals Ethel's feelings of worthlessness stemming from her
divorce. Ethel refers to the time around her divorce as "the dark ugly
side" and calls it the worst time of her life. When asked about whether
there was a connection between her feelings and the times she had
been sick, she revealed the frightening somatic ordeals she underwent
during her descent into "the dark ugly side," talking first about her
trouble with high blood pressure and then about sudden attacks of
fear.

> I've had high blood pressure problems [sighs] since about the time I was
> getting the divorce. My blood pressure shot up. And it was so high, it was
> making me really sick—health-wise. I was nervous, my blood pressure was
> high and the doctors couldn't bring it down. I was taking tranquilizers
> [sighs], and I don't like taking pills.
>   When I would get so depressed, you know, when I was going through
> the divorce, I'd just go to sleep when I got home. And maybe I'd wake up

about midnight, or whatever, and I'd get up and I'd light a cigarette. And the first puff I'd take off of that cigarette was like it hit me right around my chest. It was like a scary feeling. It was like I was scared something was going to happen. So, I'd put the cigarette out. [Laughs] Um, but that, that happened to me time and time again, you know. Like, I'll light a cigarette and, boy, it just comes over me like, "Oh, this isn't right. Something's wrong. Something's gonna happen." That I don't want to happen, you know. Uh, I don't want to be alone, I don't want to be feeling this way. [Sighs]

Typically, divorce produces acute feelings of aggrievement, but this is not so evident for Ethel. While in her experiences with these sudden attacks at night she references her distress and fear at having been left alone, Ethel's emotions about this time in her life tend to focus more on her role in depriving her children of their father. In other words, as we saw in the final phrase of the first quote, she attends, not to the loss per se or to the responsibility of others in creating the loss, but to herself as blameworthy for the loss—the hallmark of feeling worthless.

Ethel's decision to divorce put an end to five years of increasing difficulties with her husband, who, after ten years of stability, had begun to drink, to leave home for days at a time, to see other women, and to gamble away his wages rather than contribute to the functioning of the household. But her decision also plummeted her into emotional straits that were hard to negotiate, especially when her fears for her children seemed to materialize. Ethel described how her son, Mark, began skipping school and smoking marijuana.

I don't know, they keep telling me it's not a result of the divorce, but I don't know, they were hurt, very hurt. Um, Mark was fifteen. He started skipping school. At first I thought, "Oh, this is no biggie, you know. So he's skipping a couple of days of school, you know, it's no worse than that." [Lights a cigarette] I couldn't be with my kids all the time because I had to support them. I had to go to work every day.

So Mark started skipping school. He wanted to quit school. Then he wanted to go to school, but he got into pot. He was stoned half the time. And it took me a long time to realize it because I was never around it. I was never around marijuana, to know what to look for.

And that really threw me for a loop. I didn't know what to do. I tried talking to him, and he'd say, "OK, Mom. Yeah, I'm sorry. I won't do that anymore." And I would believe him. But he never quit. [Lights a cigarette] And that was hard, you know, 'cause I'd be here at work [sighs], somebody from the school would call me and say, "Well, Mark's not here. He checked out."

For a while in the beginning, I'd always tell my boss that I had to go look for him. So I'd go look for him, and I'd look for him, and I'd look for

him. Where do you look for a fifteen-, sixteen-year-old boy? [Laughs] Even
in a town this small. [Laughs]

And I'd find him, in the beginning I'd find him. And we'd get into a
fight. I'd slap him around, I was trying to shake him up. I was trying to
shake some sense into him. [Sighs] That wasn't working. I tried grounding
him, I tried everything.

Ethel's difficulties with Mark were complicated by troubles with her
daughter.

But then Sissy got to be in junior high and, holy shit, I thought Mark was
bad. Sissy was, I mean, she did everything, everything there was to do. In
that little short span between the eighth grade and her sophomore year,
when she quit school. [Sighs] God, I used to just wonder where she was at
night, you know. All the stuff that she's pulled in her short teenage years.
[Scoffing laugh]

And I . . . I don't know, sometimes I think, "God, you're so stupid, you
know, you can't see these things happening." It was during the powwow,
and Sissy was only, I don't know, fourteen, fifteen, fourteen, I guess it was.
She wanted to go to the powwow and her dad was here, so she was gonna
go with her dad. So they went. Then she told her dad that she was gonna go
home with me. I wasn't even there. [Scoffing laugh]

I didn't see her for, gosh, must have been about six weeks. She took off
and I had no idea where she was at. [Sighs] I asked her friends. Of course
her friends weren't going to tell me shit. Finally, my sister-in-law came back
from the Browning powwow and she told me that Sissy was in Browning. I
. . . I had no idea that she was gonna be in Browning. [Long pause] And
then she gets pregnant, you know. Whoa!

In talking about her difficulties with her children, Ethel takes the
blame for their behavior. Mark's misconduct resulted from the "hurt"
of the divorce as well as from Ethel's absence from the home. Sissy's
misbehavior was related, in part, to Ethel's "stupidity" at not recognizing what was going on. In sum, Ethel set off this chain of untoward
events by divorcing, and she had no one to blame but herself.

Within a year or two after these difficulties with her kids began,
Ethel started drinking. At first she started drinking just to have a good
time with her friends. Soon, however, her patterns of drinking and her
feelings about her drinking underwent a radical shift. Not only did she
begin to drink virtually every weekend, but she also began to think
that her drinking was "wrong" and began to feel "bad" about it.
Around this time, Ethel reported that she no longer drank to "laugh
around and have a good time" but that she would only drink "to get
drunk."

During this time, a number of difficulties arose out of Ethel's drinking: she lost her paycheck one night; another night she wrecked her car and ended up in the hospital for a week; she missed a significant amount of work due to hangovers or dealing with problems created by her drinking; and she worried her friends and family. Her mother told her, "When you're drinking, you're ugly. You do things that you would not do if you were sober. You're not the same person when you're drinking. I'm constantly worried about you." A friend spoke to her about his concern for her, saying that she was "on the road to destruction." Ethel reported mixed feelings in response to her friend's words, including shock that he knew about her drinking since she had never seen him when she was out, defiance that her drinking was none of his business, and relief that someone had noticed and cared about her.

Ethel described three related triggers for her drinking. First, she would drink out of "self-pity."

> I would say, "Agh, who's going to care if I'm drunk? Who's gonna care if I'm out drinking?"—you know, all that self-pity. Nothing was going right in my life, so why even try anymore? I was . . . I just wanted to give up. [Sighs]

She would also drink out of anger when she was left alone, additional evidence that "no one cared."

> Being alone is the easiest way to go out and get drunk. I'd come home from work and I'd be feeling pretty good, you know, walk in the house, there's a note on the counter. It says, "We went over here," you know. And I'd be all by myself, and I'd think, "Shit. I don't need this. I don't need to be alone." I'd think, "I don't need to be alone, I'll just go down and pick up my friend, and [sighs] we'll go somewhere where there's a lot of people."

Finally, she would drink to punish herself for everything that had gone wrong.

> So, one night I had to sit down and look at what I was doing. Exactly what I was doing, that it was getting me nowhere. And I thought, "Oh, this is a bunch of bullshit. I never had to drink before to have fun or to enjoy myself, enjoy life. So why am I doing it now? This was against all of my upbringing. I don't want my kids to do. This is something that I didn't want my husband to do. Why am I doing it now?" I mean, it's like I was still punishing myself for everything that went wrong. I was doing exactly what I didn't like. [Sighs]

Throughout these six years, starting with her father's death, through her divorce, as she dealt with her disobedient children, and as she suffered through her own drinking, Ethel felt bereaved and aggrieved at different points, but she also was battered by feelings of worthlessness, of having deserved her abandonment. At times, these feelings prevented her from seeking help from other people. "I didn't want to reach out, I guess, because I was so afraid that people would look down on me and say, 'What a screwed up woman.' " Moreover, Ethel sometimes felt too worthless even to call on God.

> My auntie was always telling me, she said, "When you need help, take your sweetgrass and burn it and pray. Pray for God's help." She said, "You used to go to church all the time and now you don't go." I told her, I said, "I don't feel like I should go to church now because I . . . I know everything I'm doing is . . . is wrong." She said, "You got it all backwards." She said, "That's when you're supposed to go to church and pray." She said, "You're lost right now and you're going away from God." So I always felt like nobody cared.
>
> The Father always assured me that I wasn't alone. He always told me, he said, "Turn your problems over to God." He said, "Sometimes it might not feel like God's listening but He is." I told him once, I said, "I feel like I'm not worthy of Him helping me." He said, "You're wrong there." And that's always stuck in my mind. He said, "Just turn your problems over to God." [Starts crying]

※

Not surprisingly, given that abandonment is one of the worst situations that any Flathead person could endure in a lifetime, the affects that accompany feeling worthless are many. As we saw in Ethel's case, there is frequently sadness, occasionally fear, and sometimes transient anger. However, there are two feelings that are most central to the experience of feeling worthless: first, there is the profound and alienating loneliness that is expressed in the assessment that one has been abandoned by virtually everyone; and second, there is the despair and self-deprecation that derives from the sense that one has been abandoned because one is somehow *unworthy* of being cared for by the members of one's networks of compassion and aid.

While Ethel reported disturbing somatic symptoms along with her feelings of worthlessness, her somatic experiences seemed to be unique. No one else whom I interviewed reported blood pressure problems or sudden attacks of fear striking in the chest in association with feelings of worthlessness, as Ethel did. While three of the six interviewees who reported feelings of worthlessness cited disturbed eating and sleeping, the others failed to report any somatic aspects to the emotion whatsoever. And in none of the cases were somatic experiences considered central to the emotion of feeling worthless. However, Ethel's somatic signs are consonant with the culturally based notion of the heart as the seat of emotion, and an epidemiology of these and similar symptoms may reveal that they are more common than my handful of interviews suggests.

Unlike feeling bereaved and feeling aggrieved, where certain types of *events* typically precede the onset of the emotion, feeling worthless seems to be in the unique position of being preceded *by other emotions*, namely, feeling bereaved and feeling aggrieved. In Ethel's case, her feelings of worthlessness were precipitated by feelings of bereavement for her father *compounded* with feelings of aggrievement surrounding her divorce. Her experiences in this regard are in no way unusual, as the following continuation of Bob's experiences illustrates. You may recall that Bob suffered feelings of aggrievement after a former girlfriend refused to loan him money or even speak to him. After that rejection, he described leaving his drinking partner and drinking whiskey alone in his car—all of which was leading up to a suicide attempt that evening.

> I don't know, I was down again. "Nobody cares for me." You know. "Nobody wants me, nobody likes me." Go on back in the bar, sat down at the bar, I knew the bartender pretty good. I was getting some free drinks from him. I went around, went in the bathroom there, go in there and sit down. I went in there, broke my whiskey bottle, and cut both my wrists and sat there. Somebody walked in and seen blood going out from the stall, and broke down the door. By that time I had went into a faint. But it happened just like that. Within a couple hours I was that down.

In Bob's case, we know that feelings of aggrievement preceded his fall into feelings of worthlessness. Moreover, we know that the immediate trigger for his feeling aggrieved, his girlfriend's rejection of him, was preceded by a similar rejection by his sister as well as a longer-term lack of money. However, as in Ethel's case, Bob's feelings of aggrievement seemed to be complicated by feelings of bereavement. Only a few years prior to this incident, Bob had undergone a profound grief reaction after a terrible car accident in which he was bedridden for a few months and lost most of the use of his right arm and left leg. At the time of this suicide attempt, Bob had slowly been regaining the use of his limbs but remained troubled by his physical disability, especially by the social implications of life as a "cripple." Bob poignantly describes his feelings of worthlessness at the time.

When the depression set in, I didn't want to see nobody. I felt like, uh, I didn't have nothing. I felt like, uh, I didn't have nothing—no home, no nothing, nobody cared. I had family, sisters, brother, whatever, but I'd never hardly see them. They didn't seem to care what I was doing. It seemed like they was just gone. I didn't see them for years at a time, sometimes. And it seemed like just me.

Thus, in both Bob's and Ethel's cases, the antecedents to feelings of worthlessness were *compounded* feelings of bereavement and aggrievement, in that order. However, the order does not appear to be the important factor, as can be seen in the case of Emmie, a fifty-year-old woman who during her first marriage felt aggrieved as a result of years of marital abuse and jealousies within her family of origin, but whose feelings of worthlessness were not triggered until the grandfather who raised her died. Moreover, it may not even be that feeling worthless results from the compounding of feeling aggrieved and feeling bereaved but simply from the chronic or pervasive occurrence of one emotion or the other. Such could be inferred from the story about the man who committed suicide after the deaths of all four of his children and the confinement of his wife to a mental institution, or the teenage boy who committed suicide, it is said, after years of poor treatment at the hands of his stepsiblings because he had a different father.

The striking aspect of accounts of feeling worthless is the shift from emotions of feeling aggrieved and/or feeling bereaved, which are limited in significance to a particular loss or rejection, to a more generalized sense of widespread abandonment and from there into a sense of personal worthlessness. In Bob's account, we saw clearly how he shifted from the specific incident "my girlfriend doesn't care for me" to "*nobody* cares for me" to an attempt to end his own life. And we saw a similar shift in Ethel's story when she got home from work to find the note saying that everyone had gone out. However, this kind of shift was evident neither in Clara's grief-loneliness following the death of her husband nor in Sophie's feelings of aggrievement about her husband's abandonment of her when he went drinking.

One only has to reread Turney-High's statement on the gravity of the taunt "You are abandoned, thrown away!" or the first three chapters of this book to realize the profound implications of complete abandonment for Flathead people. By now, it should be evident the extent to which in Flathead psychology the validity of the self is predicated on the validity of one's relationships. Within that psychology, losses, separations, and rejections have an impact on the integrity of the self in notable ways. Within that psychology, complete abandonment by others cannot be connected to anything but feelings of worthlessness about the self.

As in feeling aggrieved, both self and others are subject to scrutiny in cases of feeling worthless that come to light. However, except in cases of completed suicide, it is the self who feels worthless that receives the lion's share of scrutiny—usually in the form of chastising lectures. The chastisement that characterizes the social judgment of feeling worthless, and of the tendency of those who are feeling worthless to engage in reckless or self-destructive behaviors, is informed by the maxim that is the flip side of the psychological principle that relationships with others constitute an essential element of the self. The maxim states, "Your life is not your own; you owe your life to others." In the words of an esteemed elder,

> Well, my folks used to say, you have to believe in what your parents do, you know. There's always the devil behind you—wants you to go do this to yourself, kill yourself. Then, you don't know there's somebody behind you telling you to do it, 'cause you don't listen to your parents. You think you're the boss of yourself, "I can do this to myself." So that's all. A lot of them gets that way—they think, "Well, that's my life. It's not yours. I can do what I want to do."

From the point of view of someone who feels worthless, there are two kinds of responses to the ego damage that he or she has sustained. The first is resignation to the judgment that one is worthless, that is, suicide. The second is the putatively ego-protective attempt to disprove the judgment by trying to produce evidence that someone *does* cares. Unfortunately, neither response tends to be very beneficial. The former, if successful, ends a life that, despite overwhelming feelings to the contrary, is not worthless. The latter response often takes the form of reckless behaviors that not only put the self at risk for physical harm but also tend to perpetuate and magnify feelings of worthlessness. Moreover, these reckless behaviors tend not to elicit very agreeable expressions of caring from family and friends, as the ambivalence with which Ethel greeted the comments of her friend who communicated his concern that she was "on the road to destruction" illustrates.

Thus we can see how Ethel's drinking, for example, not only landed her in the hospital but also contributed to her sense of failure as a parent when she lost her paycheck. Similarly, during Emmie's prolonged feelings of worthlessness after the death of her grandfather, she began to drink heavily, to take drugs, and to engage in sex with many men, young and old, while she was intoxicated. The humiliation of Emmie's actions fed back into her feelings of worthlessness, thereby increasing her perceived need to drink as a mechanism to bring her into contact with people who seemed to care and to jar family and friends into the overt expressions of compassion and assistance that she needed so badly.

Given that feeling worthless proceeds out of feelings of bereavement and/or aggrievement, the communicative symbols of feelings of worthlessness are often those that attend either of those other two forms of loneliness. However, this final form of loneliness is often perceived and communicated by other, more specific signs. For example, the worthless self may present as emotionally labile, changing relatively rapidly from the irritability of feeling wrongfully rejected to the tears of grief-loneliness, or from a "good mood" into irritation. Or, as another example, the worthless self may present with "contradictory" emotions, such as when Ethel presented prolonged sadness, rather than anger, over her divorce. Other signs include diminishing participation in family get-togethers, community events, or spiritual activities.

CONCLUSION

I have described three types of loneliness in terms that show important differences among them not only in their antecedents, or triggers, but also in the way they organize the self vis-à-vis the world. In feeling bereaved, the self suffers a significant loss that others respond to with compassion and assistance. In feeling aggrieved, the self perceives an unfair loss and seeks justice through social judgment of the responsible party. In feeling worthless, the self experiences him- or herself as responsible for widespread and pervasive losses and, until final resignation, seeks to generate evidence that others care for him or her.

These differences can also be represented in pictorial form, following the idea of semantic networks developed by Byron J. Good (1977) and Byron J. Good and Mary-Jo DelVecchio Good (1982). Figure 3 shows the network of semantic associations among the three types of loneliness, revealing each as a distinct constellation of culturally marked circumstances, personal attributes, and social action. The figure shows that to translate Flathead loneliness as simply a variant on Euro-American depression would be to fundamentally misconstrue the nature of emotion as a cultural product. Translated as depressed affect or sadness, Flathead loneliness is stripped of its rich cultural meanings

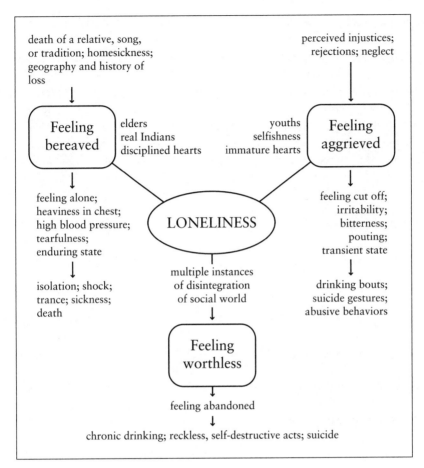

Figure 3.   Semantic network of Flathead loneliness

and becomes an impoverished term that fails to accurately attend to the complex and distinct phenomenology of feeling bereaved, feeling aggrieved, and feeling worthless. A simplistic translation would also obscure the important similarities among all types of Flathead loneliness—at the heart of which lies a fear of abandonment. Whether abandonment is caused by the death of another, is perceived as the result of the animosity or uncaring attitude of others, or stems from one's own unworthiness, the specter of separation or abandonment remains a powerful force in the emotional lives of Flathead people.

In elucidating the language of loneliness among the Flathead, I have elaborated an ethnopsychology that is rooted deeply in cultural values of belonging and social practices of reciprocity. Within this system, relationships attain a relevance for the self that transcends their importance in many Euro-American psychologies. As Sophie stated, "It's always seemed like the depressions I've been through in my life involved relationships—broken relationships or failing relationships." Flathead loneliness expresses, negatively, the cultural, social, and psychological importance of interdependence in contemporary Flathead life. The general point is that Flathead people live in a culturally constituted world that is deeply interpersonal; that their emotional lives are always concerned with relations with others; and that disruptions in relations are at best disturbing and sometimes debilitating.

Looking back to Part I, from a perspective informed by this description of belonging and the self, certain issues concerning Indian identity gain a sharper focus. First, acts of racism emerge now as acts of exclusion that question the validity of the self to belong, thus evoking loneliness. Accordingly, acts that might be motivated by racist feelings probably will not be responded to as "racist," if those acts are negligible in terms of exclusion and rejection. Second, the value structure of Flathead loneliness suggests too why racism involving children is so uniformly disparaged. Among elders and more traditional adults, serious and dangerous acts of racism induce grief-loneliness as the losses are tallied. Among youths and young adults, serious acts of racism rouse feelings of aggrievement as the unfairness of the losses is noted. But among children and others who are more vulnerable, racism triggers feelings of worthlessness, as the undeveloped self repeatedly encounters evidence that others judge him or her worthless.

This in-depth account of Flathead loneliness also helps us to appreciate what is at stake in the day-to-day negotiations of Indian identity. The stakes in the negotiation of "real Indian" identity are higher than at first glance, not only because the question about being "really Indian" fuses authentic Indian identity and proper affect but also because the question involves whether one has a right to belong or not—a question that we now know has both moral and practical implications and thus emotional implications for the self.

As a set of negotiations that at base determine the right to belong, questions of Indian identity reveal the importance of tribal traditions and survival for individual tribal members. For many Flathead people, tribe assumes its significance as a primary reference group, after family, and the termination of the tribe becomes a termination of an important aspect of the self—an orientation that nontribal Americans can

only imagine. Reciprocally, given that the meaning of belonging is buttressed by its links to the ways of "real Indians" and that those ways
are perceived as threatened, the moral valence of belonging for the individual in specific situations is buttressed.

The moral imagination with which the Flathead people create
meaningful ties among loneliness, belonging, history, and contemporary Indian identity and practices forcefully reminds us that loneliness,
as the central complaint in accounts of depression, must be dealt with
in a way that emphasizes the cultural grounding of emotion. Rather
than viewing emotion as a "functional" product of the individual's
psychobiological needs, loneliness here is cast as a culturally meaningful construct, an interpretation, that organizes the self in specific ways.
Within this perspective, to understand what a person feels in a given
situation means to understand, first, the ways that his or her culture
has structured the meaningful relations among affects, the self, and
various social actions and social situations. In other words, the first
step in understanding a person's emotion is to uncover the way that his
or her particular emotion is structured semantically in his or her local
world.

Loneliness
and Depression

Parts I and II laid the foundation for understanding the Flathead language of depression and its rich moral and complex practical meanings. Part III turns to how culture shapes individual experience and what it means for understanding depressive disorder cross-culturally.

Individual narratives of pain challenge us, as researchers and clinicians, to move beyond cultural semantics toward the creative and dynamic culturally based processes of individual experience. Chapter 5, "Speaking from the Heart," presents one man's story about his experiences with depression and suicide. As he skillfully designs his story as one of loneliness, compassion, and increasing responsibility, the narrator illustrates forcefully the role of culture in disordered experience. In particular, the telling of his story reveals culture as a set of historically and socially grounded narrative forms among which individuals choose to give voice to their experiences.

Chapter 6, "Culture and Depression," recaps what has been presented about loneliness and explores the significance of those findings for cross-cultural research into depression. Loneliness, as it appears in Flathead narratives of individual and collective experience, is an idiom that seeks to reclaim the very relationships and identities it heralds as missing, that encompasses both the meaning and the meaninglessness of pain and loss, and that, as such, is part of a larger, ongoing sociohistorical process of the demoralization and remoralization of the Flathead Indian people. Yet this view cannot be accommodated by the medical model that currently dominates American psychiatry, as embodied in the various editions of the *Diagnostic and Statistical Manual of Mental Disorders* (DSM; American Psychiatric Association 1980, 1987, 1994). The concluding section highlights the areas of tension between the two approaches to understanding depressive disorder among the Flathead, and charts a course for future research that can accommodate the insights of both approaches.

CHAPTER FIVE

Speaking from the Heart

For the poet, language is actually totally saturated with living
intonations; it is completely contaminated by rudimentary
social evaluations and orientations, and it is precisely with
them that the creative process must struggle; it is precisely
among them that one must select such or such a linguistic
form, or this or that expression. The artist receives no word
in linguistically virginal form. The word is already
impregnated by the practical situations and the poetic
contexts in which he has encountered it.
                    —*Mikhail Bakhtin, in Todorov 1984: 48–49*

As I reached the final stages in the transcription of an interview I had
conducted in the last months of my fieldwork, I was struck by the narrative that was emerging. The interview material, with only minor edit-
ing, seemed to display a rigorously organized narrative structure, and
it did not take any stretch of the imagination for me to envision the interviewee as artist, poet, or author. Imagining the interview material as
an artistic production and the interviewee as author opens up several
avenues for analysis. For one, there is the opportunity to explore the
language available to the narrator, along with its "saturation with living intonations" and its contamination "by rudimentary social evaluations and orientations," to use Bakhtin's words. In some respects, this
preliminary work has been done. I have explored some aspects of the
Flathead language of emotions and some of "the practical situations
and the poetic contexts" that impregnate that language, especially for
emotions that I regarded as somehow "like" depression.

No matter how carefully done, however, my description of general
orientations and shared values in Flathead life remains unsatisfactory.
By its very nature, it is unable to answer to an understanding of the creative process and to the unique meaning of a particular and situated
narrative, other avenues implied in an envisioning of the interviewee as
artist. To expect a generalized description to do so would be like expecting a portrayal of the shared techniques and orientations of an
artistic movement to capture the visions of individual artists. Similarly,
while we might expect to find certain shared practices and key symbols,

such as the real Indians, the Salish language and traditional spirituality, Indian-white relations, or family obligations, in almost any Flathead person's account of his or her experiences, this generalization fails to address the specific meaning, the unique force of each narrative.[1]

The narrative, or artistic product, that interests me here, however, is of a particular kind; it is a narrative that is purportedly about an individual's experiences with depression and suicide. And so, while an urge to come to terms with the creative process and with singular meaning underlies my analysis of the interview material in this chapter, my analysis also strains to apprehend *emotional* experience and the self. A generalized account of shared orientations is as poorly equipped to illuminate the intricacies of individual experience as it is to address the nature of the creative process and the construction of singular meaning. A. Irving Hallowell made a similar point nearly forty years ago: "Culture can be objectively described and for certain purposes treated as if it were a sui generis phenomenon. . . . Presented to us in this form, these cultural data do not easily permit us to apprehend, in an integral fashion, the most significant and meaningful aspects of the world of the individual as experienced by him" (1955 [completed in 1951]: 88).

My assertion that a general description of shared orientations is inadequate to the task of elucidating specific narratives about emotional experience most emphatically does not consist in some epistemological distinction between the social and the individual, the exterior and the interior, the cognitive and the affective, the cultural and the biological—those notorious dualities so common to our Western intellectual heritage. Indeed, in my view, a narrative about emotional experience must be seen as a realization or actualization of human intersubjectivity, in which the narrator attempts to persuasively construct a self and its relation to a specific social world. It is a project that is only accomplished as the narrator enters into dialogue with others, with certain life events, and with specific schemata of meaning that come to the narrator via language and the practices of family, friends, and acquaintances.

A MORAL TALE

To study the *given* in the created (for example: the
language, the already constituted general elements of
the conception of the world, the reflected real facts,
etc.) is far easier than the study of the *created* itself.

Frequently, scholarly analysis as a whole winds up
doing nothing more than making explicit all that is
given, already present and constituted before the work.
　　　　　—Mikhail Bakhtin, in Todorov 1984: 50

The narrative that forms the basis for the analysis in this chapter was
told to me within the setting of an interview about the respondent's experiences with depression and suicide.[2] I first met the respondent, Dan,
when I was introducing myself to the program directors and staff
members of the Tribal Health Department, near the start of my stay at
the reservation.[3] Dan was working as an alcohol counselor, and when
he learned of my interest in depression, he talked with me about the effects of the weather, especially extended periods of fog, on people's
emotions. I found it easy to be around Dan from the start. He was a
small and tidy man, soft-spoken but very articulate. He possessed a
sense of humor and joked easily with his colleagues and me, but at the
same time, he displayed a thoughtful, almost melancholic, air.

Dan was about fifty years old at the time of our interview and had
spent most of his life on the reservation. He was relatively well-off economically, given that both he and his wife held year-round, full-time
positions. He was integrally connected to community life, via his upbringing, his marriage into a large, well-known Indian family, his three
children, his work, and his drinking days. Dan had been sober for
fifteen years at the time I met him; before that he had been one of the
more notorious hard-core drinkers at the reservation.

Dan's narrative is an elaborate and powerful moral drama of responsibility that emerged in response to my request for an interview
about his experiences with depression and suicide. Dan's narrative thus
must be understood as structured in part by his attempts to answer to
my interests. At the same time, one of the most striking aspects of his
narrative is its high degree of autonomy from my own agenda. From
the start, Dan organizes his story not by episodes of depression or by
descriptions of isolated interior states, the direction that my questions
might have led him, but instead plunges directly into a moral universe
and a set of dramatic life events that are only loosely connected to depression per se. Depression, far from being *the* central symbol of the
narrative, plays a supporting role in a far more significant drama about
the self and moral responsibility that is woven around Dan's attempt
to commit suicide some twenty years ago.

The narrative as it appears in the following pages is the edited

product of a verbatim transcription of a two-and-a-half-hour taped interview. Fortunately, the recording was of good quality, and little was
lost in the transcription process. I had originally wanted to present
Dan's narrative in its entirety in order to retain the integrity of his
voice in the telling of his story. However, in the interests of readability,
I opted instead to present blocks of the text, interspersed with comments. My own voice appears infrequently in the narrative for two reasons: first, I spoke only rarely during the interview and then usually
only to ask for clarification on some factual matter (i.e., Where did
you grow up? How old were you then?); and second, I found that my
questions often distracted from the main text and that if my questions
(and the responses to them) were removed, the text had a greater co-
herence.

The following narrative represents approximately four-fifth's of the
original transcript, which means that the narrative that you will be
reading took Dan about two hours to relate. I mention this, and recommend reading a portion of the text aloud at a very deliberate pace,
to communicate a sense of the serious and thoughtful tenor of the narrative. The one-fifth of the transcript that was deleted consisted mainly
of my requests for information and Dan's responses to them, a couple
of interruptions, and a few sections of repetition that I judged unneces-
sary. The order of the elements of the narrative has not been altered,
nor have any significant changes been made in the relative weighting of
different themes. We can now turn to the narrative itself.

DAN'S NARRATIVE

THE ELDERS

> When I was growing up there was a lotta older, elder ones, like Mary. This
> is my grandma over here, great-grandma. [Pointing to a picture on the wall]
> And what I seen then and I don't see now is . . . there was one old lady, and
> it wasn't only her, it was different elders, people would come to the house
> and come in and sit down and they'd start visiting my grandma and them,
> they would sit around and visit. When it was time to eat, she cooked for
> whoever was there. They got done, they visited in the afternoon. She
> cooked again. Visit in the evening. Then right away, she fixed a place to . . .
> for them to sleep. And they stayed, like three, four, five days. There was
> never a question of, "Hi. How are you? How long are you going to be
> here? I'm sorry, we're gonna eat here pretty soon." They were just included
> in the family.
>
> And what we learned right away was they disciplined us. I mean, it was

just like she was my grandma, too, even though she wasn't my grandma. If I done something wrong and my grandma wasn't there, you know, I might be off running around doing something I shouldn't, she would see me and then she would correct me. And, by gosh, I had to listen because I would get a spanking if I didn't.

But now, if you notice, you come around here, the visiting isn't as, uh, important as it was back then, you know. If you go visit somebody and they're just starting with their cooking, you know, well, they let you know, "Well, we're gonna eat pretty soon." So you know you have to go. But back then, nobody ever asked. I mean, if you came, they just set a plate for you, you sat down and you stayed as long as you wanted. And one day, you'd just get up and say, "Well, we'd better go," and leave. I mean, it was just like they were part of the household—they came and went.

And growing up, there was Mary, Susan—she just died—Annie, and another old lady. There was about four or five houses in the area there where we went. And it was the same way. Whoever's house we were at at lunchtime, we went in and sat down and we were included. That's why, you know, Mary likes me so much, 'cause I was always with her kids. Uh, I was always over there playing or they were down at our house, you know. And all of them always disciplined us.

And we had so much to do around there, you know, riding horses, fishing, uh, hunting with 22s. We never had the desire to go to town. I mean, you know, we never was running to town to see what was in town, we'd hardly go at all. It was kind of a big thing for me to . . . to go to town.

Uh, and then that kinda passed on, and then my grandma told me that I needed to learn the white man ways if I was going to make it. And now, I . . . I kinda feel bad that, you know, I never paid more attention to what I had because I had a whole wealth of information, you know, right there at the house, I mean, coming and going all the time. But I didn't pay attention to that. Then I started school and started learning English—when I should have been learning our own language.

Dan frames his story of depression and suicide within the morally and affectively charged meaning-context of the real Indians. He begins his narrative with a reference to Mary, one of the most widely known and respected elders living on the reservation at the time of our interview, and follows with a reminiscence of the way of life of the traditional grandparents who raised him, focusing that description in terms of visiting, sharing, and discipline. Dan will also close his narrative with a similar, somewhat romanticized, reconstruction of the ways of the elders. In no uncertain terms, the values and wisdom of the elders constitute the beginning and ending points of the moral universe within which the events of Dan's life unfold in this narrative.

With his opening words, Dan constructs not only a subtly romanticized vision of the elders but also his own relation to them and the moral world they embody. Dan's complex relation to the world of his elders stands as a metaphorical introduction to his difficult passage to moral maturity and responsibility. Dan characterizes his relation to the elders, the real Indians, as uncertain and contradictory, distinguished by both distance and proximity.[4] He documents his ties to the elders, through kinship and upbringing, and tentatively asserts an Indian identity somewhat proximate to the real Indians for himself. However, by noting that he neither speaks the language nor knows the ways of the elders, he also asserts an opposite position highlighting his distance from that valued realm. Yet even while Dan undercuts his identity as a real Indian in these ways, he ultimately buttresses his moral character, by taking onto himself the blame for not knowing the language rather than holding someone else accountable when he confesses that he didn't "pay attention" as a child.

As Dan attributes his lack of knowledge about Indian ways to his own inattentiveness, he presages the main themes of moral maturity and responsibility in the narrative. Inattentiveness, especially in a child, is a relatively minor breach of responsibility, and, as such, it serves appropriately as an introductory foothold for the increasingly serious examples of irresponsibility that follow in the first half of the narrative.[5] However unimportant it may appear on the surface, this snippet of irresponsibility contains within it the structure of unfulfilled reciprocity that undergirds the ways that responsibility will be portrayed as the rest of the story is narrated. Inattentiveness betrays the relationship of elders to their descendants, in which elders provide wisdom to their descendants who reciprocate with attention.

GROWING UP

And, uh, then I started into sports, that's what kept me in . . . in school. Uh, I was good in basketball, football, and track. So I was accepted, you know. I could go in the Indian houses and be accepted there. But through my athletic ability, I could go to the . . . be invited to the white peoples, uh, because I was a good basketball player, football player. So, you know, I could go in either place.

So after getting into high school, being involved in sports and then realizing, you know, that I was. . . . Because all along, uh, I felt not quite as good as everybody else because we, uh, didn't have money, you know. I would go and see what my white friends had, you know. And they . . . they were always dressed nice. We always had clean clothes, but they were patched, they were old. Uh [sighs], so I . . . all through then I . . . I felt not

quite on the same level as my white friends. But then, when I started playing basketball, and football, and track, then at that level, I was as good or
better than they were. Yeah, that was mine, you know. And then, I worked
hard at it, you know. I'd spend hours playing basketball, so at that level, I
could compete, be as good or better than most of them. And, uh, so that
helped me. And by being able, I was offered a scholarship to go to, uh,
Western Montana.

A couple of points can be made about this relatively short transition
passage describing Dan's school years. First, Dan documents a separation of Indian and white communities and, in reference to those communities, argues that he was able to negotiate the two worlds—a discourse that is, perhaps surprisingly, more typical of more full-blood
and traditional Indians. Indians who have higher degrees of white
blood and who were raised in less traditional households are far more
likely to talk of the incompatibility of the two worlds, the racism of
whites, and the impossibility of negotiating a comfortable space for
themselves in this setting. Like the elders whom I interviewed, Dan
stresses the importance of harmonious social relations and asserts his
ability to get along with anybody, Indian or white.[6]

Second, when Dan notes his sense of inferiority alongside his white
friends, he gives a hint of the intertwining of material welfare and
emotional welfare that underlies the sense of "having nothing" that is
part of most of the interviews I conducted about experiences with depression. Dan locates his feelings of inferiority in the shameful fact of
having to wear clothes that did not measure up to the clothes of his
white friends. The shame of less-than-adequate clothing resides in the
complex of understandings about personal worth and the sharing of
material wealth, in which one's lack of material goods is equivalent to
not being "cared for," in which loneliness means having neither people
who care for you nor material security. As we saw in chapter 3, material poverty and affective poverty are inextricably linked, and one term
generally implies the other.

DRINKING DAYS

But then [sighs], I slipped into the drinking when I was a junior. And I
think I'm one that became an alcoholic the first time I got drunk. I mean,
the first time because, uh, we went to Post Creek down here. It's a dance
hall, where all the people used to go, all of the kids in Mission, Arlee,
Charlo, Ronan, Polson go down there and dance, and drink, and fight. And
the first time we went down there, I can remember, I looked like a "dandy."

I had a three-piece outfit on. [Laughing] I mean I was just really proud, you
know. I went down there and . . . and, by gosh, the next morning, I woke
up in the back of the car, you know. And, gee, my nice gray pants, you
know, they were all muddy, and my coat. And I sat there and I looked
around and, I was with one of my friends, and I woke him up and he said,
"Gee, what happened?" I said, "I don't know." "We musta really had fun
though, look at me," I said, "I'm just covered with mud." And so, from
that time on, you know, I never went with the intent of having one or two
drinks, I went with the intent of getting drunk. I mean, that's why I'm convinced that I was an alcoholic from the first day I started drinking.

And then I just progressively got worse, where you talk about your depression. The most depressing time with drinking is—I would be gone for
four, five days like maybe I'd get home on a Sunday, Sunday night, and
wake up in the mornings, Monday morning, sick, and then realize that my
wife, Angie, had got up and went to work, that the kids went off to school,
and that I was home with nothing to do. I mean, I had no place to go, to
belong, I didn't have a job that I could go to, I didn't belong. I couldn't go
to school. And, uh, that's where the depression would set in. I mean, and,
you know, it would get so bad you couldn't do anything. Then [sighs] I
would stay away for a while, then I would get right back into that. And
they seemed to get longer and longer.

Then I would think, "Maybe I'm not any good to anybody, to myself, to
anybody." I thought I was useless, worthless, uh, but I continued to drink. I
drank and I drank and I drank. Uh, Angie finally divorced me.

After a brief recounting of his school years, Dan takes up the theme
of irresponsibility for the second time by talking of his descent into alcoholism. Two points are especially salient in this passage. First, it is
important that one of the consequences of drinking is cast in terms of
an emotional state, depression, in which Dan reports thinking that he
was useless, worthless, and "no good to anybody." This emotion in
turn is grounded in two spheres of Dan's life world: family and work.
The reciprocal relations of self, family, and work are recurring images
in the narrative and are played out in a number of scenarios as the
meaning of responsibility is given substance.

Second, this entire period of drinking, spanning nearly twenty years,
is not described in detail but is labeled by Dan simply by the term "alcoholism." His unquestioning use of this term signals his firm location
within a community of recovering drinkers at the reservation, many of
whom participated in Alcoholics Anonymous (AA) at least during the
early stages of quitting drinking, and his own work as an alcohol
counselor. Dan's summation of the consequences of his drinking in
terms of his wife's move to divorce him represents the "rock bottom"
stage of alcoholism, a dominant motif in narratives about drinking

within the AA community.[7] Dan, however, is unwilling to end his story of drinking here. He resumes his narrative, instead, with a description of a poignant scene with his alcoholic mother, the last time he saw her alive, in which the issue of responsibility, and the term itself, is brought out overtly for the first time.

IRRESPONSIBLE DRINKING

I stopped in one night to my mom's after work. I got a job in a Missoula sawmill. I was working there and I stopped in—my mom was fifty-two years old. I stopped in on a Monday night. I just bought a new pickup. I was really proud of it and I stopped to show my grandma. They were gone. My mom had a small trailer house by there, and I stopped [sighs]. And I showed her and she wasn't interested in my pickup. She said, "Come in and have a drink." At that point she was to the point where she, uh, had to hold on to the table to get to the cupboard, and then hold on to the cupboard. And I told her, I said, "Ma, look what the hell that alcohol is doing to you." And she said, "Yeah, I know." And I said, "God, it's killing you." And she said, "Yeah." So she pulls out her fifth of vodka and I said, "I don't want any." She said, "No, you have a glass with me." Poured me a big water glass, poured her one. And she said, "That's why I like to visit with you, you never preach to me." And I said, "Yeah, but why do you do it?" And she says,"I don't have any responsibility to anybody." She said, "I never raised you kids." She says, "I left you kids when you were small. I never had a moment's responsibility to anybody."

And, uh, so after a couple of glasses of her . . . her vodka, I went to the Log Cabin, started drinking there. And then I was gone. I was off. I used to go on running drunks. I [sighs] went back to Missoula to, oh, all over, up to Kalispell. That was on Monday, I drank Tuesday, Wednesday, Thursday. My grandma had some land, she sold it and she gave each one of us some. I had that in the bank in Missoula. So, Friday morning I woke up in Polson. I thought, "Well, I can go back to Missoula and draw out some more money for the weekend." Then I went through Arlee. And I . . . I stopped at the Log Cabin, and I still had, oh, I don't know, probably three hundred dollars. And I remember clearly, walking in the Log Cabin and reaching in my billfold and pulling out a hundred dollar bill, throwing it on the bar and saying, "Give me a fifth of Canadian Club and a case of Oly." And the bartender looked at me real funny and . . . and . . . somebody was sitting there and they looked at me. I said, "Oh, and give these guys a drink, too." And the ironic part of it was, the one sitting next to me, I said, "Give him a drink." It was Woody and, uh, Woody said, "Thanks." He said, "It's too bad about your mom." And I said, "Oh, why? What did she do now?" He said, "Oh, she died last night."

And so I just turned around and I walked out, got in my pickup and I drove to my grandma's. She told me they'd been looking for me since the day before when she died. And, uh [sighs], she told me, "You better take a

shower and lay down and go to sleep and straighten up." I . . . I didn't
know when the funeral was.

And, uh, Woody took all of the change. He kept the Canadian Club and
the . . . and the case of beer. But he gathered up all my change and he put it
away. He came up to the Rosary. He came in and he said, "Here's that
money you left on the bar." You know, he could've kept it, I mean, I just
totally forgot it, but he brought it to me, gave it back.

And then, that was in November, well, my brother died in April, just
that April, and this happened in November. And then Angie told me, she
said, "You know, you're really a cold person." I said, "Why do you say
that?" She said, " 'Cause I watched you bury Kenny and I watched you
bury your mother, and you never did cry." And I said, "Well, it's because
they were doing what they wanted to do." I said, "They were happy drinking." And she said, "Well, what are you saying?" I said, "Well, what I'm
saying is when you drink, you know that, and you have to accept that when
you take that drink it might be your last."

In this powerful passage about family relations and responsibility,
Dan narrates his reason for stopping by his mother's trailer, her disinterest in his new pickup, and her avid interest in having him drink with
her. He observes her physical decline and tells her, "Ma, look at what
the hell that alcohol is doing to you. . . . God, it's killing you." She
pours the drinks anyway, and Dan, not wanting to, joins her for a couple of glasses of vodka. His mother praises him for not preaching to
her. Still, he asks her why she drinks. Her reply is telling: "I don't have
any responsibility to anybody. I never raised you kids. I left you kids
when you were small. I never had a moment's responsibility to anybody." By the middle of this passage we learn that Dan's mother dies
only days after this meeting.

This passage captures a primary mode of narrating emotional experience at the reservation: the undressed portrayal of a tragic encounter
between Dan and his mother resonates with an overwhelming pathos,
and yet terms of emotion per se are notably absent. Dan sees his
mother dying and yet is bound by his relationship with her, his own
drinking, and canons of respectful conduct not to "preach" to her. Instead of relying on a string of referents to internally located feelings,
Dan assumes that the meaning of this interaction is transparent in his
recitation of the external events.

Dan's mother's irresponsibility, like Dan's, is cast in terms of familial obligations, in this case to her children. I noted earlier that Dan's
own irresponsibility in drinking was also often cast in terms of family.
There are two illuminating differences beyond the similarity. First,

Dan's family is more than just his children. His obligations extend backward, to his grandparents, horizontally, to his wife, and forward, to his children. This is probably also the case for his mother to some degree, but this narrative strategy emphasizes gender differences. Dan's mother, as a woman, is responsible primarily to her offspring, whereas Dan, as a man, must also be more directly responsible to his elders. This follows a pattern in which it is the sons, or grandsons, who are expected to take primary responsibility for the care of aging parents or grandparents, despite the fact that it is often the case that women are performing these duties.

Second, as a man, Dan's irresponsibility is also connected in a strong way to the realm of work. At the reservation, it was not uncommon to hear elders explaining that men must be allowed "freedom" since they are the ones who "work." Again, this is in spite of the fact that it is often women who support their families economically through wage labor or by qualifying for welfare assistance. Thus while the narrative draws parallels between Dan and his mother in terms of their irresponsibilities, the parallels are enriched by differences related to the different ways that men and women are to act in the world.

In this passage, Dan also describes an interaction with Woody, a notorious drinker. Dan underscores the seeming incongruity of Woody's irresponsibility by describing his responsibility in returning the money Dan left on the bar after he heard the news about his mother. This vignette portrays this type of behavior on the part of an alcoholic as unusual, a judgment that is made more powerful by Woody's death from cirrhosis not long before our interview. This calling up of the realities of hard-core drinking is made repeatedly by Dan. The only hard drinkers that he mentions in the narrative, his mother, his brother, Woody, and Richard, were all deceased by the time of the interview. The only exception to this pattern is Dan himself.

The passage ends with a potent scene in which Dan's wife, Angie, questions Dan's emotional connection to his family by noting that he did not grieve for the deaths of his brother and his mother.[8] Dan's failure to weep is highlighted as aberrant and serves as another entry into the issue of the dilemmas of responsibility and drinking. His failure to grieve appropriately and the fact that he almost missed his mother's funeral, both powerful symbols of failed affective reciprocity, are the central representations of Dan's irresponsibility in this section of the narrative.[9]

It might be argued that, rather than irresponsibility, it is the stripping away of relationships that is the central theme of Dan's narrative so far. At some level, this is true. The phenomenology of Dan's experience is predominantly one of increasing loneliness as important relationships are severed in his continuing descent into chronic drunkenness. However, Dan's focus on irresponsibility and the moral responsibility to maintain relationships through reciprocity, rather than on loneliness per se, harkens back to the sense of dysfunctional agency that mediates loneliness in feeling worthless. By focusing on loneliness in the context of irresponsibility, Dan's story line highlights a culpable failure of reciprocity underlying the losses of self that the young Dan is suffering.

Dan's character at this point in the narrative is informed by a sense of being responsible for the consequences of one's drinking that affect one's self. This perspective will undergo dramatic revision in the second half of the narrative, in which drinkers come to be responsible not only for the consequences that affect themselves but also for those that affect others. Coming as it does in the first half of the narrative, this perspective underscores Dan's irresponsible behavior and is contrasted with the following passage, in which the wisdom of the elders is explicitly addressed.

RESPONSIBLE DRINKING

Uh, I got throwed in jail one time, when I first started drinking. I don't know what I done and I got throwed in jail. So I stayed in jail, Friday, Saturday, Sunday, Monday, Tuesday. Finally I told Angie, I said, "Go by the house and tell my grandma I'm in jail and I want to come home." So she said, "OK." So she went. So, the next day my grandpa come down, went in there and says, "I want to bail him out." So he bailed me out. So I was real happy I got out of jail. So we got my pickup and we started there and I thought, "Oh, boy!" So we got close to Arlee and I told him, "Stop in Arlee, I'll get off at the Log Cabin." And he said, "No." He said, "Your . . . your grandma wants to talk to you." And I says, "Oh, boy!" I said, "I'm in trouble, ain't I?" And he says, "Yeah, I would say that." And, uh, I said, "Well, I suppose I better go home."

And so we walked in and he went right on through, he went out the back. He had something to do out there. And she told me, "You sit down there." So I sat down there. She told me, she says, "You know, when you leave here, your Grandpa and me, we don't tell you, 'Go downtown, go to the Log Cabin and drink whatever they give you.' " She said, "What we tell you is, 'Don't drink that because you're gonna get in trouble.' But you're not listening to us. You have to go. You think you're smarter than us. You know all of these things, what we're trying to tell you not to do, you gotta go out and try and find out for yourself that we know what we're telling you." So she says, "I told him, you go down and get him outta jail, this time." "But," she says, "I'm telling you now, that was the last time." She said, "When you leave here and you go to town and you start drinking, then you better be able to accept what comes with the drinking." She said, "Whether it's dying, being in jail, going to prison, or, you know, whatever you do out there, you better be able to." And, boy, after that, when I got throwed in jail, I never would call home.

And then, like my work, you know. When I worked at first, I can remember to this day, she made my lunch. And before the people that I was gonna work with came and got me, she told me, she said, "I'm gonna tell you something now." She said, "That man is paying you his money, his good money for eight hours of your work." And she said, "And that don't mean eight hours of you looking for ways of getting out of work." She said, "If you want to take that man's money, then you better work hard for it." And that's kinda applied to, I mean, even when I was at the sawmill, you know, that's what my foreman told me, he says, "You know, I can't find a better worker than you, when you're here." He says, "But when you get ahold of that bottle, then," he said, "then you lose all responsibility." He said, "I never know when you're gonna be here." So, it's just here lately that I realized how much she's, you know, influenced my growing up.

I seen sadness in, you know, the funerals, the deaths, but I just never. . . . All I can remember is my grandma saying you can't sit around and feel sorry for yourself, you know. She says, "When things go bad, you gotta just pick yourself up and go." And I asked her about it, and she said back then they didn't have that. You know, I specifically asked her, I says, "What did you guys do for mental health?" She said you didn't have that. There was nothing for, you know, depression. I don't think she really understands what, what I'm talking about, when I talk about depression. She can't understand why you would let yourself get like that, you know, unless you like it. She said, "You must like it or you wouldn't be." She's ninety and she hasn't been sick hardly at all. And, you know, she can't understand when I say, "Oh, gee, the job gets me down and I get depressed."

But then there's, you know, this other guy I talked to about it too, and that's what he says. He says, "You allow that to happen to you." Well, he kinda said it too, that you must like to be like that or you wouldn't. . . . Uh, they felt if you didn't pray and just stayed in that, then that's your fault. That's your own choosing to be not able to do anything because you say, "No." And they say, "No, you put that in your head." And somebody tells you, "Oh, you're depressed, you can't do this," so you, you believe that. And so that's the way you're going to believe and unless you get it out of your head, you'll stay that way. You'll always be depressed.

Dan lays out the wisdom of the elders through the words of, first, his grandmother and, then, his spiritual mentor, a man we will come to know as Phillip in later passages. It is important to note that a reciprocal practice, of preaching on the part of the elders and listening on

the part of members of the younger generation, is the means by which
wisdom is assumed to pass from one generation to another. When an
elder preaches, a responsible person listens, and this is exactly what
Dan was *not* doing at the time of his life when he was so involved in
drinking. In the narrative, Dan narrates that his grandmother tells him
so explicitly.

> "What we tell you is, 'You don't drink that because you're gonna get in
> trouble.' But you're not listening to us. You have to go. You think you're
> smarter than us. You know all of these things, what we're trying to tell you
> not to do, you gotta go out and try and find out for yourself that we know
> what we're telling you."

Listening, then, implies more than the physical act of turning attention to the spoken voice of an elder. It involves obeying. The accusa-
tion of not listening thus carries a heavy moral load, for nothing is
more reprehensible in the official discourse of emotion and Indian identity than not obeying one's elders. In Dan's narrative, the dishonor of
disobeying his elders transcends the disgrace of whatever "troubles,"
that is, fighting or incarceration, he might get into when drinking. It is
Dan's disobedience toward his grandparents that is the main symbol of
his irresponsibility.

The reciprocity of wisdom and obedience that characterizes Dan's
relationships with his elders is but one form of reciprocity that undergirds this passage in particular and the narrative in general. There is
also the explicit and formal reciprocal exchange between employer and
employee that needs no further explanation—other than to note that
the arena of work is again brought explicitly into the narrative. A sub-
tler form of reciprocity is also drawn on, that is, the relationship of
caring that is said to characterize family relationships.[10] In this passage
describing the one time that his grandparents bailed him out of jail,
Dan shows how he was made to accept responsibility for the consequences of his drinking.

This outcome is not entirely typical at the reservation. Many family
members continue time after time to bail their relatives out of jail, to
take them to the emergency room after accidents or injurious brawls,
to care for their children, to supply them with money, clothing, and
cigarettes. These behaviors are most often cast in terms of the nature of
familial responsibility, a bond of caring and reciprocity that remains
unseverable even when an individual repeatedly fails to participate
responsibly. Strong disapproval often befalls family members who

choose not to "care for" their drinking relatives in these ways, who instead seek to make their drinking relatives responsible for the "troubles" that result from drinking. That Dan became responsible for the consequences of his own drinking, within a larger context of values surrounding familial responsibility, attests to the powerful persuasive ability of his traditional grandmother to cast his drinking in terms of disobedience.

So far in the narrative, Dan casts accepting responsibility for one's actions as an unproblematic step of listening to the wisdom of the elders. He would have been better off if he had listened to his grandparents as a child. His mother would have been better off if she had taken responsibility for her children. Dan's drinking would not have become so much of a problem if he had only obeyed his elders. Depression and illness would not plague him if only he would pray as he was taught. In the following passage, Dan complicates the reality of accepting responsibility by drawing on his experiences with chronic pain.

CHRONIC PAIN

Well, you see, that causes me confusion. Because, you know, if I know that, why do I allow myself to slip back into it? I know that it's in my head. But then at times, that depression can totally immobilize you. Now, uh, you know they've operated on my knees and they say they're slowly . . . that they're not going to get any better and that's the way it is. Uh, but then I keep going to doctors hoping that they'll tell me, "Well, we can do this and it'll be alright." And so I get into that frame of mind of going to the doctors and that they're controlling me. And when I went to talk to this . . . this old man about my knees, he says that, "If you believe in your faith, if you believe in the religion, you don't have to be like that." And I went for two months, great, no knee problems at all.

Then last week I was bowling and I stepped off the approach there, and I hurt my knees and I allowed my mind to slip back into thinking that way. So I constantly thought of it Friday. It got worse. Saturday, I just laid around and did nothing 'cause I thought I couldn't do anything. Sunday, the same way. Monday, I was in bed. Yesterday morning I was in bed. And Angie said, "When are you gonna call your real doctor?" And then I remember when I called him before, he says, "I've sat with you for hours and hours." He says, "And I've told you, you know, what you need to do." He said, "You need to pray. You need to use cedar." He said, "You need to cedar yourself." He said, "You have the resources right here with Dennis." He told me, "You have a lot of the people right here, like Susan." He said, "All you need to do is remember in your mind what these people tell you, what I tell you." He told me sage is good for the mind. He says it clears your mind up, you know. He said, "You'll get a lot of things going on in your mind, boil you some sage tea. Drink that." He says, "Clear your mind up."

And I found myself yesterday morning, couldn't even get out of bed. And then Angie says, "Well, what did the doctors tell you?" And I said, "Well, they said I need to stay in bed for, you know [sighs], eight to ten days. I need to go to physical therapy, uh, three or four times a week." Well, how can you do that while you're working? You can't. And so then, just her last parting thing was, "Well, when are you gonna call your real doctor?" And then, so I laid there and I thought, "She's right." But then I didn't call him 'cause I knew what I needed to do. You know, I needed to get up. I needed to build a fire, get some coals and cedar the house. And get my sage and sit there and pray and . . . and work it all out.

And I finally did it. [Laughing] Last night, we were gonna practice for an intervention and I walked in just like nothing happened. And so here I go from totally bedridden and in pain, and thinking I can't do nothing, to . . . to just thinking back to what my grandma and him and these elders have told me. You know, if you listen to people say bad things are going to happen to you, if you start believing it, then it's going to happen to you, you know. I could still be in bed right now. I wouldn't be sitting here talking to you if Angie hadn't said, "When are you gonna call your real doctor?" And it jarred in my mind, you know. The last time I called him and he said, "You know, I've sat with you and I've told you what, you have everything the Lord provided for you right here. All you need to do is use it. And that if you choose not to use it, sure, that's what's gonna happen to you." And, uh, then with the sage. I have a lot of sage. I learned from Dennis where to go to get the sage. And, uh, so then that goes back to what my grandma said. You know, she said, "That's something that you let happen to you."

But, and then that's where the conflict is because, you know, I know this. I mean I've been told by people. You know I really believe what they're telling me. But then, it's so easy to slip back into, you know. . . .

But, and then, you know, finally I went to see this old guy in Fort Hall. And he used sage, sage and cedar. And, uh, he said, "You need to pray. And you need to believe in the . . . the sage, the cedar, all . . . all these things that were put here for us to use. You need to use 'em. And you need to know when to use 'em." I called him one time. He said, "You know, you don't need to be coming down to see me." He says, "You know, we spend a lot of time together." He says, "I've told you all of the things you need to know." He said, "You just need to do 'em." "You don't need to come down here to do 'em," he said. "You have everything you need right there." He said, "There's a lot a real good people. Listen to 'em. Listen to your grandma. Your grandma's told you a lot of things." A lot of things he told me I can remember that my grandma has already told me. But I just didn't listen to her. [Laughs]

OK, I've been learning these things over the last three years. See, he prayed for me when I was drinking. My grandma asked him, "What are you gonna do? What can we do with this guy?" She said, "He's going to go

out and kill somebody or somebody's gonna kill him, or . . . or he's gonna
end up in prison, or, you know, if he keeps going on the way he's going."
And he said, "I don't know what we can do." "But," he says, "I can pray
and cedar, cedar and pray for him." "But," he says, "if he doesn't believe
it," he says, "there's not a whole lot we can do." So when he asked me and
I said, "Well, I tried everything else." You know, kinda offhand, you know.
"Sure, I'll try that, I tried everything else, you know. Nothing else worked
and this isn't gonna work either." And so he did. And I really didn't believe. I didn't connect it though.

Some moral tales display a three-part structure in which there is a
breach of responsibility followed by a crisis and the movement to a
higher level of responsibility.[11] Dan's narrative is grounded in this
structure but in a way that illuminates the inherent moral complexi-
ties of real lives through the use of digressions into mini-narratives
and the use of unresolved or failed vignettes. Dan begins by establishing the moral parameters of his world and lays out the norms that will
be violated: listening to his elders and accepting responsibility for
his actions. These norms are violated in increasingly serious ways
starting with Dan's not listening to his elders as a child and as he de-
scends into alcoholism. Dan's narration of the meaning of his mother's
death documents the lethal import of irresponsibility and furnishes a
glimpse of his expectations of what his own future would have been
like if he had not changed his ways. Dan's suicide attempt is the crisis
that follows the mounting tensions of his own irresponsibility, his divorce, and the deaths of his brother and mother. But before Dan narrates the important central crisis, he calls up a recent dilemma, his
difficulties in dealing with chronic pain. This digression into a recent
dilemma replays the issues of responsibility in a different arena from
the central one and foreshadows the difficulties of coming to a moral
position.

Dan's narration of his experiences with chronic pain represents a
mini-narrative within the larger narrative and echoes the themes of the
larger narrative. As in the larger narrative, we can see the stages of crisis, giving up in the face of an episode of chronic pain, and a chronicle
of redressive efforts, remembering the wisdom of the elders. In this
mini-narrative, the final stage, movement to a higher level of responsibility, is incomplete. Dan begins the passage by noting his confusion
over accepting responsibility for his own recovery and questioning, "If
I know that, why do I allow myself to slip back into that?" He documents his slide into hopelessness: "I allowed myself to slip back into

thinking that way." But then reports his recovery: "So here I go from totally bedridden and in pain and thinking I can't do nothing to just thinking back to what my grandma and him and these elders have told me." He concludes, "That's something you let happen to you."

Appropriately, given its placement in the first half of the narrative, Dan's dilemma of chronic pain leaves a sense that it is not completely resolved. One can easily imagine from the tone of this passage that Dan will have to struggle to remember what his grandma, Phillip, and the other elders have told him with each new episode of chronic pain. Through proximity, the incomplete resolution of Dan's dilemma is transferred to the as-yet-unresolved crisis in the larger narrative.

SUICIDE ATTEMPT

> And then I came to the point where . . . when all of those things hap-
> pened—my brother got killed, my mom died, Angie divorced me. And so I
> thought, "Well, now I can do anything I want because nobody cares. No-
> body cares what I do." So I was drinking almost every night until I got to
> the point where I was having seizures, alcohol-related seizures. Uh, so, I
> went in and I talked, well, the doctor seen me, you know. He gave me a
> medication. I don't know what kind of medication he gave me. So I saved
> it. And then I went and seen him again. And I didn't . . . I never took what
> he gave me. I went back and I got another one. Put 'em all together and I
> put 'em in the jockey box in the pickup.
>
> And I went to . . . my sister says, "Well, you can"—it was Christmas, I
> think—"come up here for dinner." Well, I had no place else to go. The
> loneliest time for alcoholics is Christmas, Thanksgiving, Easter, you know,
> when everybody's family is together and you're by yourself. Matter of fact,
> I heard that from Richard. We were sitting at the Log Cabin. He said,
> "Look around." He said, "You know, we're the loneliest people, us alco-
> holics, on days like this." He said, "Look, look who's in here, just us real
> hard-core." And [sighs] that stuck in my mind, you know, it's true. It's re-
> ally true. And I . . . I went up there, and I started to eat and I looked around
> and I thought, "No, this is her family. That's not my family." I left and I
> went to town, bought a case of beer, and I drove on and I knew I had them
> pills. And I sat there and I drank and drank and I thought, "Well, you
> know, gee. I don't have anything. There's nothing left for me. Nobody cares
> for me. I'm no good to Angie, no good to my kids, no good to anybody."
>
> So I, uh, I didn't really set out to do that but, my mind, I set them pills in
> there for a reason, that's why I never took them. And so I sat there and
> drank and drank and drank and I thought, "Well, hell. I'd be better off
> dead." And I thought, a long time. And I took those pills and I held 'em,
> and I looked at them, and I drank, and I thought, and then I drove closer to
> my sister's place. They live way out, you know. And I pulled up there and I

parked. And one of the kids seen me. I was drinking, so I thought, "Well, they know I'm drinking, they're not gonna come down."

And it was a long time I looked at them. And finally, I was kinda at peace and I took the top off, poured 'em in there, and I drank it. And then, I drank another beer and I just laid my head down. And just about that time, my sister told one of the bigger boys, "Go down there and see what he's doing." And I had the windows open, and the snow blowing in, you know. And, uh, so the boy run back up there and he said, "I don't know what he's doing. He's just laying there, sleeping." He said, "He's got all the windows open." He said, "The snow is blowing on him." And so she told him, she said, "You better run down there and see what's the matter with him." So he went down there and they got me out and they started walking me around. They got me to the doctor, and he pumped my stomach out. But, you know, I suppose, it was deep depression, you know, that I specifically got those pills for, although I didn't really plan it. I took 'em and I saved 'em and I put 'em in there. And I knew, you know, in the back of my mind, they were always there. If things got so bad I couldn't handle 'em, then I would do it. And I did. I was lucky I didn't take 'em all.

Uh, I felt that there was no one, that I was the only one left. You know, everybody else had something, you know. I had nothing. I had nothing except the beer and the pills. That's the only thing, in my mind, that I had. You know, and now my grandma was the most important thing, and she was there, but I couldn't see it. Uh, my sister, you know, she was really supportive of me. But nobody was there. I was totally by myself. It was just me. Me, the beer, and the pills. And it was real hard taking 'em out of there. But once I decided, then it was like, it was like real peaceful. You know, I took 'em, drank another beer and laid my head down to wait for whatever. And I was just lucky that, uh, you know I can laugh about it now and say I couldn't even do that right. [Laughs] But, you know, that . . . that was the loneliest, at that point, I was the loneliest person that ever was, to me. I absolutely had no one. There was no one that I could turn to, that I could talk to.

[T: How long do you think you had been in that depression?] Month. Probably took a month to lead up to it, to go in the bar and look around in the bar and laugh, with that hollow laugh. You know, I was laughing but I wasn't laughing. I mean, I could sit in the whole bar and be alone. You know, there's people all over. You'd want to sit and visit, I'd sit and visit with you and drink with you, but I wouldn't be there. I'd be sitting beside you and talking but my mind was not there, you know. My mind was off, I had everything I really wanted but I just didn't know what I had. I did not know that's what I wanted until I lost it. And then I felt I just totally lost it altogether. It was . . . it was gone, you know. I had all along what I was looking for. I didn't realize it until I lost it. And I felt I lost it totally. So, you know, I could go in the bar and laugh and have fun, tell jokes, but I wasn't there. It was just, you know, 'cause my mind was going.

And it was probably a month from the time I, you know, realized, well, Angie was serious this time. You know, because she was always going to do it before. She'd kick me out for two weeks and then I'd be back. And then I thought, "Whoa. I finally got what I wanted. And now I look around me and that's not what I wanted." I'd look at the TV and think, "I used to watch this at home. I used to sit in my chair and watch this and really enjoy it. And laugh with the family. And now, what am I, where am I? I'm sitting in the bar."

At work, you know, I don't know how I used to make it to work, sleep somewhere, just anywhere, you know. And I'd wake up and still be half drunk and go to work. And I'd still make it to work and work, you know. And, in all the time I was working, you know, when it come lunchtime, you know, I'd always hurry 'cause I was hungry. Well, I wasn't hungry. You know, I had no appetite. I was down, jeez, I lost, God, I lost a lot of weight. Come four, three-thirty, three o'clock, no, we got off at three-thirty. Three-thirty, jeez, I used to be out that door. We used to race to get out that door to get home. And, so then, pretty soon I was standing there watching those guys. And that, and I'd say, "Well, look, you know, here they are. They're all racing because they got somewhere to go. I don't have anywhere to go." You know. And I'd be fooling around in the mill and I'd be talking to the foreman, walking around talking to him. And he asked me, he said, "What's the matter with you?" And I said, "Oh, my wife divorced me." He said, "Oh." He said, uh, "You just haven't been the same." And I said, "Well, don't have anything left, you know." He said, "Well, where you staying?" I said, "I stay with my grandma or wherever I end up, you know." And he said, "Well, that's pretty tough right at first." But he said I would get over it. But I . . . I didn't.

Dan has now reached the central portion of his dramatic narrative. Here he tells about his attempt to take his own life, some twenty years ago. Not surprisingly, Dan's suicide attempt is enacted outside the house of his sister's family. Parking within viewing distance from the only relations left to him, Dan has chosen a stage for this social drama that underscores the degree of damage sustained by his social and psychological world.

Dan describes this period of his life primarily as one of loneliness. He says, "I was the loneliest person that ever was." He narrates how no one cared for him, how he had nothing, how he was totally by himself. The loneliness that Dan narrates is a statement about the ways in which he is and was related to the world and not simply an expression of an interior state of emotion. Statements of feeling lonely, feeling that no one cares, of having nothing, are central to every interview I conducted. Loneliness symbolizes the worst fate that can befall a human being. It is what underlies the dread of relative's deaths, the horror of a prison sentence, the fear of angering one's friends, the re-luctance to live off the reservation. Dan's description of his suicide attempt calls up these shared meanings of loneliness and is grounded in the specific losses of his mother and brother by death as well as the loss of his wife and children by divorce—losses that are revealed by Dan in staccato fashion in the opening to this segment of his story.

Even though Dan has reached the central section of his narrative, the meaning of his suicide attempt remains incomplete. The loneliness that he describes is a statement about his place in a world in which others are no longer there for him. But loneliness is grounded in the essential reciprocity of relationships, and the other side of the story of his disconnection from the world, the side in which he is responsible for the loneliness of others, has yet to be told and assessed. Dan does this primarily in a passage describing the completed suicide of his nephew, John. But before he describes John's suicide and completes the meaning of his own attempt, Dan highlights his movement toward increasing responsibility, especially in the area of spirituality.

INCREASING RESPONSIBILITY

You know, I just feel real lucky that Angie took me back. So, you know, I know what that depression can do to you, uh, if you allow it to get ahold of you. Like with John's suicide, that month when I sat home, I just let myself slip back into that. And I sat there and I thought, "Maybe John did the right thing." And I thought, "Oh boy, I'm in trouble. I'm in trouble."

And so, then that's when I went to see Dr. O'Hara in Missoula. So, you know, I've had good, good training. But, you know, Dr. O'Hara, he said, when you begin to have that depression, something physical is gonna happen to you. Then what I got from my grandma and them other ones, is nothing will happen to you if you don't let it happen to you. You know, if you realize right away you're getting into that, you need to pray, you need to burn sage, burn sweetgrass, or, you know, whatever you believe in. Uh, cedar or, you know, sweat. You know, you do that to get that off your mind and you don't get depressed.

[T: Did O'Hara give you medication?] Hm-mm. No, he wanted me on Amitriptyline, but they put me on that for my knees and I couldn't . . . I just don't like to take drugs, you know, it just covers up the real. But, what they say is, "We have everything growing right here, what you need to take, whatever is bothering you." And, you know, we're slowly losing it, you know. Even me, you know, I should have been learning that a long time ago, instead of starting now.

And, uh, I've noticed all of the things I went through lately, you know, with John, uh, my knees, I never once have considered drinking again. So, I feel real lucky. I never say, "I'll never drink again, you know." I'm not gonna set myself up by saying I'll never. And, you know, I often said that I

never really was tested but here lately I think I have. And I think I've been
tested real severe. But then, then I have to pray and give thanks that, you
know, I've been able to handle the things that's come up. But, uh, the main
thing is, what I feel, is in this depression, we need to learn from the elders
that we allow it to take control of us. That's what . . . that's what the
young ones, now I say young, you know, now I'm an old elder. [Laughs]
Yeah, I'm an old man now. I look back and I just didn't listen, you know. If
I woulda listened, it would've saved me a lotta heartache and pain. If I
would've just listened to these old . . . look at 'em all around here. [Pointing
to portraits of elders on the walls]

[T: What's the longest period of time you've gone without being depressed?] [Sighs, long pause] Probably a year—the first year I realized that
religion, you know, when I first started looking at religion. You know, all
along I said, "Oh, yeah. Religion's a really important part of recovery." I
knew that intellectually but . . . but it wasn't for me. It was for them. You
know, I could tell them, "You need to look at spirituality in recovery."
Well, that was easy for me to tell them, but I wasn't doing it myself. And
then when I started going in the mountains and really sitting there, supposedly going fishing, you know, and looking—the water, the trees—really getting in touch with everything—the rocks, the birds, whatever—then really
feeling at peace. And then realizing I was finally understanding what spirituality was talking to Dennis, coming and talking to Dennis. And Dennis
said, "That's where it's coming out for you is in the mountains and that's
good." Talking to Louie, talking to this Phillip, and my grandma, and
finally realizing, you know, this is where it was. And for a year there I was
really happy.

This passage begins with Dan recalling the suicide of his nephew,
John, six months before our interview. As Dan reports the effect that
John's suicide had on him, he prepares the way for a reassessment of
his own suicide attempt in terms of his responsibility to others. Although the shift in the meaning of his own suicide attempt from ego-
centered loneliness to irresponsibility toward others is so far incomplete,
its eventuality is also facilitated by statements about his increasing
responsibility for his drinking and for his emotions. With regard to
drinking, while Dan claims that he cannot say that he will never drink
again, he nonetheless asserts his abilities in the face of painful life
events to avoid drinking. In a statement about taking responsibility for
his emotions, Dan comes close to claiming a position of wisdom for
himself, albeit jokingly.

But, uh, the main thing is, what I feel, is in this depression, we need to learn
from the elders that we allow it to take control of us. That's what . . . that's
what the young ones, now I say young, you know, now I'm an old elder.
[Laughs] Yeah, I'm an old man now. I look back and I just didn't listen,

you know. If I woulda listened, it would've saved me a lotta heartache and pain. If I would've just listened to these old . . . look at 'em all around here.

Another way that Dan documents his increasing maturity and responsibility lies in his assertions about the role of spirituality in his life. Dan asserts his spiritual growth and documents it with reference to talks he has had with Phillip, his grandmother, and two spiritual leaders of the community, Dennis and Louie. Spirituality is a master metaphor in marking maturity and responsibility in much of the talk one hears at the reservation. So again, Dan draws on the surplus meaning of a symbol to construct the meaning of his own life. There is an implicit aspect to spirituality that needs to be drawn out at this point. Spirituality, like loneliness, is a statement about reciprocity, a reciprocity between a world of power and an individual. Unlike symbols of maturity in mainstream America, Indian spirituality is a symbol celebrating interdependence, in this case between humans and spiritual beings. This calling up of the importance of reciprocity, through his narration of spiritual growth, is entirely in keeping with the shift that we will see from the first half of the narration to the second, from irresponsibility to responsibility, from concern with the self to concern for others.

This passage marks most dramatically the shift from irresponsibility to responsibility, the shift from self to others, that constructs the meaning of Dan's life experiences, where he was and where he is at the time of the interview. The remainder of the interview is in some sense a mirror image of the first half, with stories of irresponsibility matched by stories of responsibility. Dan follows this transition passage with an explicit detailing of the new meaning of his suicide attempt.

A "SELFISH" SUICIDE

Well, getting back to what my grandma said, now I have to accept what the consequences of my actions were. And at that point, that was the way I was going to accept it. And, see, at that point, I never once considered anybody else. I was the only one involved in this. There was nobody else involved in it. It was me. "I'm the one that's gonna take these pills. I'm the one that's going to die. Everybody's gonna be better off when I'm gone." I never once considered what it would do to my children, Angie, anybody else. You know, any of all the people around me, I never once considered my grandma. I don't know how she would have, you know, what she would've done because, they always tease me about me being the favorite. You know, they say, "Well, yeah. You're her favorite." And, you know, now, I would never do anything to hurt her. But at that point in my life, I never even considered her when I was making that decision. She never once crossed my mind.

I could identify with how alone John felt that morning he stood here and faced that wall. Angie said, "My God, I don't know how he . . ." And I knew. I knew what he was thinking. I knew how alone he felt. How, you know, there was nothing else. That was the only thing left to do. And probably when he, just before he pulled the trigger, he was at peace, you know. It's hard coming up to that, you know, you think about it, but it's a really hard thing to . . . to actually bring yourself to do it. You know, how many times I reached for that, then, "No," and I'd drink. Just, you know, and then finally taking it, and holding it and looking at it, and I thought, "Well, this will do it." You know, and then, "No, I can't do this. Well, there's . . . there's nobody. There's just me. Just me and the pills and the beer." And to finally take that cap off. And then when you do it, and then, and then it's peaceful. It's just . . . and I drank my beer and laid my coat on there and just laid down there and I thought, "Well, well, it's done now, you know. I'll just lay down and go to sleep and all of the pain, the hurt, and the loneliness will be gone. You know, I won't . . . I won't have to go through that anymore." And so at that time, you know, you think you've made the right choice.

I thought I made the right choice. But it's, you know, from doing it and then learning and then, now, with John, now, there's to realize how selfish, you know, that's the most selfish thing you can do to somebody. That's the most selfish thing I coulda done to Angie, whether she divorced me or not. My grandma, she would still be. . . . Uh, my children, I don't know how my children would be now, years later, you know, when it's over. To see the ripple effect of John's suicide, I mean, that's still going on, the effect that it has. And to where at that point, you're the only person.

It's not an option for me. Yeah, that's not an option because I've seen both sides. I came so close myself, to thinking that it's totally me, you know, I'm the only one that's gonna be hurt by it. To seeing how many . . . just the wide variety of people that are just devastated by that. And that, you know, it takes so long, I mean, it's so, so long-term. I mean that's what I'm finding out with John's, I mean, first you're in shock, and then grief, and then sorrow, and then blaming, and then denial and, you know. You don't go through it like a textbook. I mean, jeez, we're just flip-flopping back and forth yet. I mean this is October, John committed suicide in early April and it's still having effects. And just when I think, "Well, things are kinda settling down, people are working through it," somebody else'll go off on . . . on a different tangent, you know. And then watching Angie going through to the acceptance part and then all of a sudden, for whatever little reason, you know, it will set her off. And she's right back, exactly right back to when . . . when she realized John was dead. And, so, from looking at it from the view I had of when I was going to do it, to watching John complete it, now it wouldn't be an option for me. I would not do that to . . . to . . . I mean, it makes you realize the friends, I mean, not only

Angie, uh, my boss, my co-workers, my friends, they're there, you know. People I work with, uh, these people here. Even you.

The transition of the meaning of Dan's suicide attempt is complete now. Dan says quite clearly, first in reference to John but then about himself, that suicide is "the most selfish thing you can do to somebody." Because he is more responsible now, Dan can say straight out, "It's not an option for me."

Dan's drinking was resolved in the previous passage; his suicide attempt is resolved in this one. The world has shifted from one in which others are responsible to him and he is responsible for himself, to one in which he is responsible to others. And it is a wide range of others, a range that includes even the interviewer.[12] Just how wide this range will be is the dilemma of the next passage in which Dan narrates the profound impact John's suicide had on his job as an alcohol counselor. Dan was put in a particular position of having to follow certain professional procedures in the unfolding of John's suicide, procedures that later came back to haunt him in his new role of responsibility.

NEW DILEMMAS OF RESPONSIBILITY

I didn't really think right to the minute I listened to him on the phone and I knew he was dying, you know, and I told him, I said, "John, dammit, hang on." I said, "I'll be right there." When I hung the phone up, I knew he was dead. And I could not accept it. I couldn't believe it. And I jumped in the car and I went rushing down there, you know. I mean, you know, I still have flashbacks of pulling onto their yard and seeing my brother-in-law holding somebody on the lawn and thinking, "Good, it's John. You know, they got him out of the house. Now they got him out there, it's the police cars now, well, they're gonna load John up and they'll take him to jail. And then we'll take him to Three North or whatever kind of help he needs, we can give it to him, you know." And yet knowing, knowing already when I listened to him on the phone, you know, he was going to be dead when I got there. And . . . and . . . and yet not accepting it. And then realizing it wasn't John, it was Ray. And I thought, well, you know, he's alright yet. I'll go up. And meeting Joe coming down and Joe grabbing me and saying, "No, you don't want to go up there." And then pushing Joe away and saying, "No, I'm going." Then going up the stairs, you know, to . . . to talk to John, I guess. And, uh, the cop and them grabbing me and saying, "No, don't go in there, it's too late." So it was, it was a terrible . . . it was a terrible shock.

And I talked with my brother-in-law, you know, about the guilt of, you know. I knew all of the procedures we had to go through, and going through those procedures but yet thinking, "If I would've went to him

immediately insteada waiting to call Tribal Police, waiting for them to get
there, would there have been a different outcome?" And O'Hara's response
to that, "Yeah, there could've been a very different outcome. You could've
been dead. You *and* John." Because John was very mean when he was
drinking. He was, he was mean. And O'Hara said, "OK, let's play that
back. OK, you get that phone call, you jump up, you run up there, and
John shoots you. OK. When John realizes it, 'Well, OK,' then, he shoots
himself." "Or," he said, "let's play it, he shoots you, you're dead and then
he decides not to shoot himself. OK, they take John to jail, then how would
Angie feel? How bitter Angie would be towards everyone. Towards your
job." Towards the type of work I do.

Did he tell you what he told me? He says, "You know," he said, "The
system you work in just eats you up." He said, "It'll eat you up and spit
you up and there'll be somebody right there to take your place." And he
said, "And they'll be in line to take your place." He said, "So, you need to
realize how much you give, you know. You can only give so much." And he
told me when I first came in he thought I was to the point where I had given
too much and I would never come back in this field again. He said, "I
thought you were totally burnt out." He said, "I didn't think you could go
back."

But, it was when my cousin, he came back and he spent some time with
me. We spent a lot of time, him and his boy, fishing. And that was just before I went down to see Phillip and I told him, I said, "I'm gonna be on the
way down there to Fort Hall." And then they left Saturday because I was
gone. You know, they usually go fishing on Saturday. I said, "But I need to
do this." And he said, "Yeah, I know you do."

And on Monday, you know, Phillip told me, he said, "The type of work
you do," he said, "you don't hardly ever see the results, for a long time."
He says, "It'll be a long time before somebody will come to you and say to
you, 'Remember when you said.' " He said, "It won't begin right then." He
said, "Way down, when they do decide to make that change." He said, "It
will be something you said." He said, "You may never know what you said
made a difference to them, but it did, and it'll change their life. And it's
gonna change the kids, their kids'." He said, "And you, you're not going to
see that." And [sighs] so he said that. He said, "Your work is very, very important." He says, "I know, probably a lot of people right there that won't
agree with it. They'll think you're, well, like what they say, all we do is go
around and drink coffee." That's what I've heard, you know, "That's all
you guys do is sit, you're on tribal payroll, and just drink coffee all day
long." They're not into the . . . the crisis, you know, what we do. But then
there was three things. Phillip telling me that on Sunday, he says, "You
know, you need to make up your own mind." "But," he says, "I need to tell
you, what you guys are doing on the reservation now is going to affect it
down the road." He said, "And I think you guys are doing a good job." He
says, "I can come back and I can see the differences. I look around and see,
'Oh, this person's not drinking now, you know. This person's not drinking.' So I can go back and see." He said, "I can see the change, you can't."

So that was on Sunday. And then on . . . on Tuesday, I got a phone call from my cousin. He says, "You know, I was driving home and I told my boy, I says, 'When we come back, he's not gonna be working for that program. He's gonna be gone.' " He said, "I think he's already made up his mind." So, he says, "I'm not one to tell you what you should do or what you shouldn't do, but I think you guys are really doing a good job there." And he said, uh, "You're good at it." He said, "So, do what you think you have to do."

And then I sat there and listened to that. And then just watching the national news on the TV. You know, just happened to glance up, and, uh, the rate of teenage drugs and alcohol use over the last five years has went down. And so I thought, "Gee, here's three . . . three different things telling me, 'Yeah, we are making a difference.' And so, yeah, it is important that I continue, you know, as long as I can."

In this passage, Dan narrates another recent moral dilemma of responsibility that stands in counterpoint to the moral dilemma of chronic pain. In the case of chronic pain, the dilemma remains unresolved. In this case, Dan tells of the ultimately resolved dilemma of responsibility in relation to his work as an alcohol counselor. Dan describes how the death of his nephew affected his thoughts about his work, making him call into question whether the pain and turmoil of unsuccessful interventions undermined any good he could do. With the support of Dr. O'Hara, his medicine man, his cousin, and a television news program, Dan decides to continue with the struggle.

An implicit part of this struggle reflects the new moral arenas that Dan has moved into: now that he is responsible to others, how does he resolve the potential conflicts between his responsibilities to different groups of others, in this case, family and work? That it was a member of his family, a nephew, who represents "unsuccessful intervention" heightens the conflict between Dan's responsibilities to his family, primarily his wife, and his clients. At first, Dan feels guilty for following the established procedures outlined for counselors in dealing with suicide attempts, and he wonders whether the outcome might have been different if he had responded instead simply as a family member.

When Dan takes us out of the loose chronology that structures his story about drinking and his suicide attempt by calling up the two recent dilemmas, he highlights the continued significance of moral decision making in his day-to-day life. And yet Dan glosses these difficulties in the final sections of the interview by returning to a simpler moral decision, that of learning the language, and by closing the narrative with another reminiscent look at the ways and wisdom of the elders.

THE ELDERS

Another thing that this Phillip told me. He says, "You know, the first thing you need to do is learn your language." He said, "So when you pray, it's clear." According to his old grandmother, if you listen to white man, white man will tell you one word that can mean many things. And that when you pray in Indian, it's clear what you mean, you know, everything is understood. Whereas if you talk in English, one word might mean a whole bunch of completely different things. And he said, "Are you hearing what I'm saying?" And I said, "Yeah. I think so." And I said, "Yeah. I'm going to do that."

But ... but it's really good to listen to him, you know. And time ... time for him, there's no time. He mentioned one day, he says, "Well, tomorrow morning I gotta go see So-and-so." When he comes back, everybody wants to visit with him and have some of his time. Well [sighs], I felt I was monopolizing his time because he was staying with us. And we'd visit from the time he'd get up, you know, until one, two o'clock in the morning. And, so he mentioned that he had to see somebody in Arlee, tomorrow morning. So we got up and had breakfast and we had coffee and we were talking. And so finally, got to be about quarter to eleven, you know. And I looked at this [points to his watch], talking, and I looked at this. So he turned and said something in their language to his wife and she started laughing. And, I says, "What did he say?" And she started laughing. She said, "Well, he thinks it's real funny. He told me, 'It's not bad enough that your watch controls you.' He says, 'Now, he's trying to get his watch to control me. He's trying to tell me I should be somewhere at a certain time.' " And I said, "Well, I was just ... he said that he needed to go see somebody in the morning, and it's getting to be eleven o'clock, you know." And she says, "He goes when he's ready, you know. He knows when you're done saying what you need to say. He knows, then he'll go. But if you're talking about something important, he's not going to get up and go, say, 'I have to go,' and leave you half finished with what you really want to say and then go off and see somebody else. He stays until he knows that you said what you need to say. And then, then he'll go. If it's this afternoon, you know, he'll still go."

And also that first thing I told you about, you know, when they go to your house, come in and sit down and visit when it's time to eat, we eat. And my grandma, I never heard her say, "Well, how long are you gonna stay?" You know, they start visiting, they'd visit and then when it became time to eat, she would get up and cook. And she'd never ask you if you were staying. It was just understood that you were gonna stay and eat. And if you were still here when it was time to go to bed, then she fixed your bed and you stayed, you know. And, uh, there was never any set time, you know. You stay one day or you stay two days. There was never any question. And one day they got up and say, "Well, we have to go" or "I have to go." And then they went. And it wasn't like, "Good-bye." They just left.

And now they're back again, you know. So, you know, you just came and went. And it was just like they were part of the family.

So, I don't know what we've lost, you know. Uh, maybe we get involved in too many things. I don't know. You know, you think about it and it's hard to explain. You know, now you can just jump in your car and go. There's no reason for not visiting. And back then, you know, they had to, well, most of them walked. And you'd see 'em coming and seems just like that old lady, just grandma, you know. "Grandma's coming again," and . . . and she'd move in and sit in her favorite, you know, she had her place to sit. And when she was there, you didn't dare sit in there 'cause she had a cane and she wasn't above giving you a good rap with that cane, you know. If I got too noisy, if we got to playing too loud, you know, she'd just reach over with the cane and crack you one and . . . and you knew to be quiet. And it was just accepted, you know, because it was grandma, you know, you didn't sit in grandma's spot. You know, although it coulda been mine all the time she wasn't there. But when she was there, that was her spot, you know.

CONCLUSION

With a final panegyric for the ways of the elders that echoes the themes of visiting, sharing, and discipline that reverberate in his opening statements, Dan brings his story about the struggle of responsibility, about a moral coming of age, to a close. It was this framing of the entire narrative within the moral parameters of the real Indians, this evidence of the structural virtuosity of Dan's narrative, that struck me so forcibly at first. Dan's suicide attempt derives its meaning in part through its structural opposition to the ways of the elders. In a deft twist, the structural *centrality* of Dan's suicide attempt in the narrative creates and highlights its moral *marginality* as it is distanced from and opposed to the elders and the defining moral boundaries of the narrative. The meaning of Dan's suicide attempt is enhanced through its structural equation, at the double center of the narrative, with the completed suicide of John, Dan's nephew. Through this equation, Dan constructs the meaning of his suicide attempt, shifting its significance from its original meaning of loneliness to its final and truer meaning of selfishness and irresponsibility.

The message of moral responsibility is also conveyed through an overarching bifurcation of the story and a bracketing of the suicide attempt by two recent moral dilemmas. The first half of Dan's narrative is a story of irresponsibilities of increasing significance that foreshadow his suicide attempt. The second half is a story that documents Dan's movement toward increasing responsibility. The centerpiece of the narrative is bracketed by two dilemmas of responsibility that were salient in Dan's life at the time of the interview: his struggle with chronic knee pain and his struggle with demoralization in his work as an alcohol counselor. The first dilemma remained unresolved at the time of the interview and, through its position in the first half of the narrative, reinforces the two-part division of the narrative. This is especially visible in contrast to the more resolved dilemma of responsibility, Dan's demoralization with his work, in the second half of the narrative.

Dan's adeptness at structuring his narrative is matched by a felicitous positioning of his story within a universe of narrative styles. If it seems at times that I explain too much of the "given" at the expense of the "created," to use Bakhtin's terms, it is because Dan uses the "given" so subtly that it must be understood before the creative singularity of his narrative can be fully appreciated. For example, it is not insignificant that Dan's narrative has elements of an AA recitation, given his work as an alcohol counselor and his own nondrinking status. However, his narrative actually resonates more fully with the pathos of a different style of narrative: the mea culpa laments that are delivered by certain men of Dan's age (and an occasional woman) at some traditional gatherings and memorial feasts. In these laments, the speakers reveal their deep sadness over the pain they inflicted on their elders by being disobedient and mourn the loss of the wisdom that resulted from not listening to their elders. At times, Dan's narrative style also approaches, but never fully reaches, the style of reminiscent preaching of the elders. In keeping with the pathos of moral maturity, anger is entirely absent.

The result of this diverse situating of Dan's narrative style is not an incongruous and confusing hodgepodge but an evocative and convincing story. In it, Dan's choices of narrative style ground his assertions about who he is in plainly evident social reality. Starting with indisputable facts, Dan constructs a credible self that lends strength to his other assertions. Dan, as the narrator, is male, around fifty years of age, raised by his traditional Indian grandparents, nondrinking, and working. With this authoritative self in place, Dan moves on to create himself, again as the narrator, as repentant, obedient, and morally responsible. Dan's present authority reinforces his interpretation of who he was twenty years ago and, perhaps, who he will be twenty years hence.

In addition to his abilities to construct a strong narrative organization and an equally powerful authoritative voice, Dan reveals his mastery of symbolism. He sets up potent symbols of responsibility, and failed responsibility, to give substance to his story of moral growth. In the analytic sections interspersed throughout the text I have tried to describe the force of these symbols, such as his lack of appropriate grief at the death of his mother or his disobedient disregard of his grandparents' words, on the negative side, and his increasing spirituality or his continued work as a counselor, on the positive side. Responsibility in Dan's narrative is not defined by an abstract list of discrete behaviors, either obligatory or to be avoided, such as going to church regularly or not drinking. Instead, Dan's representations recall the implicit reciprocity of the first definition for *responsible* in *Merriam-Webster's 1993 Collegiate Dictionary*, 10th ed. (1993): "liable to be called on to answer." In his story, he repeatedly relies on the tacitly understood process of give-and-take in all relationships. The responsibility, or irresponsibility, of Dan's behavior, and the behavior of others, unfolds within contexts of concrete and specific relationships of reciprocity and is judged implicitly against the benchmark of the ways of the elders.

Dan's narrative, like many works of art, can probably be appreciated without a full awareness of the aesthetic vision and the array of techniques brought to bear in its creation. As with most artwork, however, our understanding and respect deepen as our familiarity with the particular language used by the artist grows. An analysis that maps out Dan's narrative skills, the way he expertly crafts the structure of his narrative, adeptly situates his voice within a universe of narrative styles, and masterfully selects powerful symbols, gives new depth to our appreciation of the creative force of Dan's story.

Dan's narrative is an engaging story, informed as much by who Dan is now and who he wants to be as who he was twenty years ago when he tried to kill himself with an overdose of pills. Dan's drinking, his suicide attempt, and his difficulties with depression become the material with which he sketches who he is today through contrast with who he was twenty years ago. Equally, Dan's chronic pain, spirituality, abstinence, and employment become the contrastive material with which he sketches who he was twenty years ago. The contrasts between the younger Dan and the present Dan reveal his story to be one of moral growth. At the same time, the placing of the present Dan within a subplot in which he slides easily into an existential rethinking of suicide

imparts a fragility to the present Dan—showing that the work to fashion a positive self is a continuing, difficult, and never-ending effort.

The artistry of Dan's story should not, however, blind us to important differences between his narrative and a work of art. First, unlike a
fictionalized representation that is consciously created to produce an
aesthetic response, Dan's narrative is a reporting of real experiences.
Even though Dan created and constructed this narrative, he did not
make up the story. Dan's narrative was produced in response to my request for information; it was not designed for my enjoyment or enter-
tainment. Second, unlike a work of art that is given permanency by its
creator, Dan's narrative was fixed in writing not by Dan but by me.
These caveats implore us to go beyond an understanding of Dan's narrative as simply "a good story." We must continually strive to grasp
the phenomenological essence in the story while recognizing that narratives reflect but fixed moments in the dialectical processes of self-
creation.

CHAPTER SIX

Culture and Depression

Why is it said by some within the Flathead community that 70 to 80 percent of their people are depressed? Why do Flathead accounts of depression resonate with positive moral meanings as much as they do with individual pain? Reflecting on Dan's story, on Ron's wake, and on early Indian-white history, it is clear that the answers to these questions lie in the ways that Flathead culture makes sense and meaning out of loss and sadness.

Specifically, sadness and loss are nested within a rich language of loneliness, which in turn is nested within an ideology and praxis of belonging. Belonging itself, through the valorized affects of pity and compassion, is nested within a prominent discourse extolling the ways of the ancestors, the "real Indians." In turn, the discourse on the "real Indians" is paired to the rhetoric of the "empty center" in the charged setting of authentic Indian identity in today's world. Finally, the issues of contemporary Indian identity are embedded within the morally imbued Flathead response to a century and a half of threat posed by ignorant, sometimes hostile, outsiders. In effect, Flathead culture ties loss to practices in which loss, as loneliness, is worked into pity and compassion and, therefore, into responsibility toward others. Ideally, for Flathead people, losses are not to be avoided and forgotten but should remain in their hearts as reminders to have pity on others. Thus Flathead people discipline their hearts to remember their pain and yet to transcend it.

What is to be made of what we have learned about Flathead loneliness? While I believe wholeheartedly that individual readers can

explore Flathead notions, such as those of the interdependent self and
social responsibility, to expand and enrich their understandings of
their own paths through life, I also believe that this investigation can
speak potently to three important areas of academic concern: first,
how to conceive the relationship between culture and emotion; second,
how to understand the similarities and differences between Flathead visions of loneliness and DSM formulations of depressive disorder; and,
third, how to imagine the connection between culture and depression
in ways that promote better research and clinical practice. I will address each area in turn.

CULTURE AND EMOTION

The preceding chapters have detailed the centrality of loneliness, as
a key symbol, in contemporary Flathead culture. Within a symbolic
world that posits belonging as essential for individual and group survival, as well as emblematic of valued but threatened traditional ways,
loneliness is the emotional glue that binds selves to others by forging
bonds of pity, aid, and exchange. In individual narratives, loneliness is
a powerful idiom that draws on the deeply moral meanings of the
larger Flathead discourse on loneliness. As Dan's story reveals, loneliness in narratives of individual experience speaks to issues of moral
worth, Indianness, and the importance of belonging. Consequently,
loneliness, as an idiom of disordered identity and disrupted social relations, can carry tremendous force to effect changes in a person's status and social relationships.

Based on responses to various presentations I have made over the
years on Flathead loneliness, I imagine that some non-Flathead readers, even at this point, may find it easy to equate Flathead loneliness
with their own experiences of loneliness. As a first step toward understanding Flathead loneliness, the assimilation of other's experience to
one's own is commendable; yet it is not adequate for a rigorous accounting of the phenomenology of loneliness for Flathead people. To
accomplish the next step in understanding, I suggest a careful (re-)con-
sideration of the ethnographic material. Those who have felt loneliness
after losing a close friend or relative may want to reflect that that experience probably did not entail the mobilization of one's network of
family and friends for a set of death rituals ending in a give-away. Nor
was that experience of bereavement somehow similar to the loss of a
traditional song that one used to hear as a child. Nor is that loneliness

mapped onto the landscape in sites associated with the deaths of relatives, or the erosion of the tribe in the face of external forces. Those who may have felt loneliness at other times may want to reflect that it probably did not have connections to values of material exchange and reciprocity, to a perceived breach in valued traditions, or to a moral responsibility to transform personal pain into social responsibility. In sum, Flathead loneliness entails moral meanings and social forces that are probably not entailed in the loneliness of non-Flathead readers.

It would not be surprising if many Euro-American readers do, in fact, have difficulty in understanding the cultural specificity of Flathead loneliness. As Shweder cautions, "The process of understanding the consciousness of others can deceptively appear to be far easier than it really is" (1993: 428). Understanding some of the reasons why the emotions of others should be so "deceptively" easy to translate (as a variant of one's own emotions) is illuminating for the vision of culture and emotion that I am advancing here. In this vision, emotions are socially negotiated interpretive responses that derive their meaning from a culturally constructed moral rhetoric of the self. In turn, that rhetoric of the self derives its significance, and is reinforced, within historically informed social contexts.

From this perspective, Flathead loneliness is an interpretive response to a perceived situation of separation or abandonment. Separation and abandonment derive their significance for the self from a morally charged cultural vision of the self. In that vision, belonging is crucial for the self, and the acknowledgment of one's interdependence, through depth of feeling and displays of generosity, marks maturity and Indianness. The history of threats to the Indian family and Indian ways has heightened the valence of belonging, thus lending a special force to claims of loneliness, especially those relating to obligations of caring and sharing and to "real Indian" identity. By virtue of its historically informed valence, a claim of loneliness is not a simple claim for an interior experience. Loneliness is, instead, a claim with important social and moral meanings for self and others. With so much at stake, the validity of claims of loneliness, and what to do about them, can be subject to social negotiation.

The emotion of loneliness must, therefore, be understood in terms other than as a "cultural" variant on Euro-American loneliness. But why is the emotional experience of Flathead loneliness so deceptively easy to assimilate as a slightly reshaped version of Euro-American loneliness? To begin with, the uniqueness of loneliness among the Flathead people may be obscured for English speakers because Flathead people also speak English. Rather than appearing as a foreign phrase in italics, Flathead loneliness appears identical on the page to Euro-American loneliness. Yet even when we take account of the vastly different cultural meanings and social and historical associations of Flathead loneliness, why is it still difficult to apprehend Flathead loneliness as concept and experience? The problem lies at an even deeper level: the construction of emotion in Euro-American culture as a "natural" psychobiological phenomenon narrows the questions that are regarded as essential for a good understanding of emotion cross-culturally.

In her provocative essay entitled "Depression and the Translation of Emotional Worlds," Catherine Lutz deconstructs the ways that emotion is often conceptualized within Euro-American culture (1985). While acknowledging the undeniable presence of distinct subcultures within the broader Euro-American culture, she nonetheless posits widely shared interpretations of emotion that are manifested in popular accounts, clinical understandings, and social scientific theories of emotion. In her analysis, Lutz argues compellingly that within Euro-American culture, emotion is understood as a psychophysiological event whose ultimate reality resides in the internal feelings experienced by an individual. As Lutz notes in her book, this perspective on emotion sets up feelings as beyond personal responsibility, counter to rationality, and precultural (1988: 78–79). In a more recent essay, Lutz also explores the ways in which emotion is constructed in Euro-American culture as within the province of the "female" (1990).

I argue, as does Lutz, that this perspective on emotion can render Euro-American readers, lay, clinician, and social scientist alike, blind to the ways in which the emotional lives of others are experienced. In particular, this understanding predisposes us to imagine that only those aspects of another's experience which differ from our own are "cultural." More than a few times, when colleagues and friends have reviewed portions of manuscripts on Flathead loneliness, I received comments along the lines of "Well, *I've* felt like that." The implied question is, "Why have you included 'natural' or 'noncultural' emotions like mine in your cultural analysis of Flathead loneliness?" Such comments reveal a culturally patterned privileging of Euro-American emotions as the gold standard against which the emotions of others are understood. These comments also reflect an unconscious exoticism of the emotions of others as "cultural" in comparison to our "natural" emotions.

Equally important, however, the Euro-American vision encourages a narrow understanding of emotion that essentializes it as an interior state, relegating its social effects, historical roots, and moral overtones to epiphenomena. It is a vision that sets up interior feelings as the most important part of emotional experience, and it is a vision that erases the possibility that other aspects of emotions may be central to the experience.

This view of emotion as essentially about interior feeling states and as a "natural" or precultural phenomenon flies in the face of the evidence on Flathead loneliness, but it is a view that has a long history in Western social thought—even in theories that account for the self in social terms. Arguing at the turn of the last century against the environmental and biological determinism of evolutionary theory, George Herbert Mead put forward the radical proposition that social experience is the precondition of the self and not vice versa: "The process out of which the self arises is a social process which implies interaction of individuals in the group, implies the pre-existence of the group" ([1934] 1962: 164). Mead's formulations on the social origins of human nature, along with the works of Emile Durkheim and Marcel Mauss in Europe and John Dewey stateside, helped to transform prevailing social science notions ascribing preeminence to the individual. In Mead's understanding, an individual becomes an object to himself, or in other words develops a self, only by taking on the attitudes of others toward himself within social contexts in which both he and they are involved, a process tied intimately to linguistic symbols. As selves develop and mature, they can know themselves outside of specific interactions through the incorporation of the attitudes of the social groups to which they belong as the "generalized other." According to Mead, the self is emergent in a social process involving reflexivity (or self-consciousness), interaction, and symbolization.

Within this intricate social psychological framework, Mead criticized Charles Darwin's notion that acts of emotional expression and human languages of emotion exist to reflect and convey an organism's awareness or consciousness of an emotion. Specifically, Mead countered Darwin's idea by noting that the social act precedes individual consciousness. Moreover, Mead contended, the "inner attitude" is only one part of an emotional gesture, whose meaning also includes the response that the gesture engenders in the other, and the product of the interaction that was initiated by the gesture.

Yet despite the thoroughly social nature of the self in Mead's view and his condemnation of Darwin's take on emotional expression and language, Mead retained a notion of affect as separate from cognition and reflective of physiological and instinctual bases of human nature. Writing about the self-reflexive nature of the self, Mead implied the role and nature of affect in his theory:

> Emphasis should be laid on the central position of thinking when consider-
> ing the nature of the self. Self-consciousness, rather than affective experience
> with its motor accompaniments, provides the core and primary structure
> of the self, which is thus essentially a cognitive rather than an emotional
> phenomenon. . . . Cooley and James, it is true, endeavor to find the basis of
> the self in reflexive affective experience, i.e., experiences involving "self-
> feeling." . . . [But] the individual need not take the attitude of others toward
> himself in these experiences. (1962: 173)

For Mead, then, emotion remains presocial, separate from cognition, and, as such, is not implicated in reflexivity or the self. It is a position that keeps separate the "social" self and the "feeling" self.[1] In
essence, Mead's position on emotion is one that underlies almost all
but the most recent works on culture, self, and emotion. Certainly, the
field of culture and personality studies relies on a division of the self
into the social and the psychological. From the 1930s, with the pio-
neering studies of Ruth Benedict and Margaret Mead, through to the
1970s and 1980s, with the psychodynamically inspired research of
Robert LeVine, Mel Spiro, and Robert Levy, the perspectives of culture
and personality studies have, by far, been the most influential on anthropological thinking on culture and the self. An examination of the
major tenets of culture and personality theory helps to explicate,
through one more set of contrasts, the alternative vision that informs
my interpretation of Flathead loneliness.

Basic to the entire school's thought is the assumption that there are
psychological differences between populations that can be traced to
differences in cultural and social processes. These assumptions are revealed in the receptivity of culture and personality theorists in the
1940s through the present to the clinical/psychodynamic focus on early
childhood experience. The assumptions about culture and personality
are also revealed in statements such as "the Dobu are more competi-
tive and less cooperative than the Zuni" (Benedict 1934, cited in
Shweder 1979: 286), in which cultural differences are cast as differences in modal personalities.

Within the culture and personality field, despite the emphasis on the
cultural variability of "personality," emotion retains a unique precul-

tural role whose appearance signals a cleavage between the individual and his or her social world. The expression of emotion allows the researcher an opportunity to penetrate the "social surface of personality" to discover the deep psychological mechanisms of personality in culture (LeVine 1982: 227). For culture and personality researchers, emotions reflect a deeper reality, which, depending on the investigator's theoretical bent, is constituted of motives and defensive reactions against conflicts; of stresses and attempts at stress reduction; or of structured personality dispositions and efforts to maintain certain self-representations.

Regardless of the various terminologies, however, emotion is understood as both a functional product of individual personality and as a universal human experience. These assumptions translate into a style of research and analysis that draws easily on the work of Paul Ekman and others who posit the universality of certain basic or primary emotions, such as anger, sadness, and happiness (Ekman, Sorensen, and Friesen 1969; Ekman, Friesen, and Ellsworth 1972). Not surprisingly, we find within this subdiscipline that the emotion terms of others tend to be translated in terms of Euro-American emotion terms, which then fit easily into a dynamic framework of personality. This strategy undergirds, for example, the continued research into the presence or absence in different societies of the supposedly universal emotions of "guilt" and "shame" or the supposedly universal affective dynamics of the Oedipal complex.[2]

The field of culture and personality studies has come under criticism, seemingly from its inception. In the 1940s, culture and personality researchers were criticized for the lack of empirical grounding for their claims about "national character," as well as for the general haziness about their research and analytic methods. Around the same time, culture and personality theorists had to deal with criticisms of the notion of childhood determinism of adult personality. More recently, as the fields of anthropology and psychology have come to question the very notions of culture and personality, respectively, culture and personality theorists have had to respond creatively to the increasingly complicated and contentious nature of the basic terms of their perspective (Shweder 1979).

Perhaps the most important questions for culture and personality for this discussion on emotion, however, are posed by the field of ethnopsychology. Emerging in the late seventies and early eighties out of the Boasian tradition of strict and methodical ethnography, the phenomenological perspective of Hallowell, and the interpretive stance epitomized in the writings of Clifford Geertz, the field of ethnopsychology aims to explicate and translate the terms in which personal experience is organized in other cultures. The process for translating emotions terms, however, is fundamentally transformed from the process evident in culture and personality studies. Rather than translate the emotion terms of others into Euro-American terms, the latter play a circumscribed, increasingly scrutinized, role. For an example of the former approach, it is instructive to review Levy's exposition on Tahitian "anger." He writes that for the Tahitians,

> the ordinary word for anger is *riri*. . . . Extreme rage is *hae*, when according to Poria, "The person wants to devour you." . . . Oro, asked his thoughts about anger, describes the unpleasantness of the experience of being angry. "[Anger] isn't a good thing. . . . Because of that thing [the anger] you become weak. . . . Flora adds that unexpressed anger will turn one's hair white. (Levy 1973: 284)

Despite the seemingly odd associations of whitened hair, weakness, and the desire to eat the object of one's anger, Levy takes the local Tahitian terms *riri* and *hae* and translates them with ease (the deceptive ease that Shweder cautions against) into variants of Euro-American "anger" and "rage."

In contrast, ethnopsychologists tend to use Euro-American terms as bracketed approximations for others' terms and tend to retain the local term in subsequent discussion rather than switch over to the Euro-American term that is the local term's supposed functional equivalent. For example, in writing about everyday sentiments among the Ifaluk, a Micronesian people, Lutz writes,

> The implicit poetry in Ifaluk emotional understandings is nowhere more evident than in the concept of *fago* (compassion/love/sadness). . . . *Fago* speaks to the sense that life is fragile, that connections to others are both precious and may be severed through death or travel, that love may equal loss. *Fago* is uttered in recognition of the suffering that is everywhere and in the spirit of a vigorous optimism that human effort, most especially in the form of caring for others, can control its ravages. (Lutz 1988: 119)

The transformation of the translation process has had several effects on the anthropological conceptualization of culture and emotion. First, it has allowed researchers to be more cognizant of how the emotion terms of others may be semantically associated with elements of social reality that have little to do per se with the internal individual feelings that define the fundamental reality of emotion terms in Euro-American culture. So, for example, Geoffrey White, in his exploration of "personality" descriptors among a Solomon Island people, was able to apprehend the unanticipated finding that almost all such terms and phrases were characterized by an interpersonal and relational logic (1980, 1992*b*). In a related manner, the rich semantic associations of emotion terms are attended to as central to their interpretation rather than as exotic or quaint appendages. Michelle Rosaldo, for example, finds that *liget* among the Ilongot in the Philippines, an emotion term that she loosely glosses as Euro-American 'anger' or 'passion,' is associated with weighty hearts, vitality, headhunting, and the notion of 'unfinished bachelors' (1980). Similarly, Lutz finds semantic connections between 'fago' and maturity, nurturance, calmness, and chiefs, priests, spirits, and God (1988). Rather than peripheralize or erase the relational aspects of emotion, or their seemingly incidental associations, each of these authors takes pains to document the semantic logic underlying emotion terms and their cultural associations.

The transformation of the translation process has had a second effect on the anthropological conceptualization of emotion and culture. Rooted in a disciplinary refiguring of the nature of language—away from the mentalism and concrete referentiality inhering in a vision of language as a static superstructure that reflects the objective world and toward the interactionism and referential fluidity of Wittgenstein's language games and Bahktin's dialogics—the transformation of the translation process has been accompanied by a shift from the presentation of emotion terms as cognitive phenomena to their presentation of emotion terms as discursive phenomena. Rather than as elements of a timeless, seamless worldview, emotions are presented as commonly used discursive pathways within historically shaped, continually reconstructed, and sometimes disputatious everyday worlds.

Reflecting the focus on emotion as discursive phenomena, researchers have begun to attend to the dominant discursive practices and contexts that semantically unite emotion terms with their associated meanings. Thus Rosaldo notes the linking of 'liget' with its cultural and social meanings in oratories about marrying and killing that are delivered in ritual settings by esteemed male elders (1980). In a detailed analysis of Bedouin sentiments, Lila Abu-Lughod grounds their meaning in the poetic productions of women and men in public and private contexts (1986, 1990). Similarly, in his recent book on narratives of identity in a Solomon Island society, White finds the meaning of history, identity, and emotion in their reciprocal associations in the epic story lines of shared history narrated at large feasts and the shared motifs of individual accounts of conversion (1992*b*). Rather than present the meaning of emotion terms as abstract entries in a dictionary of local terms, these authors present the terms' meaning as produced and reproduced in discourse in important social contexts.

This image of emotion as discursively produced has created within anthropological writing an openness, if not a mandate, to attend to the pragmatic, political, and historical dimensions of emotional experience. In a recent compilation of works, Lutz and Abu-Lughod applaud an emerging interest among students of ethnopsychology to examine the ways in which power relations and discourses of emotion are tied together (1990). They call for analyses that reveal not only "the way power relations determine what can, cannot, or must be said about self and emotion, what is taken to be true or false about them, and what only some individuals can say about them" but also "how emotion discourses establish, assert, challenge, or reinforce power or status differences." At the forefront, we find Lutz's analysis of Euro-American emotion discourse, in which she discerns an association between "emotion" and "the female" and a concomitant rationale vindicating the hierarchy of men over women and the legitimacy of control over women (1990).

Throughout the social pragmatism of G. H. Mead, the psychodynamic tenets of culture and personality theorists, and the most recent ethnopsychological formulations on emotion as discourse runs the theme that the self is "incomplete" and must be socialized into a culturally meaningful world to become fully human. Yet each of these theories of self and society differs substantially in the role that they assign to emotion. And it is only in the most recent research and writing that emotion is imagined as culturally constituted. For G. H. Mead and others, emotion, as a noncognitive phenomenon, remains outside of the social processes of symbolically structured interaction and self-reflexivity. For many culture and personality theorists, emotion, as a principal feature of personality dynamics, enters into social and cultural processes as universally interpretable reflections of the degree to which an individual has been socialized into society, or the degree to which a society has trespassed normal human limits.[3]

For both social pragmatists and culture and personality theorists, emotion looks very much like the image drawn by Lutz in her analysis of emotion in Euro-American culture, in which emotions are precultural, prerational, psychobiological events whose ultimate reality in-heres in the feelings experienced by individuals. This image has shifted radically for most ethnopsychologists, for whom emotions are cultur-ally based discursive pathways that no longer simply reference inter-nal feeling states. Within this alternative perspective, emotions instead offer common culture-specific interpretations of social action and pro-vide culture-specific motivations for social action—all in a language that is tightly bound to relations of power.

My treatment of the Flathead emotion of loneliness in the first five chapters of this book fits most comfortably within this last approach. With an emphasis on Flathead loneliness as a symbolic medium that is used by Flathead people to interpret the actions of others, as well as their own, my treatment is far from the presocial perspective on emo-tion offered by G. H. Mead. Similarly, my attention to the broad social and cultural meanings of Flathead loneliness, rather than to its narrow functional meaning for the individual, distances me from traditional culture and personality theory.

However, recent formulations on culture, self, and emotion are not problem-free from the perspective of the Flathead material. In particu-lar, I want to raise two related issues plaguing the most recent formu-lations: the loss of the psychological actor and the appearance of the political actor in her stead. Let me address the latter first.

At some level, the Flathead material on loneliness is conducive to the type of political and pragmatic analyses called for by Lutz and Abu-Lughod, among others. The extended discussion of Flathead death rituals in chapter 3 reveals an association of the Flathead ideol-ogy of self and emotion and power relations. Within the wakes, as the discourse on loneliness is reproduced, certain affects and behaviors are sanctioned and certain individuals are set up as the arbiters of proper affect and behavior. Embodied in the speaking of the elders and prayer leaders, the discourse on loneliness and pity makes evident the moral standards of a close-knit group that not only bears but fortifies the au-thority of the most powerful members of this community. The dis-course on loneliness and pity sets up the prayer leaders, the elders, the "real Indians," and men, more generally, as judges of the adequateness of depth of feeling and appropriateness of certain acts of social respon-sibility. Not unexpectedly, it is generally held that these community members are most affected by feelings of loneliness. Moreover, the trend in which wakes and memorial feasts are increasingly being conducted only by the more "traditional" families reinforces and perpetuates the hierarchical structure not only of the elders and prayer leaders but also of the "real Indians."[4]

This setting up of given individuals as paragons of virtue and thus imbued with the authority to judge the actions of others is part and parcel of the ideology of loneliness and is important to grasp. However, as the second half of chapter 3 showed, it is equally important to understand that this ideology of loneliness provides the terms within which the actions of fathers and mothers, sisters and brothers, girlfriends and boyfriends, friends and cousins are assessed *by each other*. In other words, while the words of the elders, the prayer leaders, or the "real Indians" may carry tremendous force in many contexts, accusations of stinginess or selfishness by friends or relatives are not meaningless. The discourse about loneliness opens a space that can be used by individuals in everyday contexts for controlling others—and this is by far the more important aspect of the link between power relations and the Flathead ideology of loneliness and pity.

However, and this is my main point, the political dimensions of the Flathead discourse on loneliness are not central to its cultural construction either, appearing more as a by-product of the more dominant moral meanings of that discourse. Within the wakes, loneliness plays an important role in helping to construct the Flathead vision of the individual as embedded in relations of reciprocity and as effectively lost without those relations. Loneliness describes the horror of being alone and the fear of being outside networks of kinship and friendship. As a condition that arouses the pity of others and to which compassionate help is directed, loneliness is a complaint that holds the potential to mobilize relatives and friends, but it holds that potential because it connects in powerful ways to the notion of the right way to live. Loneliness signals a break in a valued way of life and derives its force to motivate individuals and groups precisely because it deviates from the proper orientation for Flathead people.

To cast the Flathead discourse of loneliness in political terms is to fundamentally misconstrue its moral essence—a process that, in turn, miscasts human agency and motivation as uniformly willful and characterized by rational self-interest. This willful, rationally self-interested political actor is very much at home in current anthropological theorizing, whereas the moral actor scarcely has a place to hang his or her hat—a situation fully consonant with Charles Taylor's depiction of "modern epistemology" (1989). In *Sources of the Self*, Taylor discerns within modern Western thought an unacknowledged moral perspective characterized by a valuation of the "ordinary life" and a concomitant distrust of any form of elitism. Yet despite its own moral underpinnings, the distrust of the "higher good" within modern Western thought leaves us mute, without a language to discuss or even acknowledge the moral contours of our own universe. Correspondingly, Euro-American philosophies and human sciences are imbued with a naturalist and utilitarian temper that forces us to imagine the practical principles and processes of production, reproduction, and power relations as basic to human life everywhere, while at the same time it compels us to marginalize morality (and spirituality) as optional.

The reproduction of this perspective in the privileging of the political actor in anthropological writings on culture, self, and emotion is disturbing on several counts. First, it reflects the degree to which we remain culturally blindfolded to the lived realities of others, despite our extensive interactions with those who, unlike ourselves, live in "enchanted" or moral universes. Second, it suggests a new referentiality for emotion terms (i.e., these terms are *really* about gender relations) that hinders our movement toward understanding emotional experience in discursive, and nonreferential, terms. Third, it relies on the notion of a culture-free practical reason that the discipline as a whole has been railing against, from the early efforts of Lewis Henry Morgan on the cultural grounding of family and kinship ([1877] 1974), to Marshall Sahlins's sophisticated critique of culture-free economic rationality (1976), to the contemporary works of ethnopsychologists intent on disclosing the cultural specificity of the meaning of emotion terms.

Equally disturbing in many of the newer, discourse-oriented works on culture, self, and emotion is the loss of the psychological actor. Attributable to the admirable attempt to avoid ethnocentric theorizing about the psychological experience of others, we have nonetheless at some level lost the central object of our study. The cross-cultural study of emotions ascertains that emotions often have more to do with their various semantic associations and interpersonal relations than with interior feelings. As a result, we no longer see the psychologically driven actor expressing and resolving conflict in ritual settings, or even the Goffmanesque actor maneuvering to put his best face forward. The loss of the psychological actor among researchers motivated to understand personal experience in the context of culture explains, perhaps, our willingness to embrace the political actor—for in that embrace we can retain a vision of human agency.

Retrieving the psychological actor may prove to be the thorniest dilemma of all for a discursive approach to culture, self, and emotion. Implicit in the approach is a severing of the referential ties between words and things that leaves us adrift about the correspondence between cultural terms and their meaning for psychological experience. This is not to say that cross-cultural researchers believe that emotion discourses are ideologies that remain unconnected to social action or the phenomenal experience of the self. Instead, it is to say that researchers are less and less comfortable with the notion of a one-to-one correspondence between linguistic symbols and given psychological realities and more attentive to the contextual and dialogic nature of the processes by which an event becomes "emotionalized."

If we are to move beyond butterfly collections of different cultural ideologies of self and emotion, beyond accounts that simplistically assert universal psychological or political functions behind local terms and practices, and toward a reincorporation of the psychological actor, we must do so in terms attentive to cultural processes of meaning making. As a first step, we must attend to culture-specific languages of emotion in all their richness, taking care not to exclude culturally salient aspects of given terms or classes of terms as we translate them into Euro-American terms. As a next step, we must attend to the discursive contexts within which these terms appear and have force. Here, too, we must take care to translate the evident power and forces of such terms in empirically accurate ways, because it is only in this step that we can discover the contours of self/other and motivation as they are constructed in these other ideological systems. Finally, we must return to individual life accounts to discern the specific ways in which emotion terms have psychological meaning for the individual. But in incorporating human agency into our analyses of conscious and unconscious motivations in individual narratives, we must be careful to avoid culturally ungrounded psychological functionalism or political reductionism. One way to do so would be to recognize that narrated selves are necessarily constituted in cultural terms whose force is primarily moral, in the broad sense.

Each of these steps contributes an essential element to a picture of emotions as socially and culturally grounded interpretive responses. This picture in turn helps to inform our understanding of healthy psychological functioning within a given culture. It also forms an essential backdrop to the adequate understanding of pathological functioning within a given culture and the relation between local systems of mean-

ing and Euro-American formulations of psychiatric disorder, the topic
of the next section.

LONELINESS AND DSM-DEFINED
DEPRESSIVE DISORDER

While virtually everyone I interviewed about "depression" spoke
about their loneliness, not everyone who experienced loneliness met
DSM criteria for a depressive disorder. In itself, this finding is not surprising. Even within a group of Euro-American interviewees, we would
not expect all respondents who reported dysphoric mood to be suffering from a diagnosable depressive disorder. Indeed, while the DSM-
III-R (1987) characterizes major depressive disorder and dysthymia as
essentially disorders of "mood" or "affect," a diagnosis is not generally made unless the diagnostician discerns an associated cluster of additional signs of disorder. In other words, a depressive disorder is a
syndrome that encompasses more than depressed affect.

When I went off to the field, I had been trained in the use of the
DSM-III (1980) to diagnose and assess depressive disorders. And that
version of the DSM provided the basis for my investigation among the
Flathead people of the cultural meanings of Euro-American criteria for
depressive disorder. Since that time, the American Psychiatric Association has issued both the DSM-III-R (1987) and the DSM-IV (1994).
The revisions of the manual since the time of my research raise the
question about whether my findings have relevance for current formulations of depressive disorders.

A comparison of the three sets of criteria for major depression reveals only minor differences (see table 2). First, the DSM-III-R and the
DSM-IV each combine DSM-III A and B criteria to avoid duplication
of "loss of interest or pleasure in usual activities." Second, the authors
of the DSM-III-R have inserted the phrase "most of the day, nearly
everyday" for the two mood criteria (1 and 2), and the phrase "nearly
every day" for the remaining criteria (3 to 8), with the exception of criterion 9 dealing with thoughts of death and suicidality—a change that
remains with the DSM-IV. Finally, the authors of the DSM-IV have
added criterion C so that impairment will be a necessary aspect of a diagnosable disorder. From my perspective, despite amendments, criteria
for depressive disorder remain essentially unchanged across the three
manuals.

TABLE 2 A COMPARISON OF DIAGNOSTIC CRITERIA FOR MAJOR DEPRESSIVE EPISODE ACROSS THE DSM-III, THE DSM-III-R, AND THE DSM-IV

DSM-III Criteria	DSM-III-R Criteria	DSM-IV Criteria
A. Dysphoric mood or loss of interest or pleasure in all, or almost all, usual activities and pastimes. The dysphoric mood is characterized by symptoms such as the following: depressed, sad, blue, hopeless, low, down in the dumps, irritable. The mood disturbance must be prominent and relatively persistent, but not necessarily the most dominant symptom, and does not include momentary shifts from one dysphoric mood to another dysphoric mood, e.g., anxiety to depression to anger, such as are seen in acute psychotic turmoil. (For children under six, dysphoric mood may have to be inferred from a persistently sad facial expression.)	A. At least five of the following symptoms have been present during the same two-week period and represent a change from previous functioning; at least one of the symptoms is either (1) depressed mood or (2) loss of interest or pleasure. (Do not include symptoms that are clearly due to a physical condition, mood-incongruent delusions or hallucinations, incoherence, or marked loosening of associations.)	A. Five (or more) of the following symptoms have been present during the same two-week period and represent a change from previous functioning; at least one of the symptoms is either (1) depressed mood or (2) loss of interest or pleasure. Note: Do not include symptoms that are clearly due to a general medical condition, or mood-incongruent delusions or hallucinations.
B. At least four of the following symptoms have each been present nearly every day for a period of at least two weeks (in children under six, at least three of the first four).	(1) depressed mood (or can be irritable mood in children and adolescents) most of the day, nearly every day, as indicated by subjective account or observation by others	(1) depressed mood most of the day, nearly every day, as indicated by either subjective report (e.g., feels sad or empty) or observation made by others (e.g., appears tearful). Note: In children and adolescents, can be irritable mood.
(1) poor appetite or significant weight loss (when not dieting) or increased appetite or significant weight gain (in children under six, consider failure to make expected weight gains)	(2) markedly diminished interest or pleasure in all, or almost all, activities most of the day, nearly every day (as indicated by subjective account or observation by others of apathy most of the time)	(2) markedly diminished interest or pleasure in all, or almost all, activities most of the day, nearly every day (as indicated by either subjective report or observation made by others)
	(3) significant weight loss or weight gain when not dieting (e.g., more than 5% of body weight in a month), or decrease or increase in appetite nearly every day (in children under six, consider failure to make expected weight gains)	(3) significant weight loss when not dieting or weight gain (e.g., more than 5% of body weight in a month), or decrease or increase in appetite nearly every day.

(2) insomnia or hypersomnia
(3) psychomotor agitation or retardation (but not merely subjective feelings of restlessness or being slowed down) (in children under six, hypoactivity)
(4) loss of interest or pleasure in usual activities, or decrease in sexual drive not limited to a period when delusional or hallucinating (in children under six, signs of apathy)
(5) loss of energy, fatigue
(6) feelings of worthlessness, self-reproach, or excessive or inappropriate guilt (either may be delusional)
(7) complaints or evidence of diminished ability to think or concentrate, such as slowed thinking, or indecisiveness not associated with marked loosening of associations or incoherence
(8) recurrent thoughts of death, suicidal ideation, wishes to be dead, or suicide attempt

(4) insomnia or hypersomnia nearly every day
(5) psychomotor agitation or retardation nearly every day (observable by others, not merely subjective feelings of restlessness or being slowed down)
(6) fatigue or loss of energy nearly every day
(7) feelings of worthlessness or excessive or inappropriate guilt (which may be delusional) nearly every day (not merely self-reproach or guilt about being sick)
(8) diminished ability to think or concentrate, or indecisiveness nearly every day (either by subjective account or as observed by others)
(9) recurrent thoughts of death (not just fear of dying), recurrent suicidal ideation without a specific plan, or a suicide attempt or a specific plan for committing suicide

Note: In children, consider failure to make expected weight gains.
(4) insomnia or hypersomnia nearly every day
(5) psychomotor agitation or retardation nearly every day (observable by others, not merely subjective feelings of restlessness or being slowed down)
(6) fatigue or loss of energy nearly every day
(7) feelings of worthlessness or excessive or inappropriate guilt (which may be delusional) nearly every day (not merely self-reproach or guilt about being sick)
(8) diminished ability to think or concentrate, or indecisiveness nearly every day (either by subjective account or as observed by others)
(9) recurrent thoughts of death (not just fear of dying), recurrent suicidal ideation without a specific plan, or a suicide attempt or a specific plan for committing suicide

TABLE 2 (continued)

DSM-III Criteria	DSM-III-R Criteria	DSM-IV Criteria
C. Neither of the following dominate the clinical picture when an affective syndrome (i.e., criteria A and B above) is not present, that is, before it developed or after it has remitted. (1) preoccupation with a mood-incongruent delusion or hallucination (2) bizarre behavior	B. (1) It cannot be established that an organic factor initiated and maintained the disturbance. (2) The disturbance is not a normal reaction to the death of a loved one (Uncomplicated Bereavement). **Note:** Morbid preoccupation with worthlessness, suicidal ideation, marked functional impairment or psychomotor retardation, or prolonged duration suggest bereavement complicated by Major Depression.	B. The symptoms do not meet criteria for a Mixed Episode. C. The symptoms cause clinically significant distress or impairment in social, occupational, or other important areas of functioning.
D. Not superimposed on either Schizophrenia, Schizophreniform Disorder, or a Paranoid Disorder.	C. At no time during the disturbance have there been delusions or hallucinations for as long as two weeks in the absence of mood symptoms (i.e., before the mood symptoms developed or after they have remitted).	D. The symptoms are not due to the direct physiological effects of a substance (e.g., a drug of abuse, medication) or a general medical condition (e.g., hypothyroidism).
E. Not due to an Organic Mental Disorder or Uncomplicated Bereavement.	D. Not superimposed on either Schizophrenia, Schizophreniform Disorder, Delusional Disorder, or Psychotic Disorder NOS.	E. The symptoms are not better accounted for by Bereavement, i.e., after the loss of a loved one, the symptoms persist for longer than two months or are characterized by marked functional impairment, morbid preoccupation with worthlessness, suicidal ideation, psychotic symptoms, or psychomotor retardation.

SOURCES: American Psychiatric Association, Diagnostic and Statistical Manual of Mental Disorders, Third Edition, Washington, D.C.: American Psychiatric Association, 1980. American Psychiatric Association, Diagnostic and Statistical Manual of Mental Disorders, Third Edition, Revised, Washington, D.C.: American Psychiatric Association, 1987. American Psychiatric Association, Diagnostic and Statistical Manual of Mental Disorders, Fourth Edition, Washington, D.C.: American Psychiatric Association, 1994.

As noted earlier, while the DSM depicts depressive disorders as primarily affective disorders, there must nonetheless be present other associated signs of disturbance for a diagnosis of depression to be made. Specifically, an individual would need to present with at least four symptoms in addition to mood disturbance. As shown in table 2, these additional symptoms range from somatic complaints, such as appetite and sleep disturbance or fatigue, to cognitive complaints, such as difficulty concentrating or preoccupation with thoughts of death or suicide. The issue to which this section is directed is whether DSM criteria for depressive disorder accurately capture important distinctions among Flathead individuals—between those who experience normal loneliness and those who experience a profound and pathological disturbance of mood that "colors the whole psychic life" (American Psychiatric Association 1987: 213). Rather than ask whether Flathead people experiencing loneliness meet DSM criteria for a depressive disorder (a question that ignores the difference between affect and affective disorder), we must ask whether those who meet the criteria are truly disturbed and whether those who do not meet the criteria are correspondingly well (a question that compares disturbance with disturbance and wellness with wellness). For those trained in the use of psychiatric instrumentation, the question might well be phrased: How well does the DSM formulation do in helping clinicians and researchers avoid making diagnoses that are falsely positive or falsely negative?

The question is ultimately one of validity: Are DSM criteria, born out of Euro-American culture and biomedical traditions, able to accurately determine pathology among individuals from a distinct cultural heritage? Unfortunately, the answers are not straightforward—in part because before we can address the question of validity we must first deal with the thorny question of what to use as a yardstick against which to measure the validity of DSM criteria. The question is thorny because it is standard practice in psychiatric research to use clinician judgment, especially if channeled by the reliable use of DSM criteria, as the gold standard for detecting and assessing psychiatric disorder. This undoubtedly works well within most intracultural research programs. However, when the question becomes one of assessing the cultural validity of diagnostic criteria, an alternate yardstick for assessing pathology must be developed.

The yardstick that I used in assessing the pathology of a given individual's experience of loneliness was a set of qualitative distinctions that grew out of my training and my fieldwork. In essence, I determined whether or not a person was reporting "pathological loneliness" on several bases that include subjective accounts of distress, the atypical usage of Flathead idioms, subjective accounts or evidence of disordered social relationships (whether in terms of affection or material reciprocity), the extent of help-seeking for reported distress, and family or community judgments about the individual. While not standardized to the degree of the DSM, I believe that these cultural criteria maintain the integrity of local assessments of pathology and at the same time provide a functional resemblance to assessment criteria that Euro-American clinicians typically use in their daily work.

I applied this yardstick to twenty case studies of loneliness/depression that I collected during my field research.[5] Among the cases I reviewed, there were respondents who met criteria for a depressive disorder but who evidenced little or no pathology according to the cultural criteria noted above. There were also respondents who met criteria but whose narratives of loneliness included locally significant signs of distress that the DSM criteria failed to capture. Finally, there were respondents who at some level of accuracy could be diagnosed with a depressive disorder with DSM criteria but for whom an assessment of the severity or pathology of individual symptoms or symptom patterns could easily be misjudged.

Nancy, for example, was a sixty-one-year-old woman who met criteria for dysthymia and who had been prescribed antidepressants by a physician whom she saw for her diabetes. However, instead of eliciting concern from members of her family and the community, her sad and resigned demeanor tended to be admired and emulated. During our interview, Nancy described depression in terms of her heart feeling bad and attributed her feelings to a number of situations ranging from illness and pain to the difficulties of parenting, marriage, and other family relationships and the passing of the ways of the old Indians. She reported a fair number of depressive symptoms, including tearfulness, poor appetite, difficulty in falling asleep until early morning, feeling "drained," worrying about any pain she had caused her loved ones, thinking about "bad things," feeling unsure of what to do, and frequently feeling fearful that something bad was going to happen. While not constant, these feelings never left her for long. She described these feelings, in fact, as simply "part of life."

Despite the clear presence of depressive symptoms, however, a diagnosis indicating pathology seems unwarranted for Nancy since she met none of the cultural criteria for pathology. Moreover, to medicalize her presentation would be to completely misread her embodied memorialization of tribal losses and her Indian identity. The problem seems to be reversed for Rachel, a thirty-two-year-old woman who, failing to meet the criteria for major depression, nonetheless presented a history of repeated and profound disturbances of mood that colored her whole psychic life. Rachel described several discrete periods in her life during which she experienced feelings of loneliness and being overwhelmed by family responsibilities, difficulties in sleeping, and frequent thoughts about suicide. During these periods, Rachel sought help from a wide circle of helpers and usually sought inpatient hospitalization from a psychiatrist. She described these times in her life as always precipitated by troubled relationships. In fact, throughout the interview, Rachel tended to focus her narrative on situations and instances that showed how she had been mistreated by her husband or other family members, rather than on her internal feelings.

Rachel's tendency to report distress in situational and relational terms is perfectly consonant with her cultural heritage, but it results in her use of an idiom that is not acknowledged by DSM criteria. Her pain, if it could be heard at all, would be understood in terms of a series of adjustment disorders (with mixed emotional features) or, more likely, as a personality disorder (borderline)—neither of which recognizes the normative character of Rachel's relational complaints or the inherently relational dimensions of mood disturbance in Flathead culture.

Some of these same issues appear in a more complex case involving Earl, a thirty-one-year-old man who easily met DSM criteria for major depression but whose symptoms reflected a complicated pattern of pathological and normal functioning. Earl was recently separated from his second wife, to whom he had been married for about a year. Their separation was precipitated by difficulties arising from custody of their respective children from previous marriages, his drinking, and her "jealousy." The situation was compounded when Earl's wife suffered a miscarriage within a week after their separation—a troubling event for both of them. Noting that he had experienced "total fulfillment" with his new wife, Earl had a hard time talking about anything other than his relationship with her for any length of time throughout our interview.

Earl had complained of profound feelings of depression when we had met the previous weekend and had been very interested in being interviewed. He also acknowledged current difficulties with drugs and alcohol. During our interview, he described crying easily and feeling depressed, hopeless, and fearful of being alone. He also reported anhedonia and a nearly complete loss of interest in his usual pursuits, citing the fact that he had not fished, played basketball, or visited his sons for at least nine months. Earl described himself as feeling tired and totally lacking in energy, saying that "it took everything just to walk a few feet." Earl reported initial insomnia resulting in three to four hours of sleep a night. He described how he did things "automatically" and how "the world was heavy" on him. He complained of loss of appetite and reported a weight loss of thirty-five pounds over the past five months. He also reported recurrent thoughts of death and suicidal ideation: he had prayed for death and had thought about dying in a car crash, walking on the highway, and battling with a bear up in the mountains. However, he denied having any suicidal intent, or having a plan. Although Earl described an insidious onset of his symptoms about one year previous to the interview, it seems more likely that he had experienced a temporary respite from his afflictions for a period of a few months not quite a year and a half ago when he met and married his second wife. He denied elevated or expansive mood, or increased energy.

Earl's presentation was complicated by mood-congruent "bizarre thoughts," including foreknowledge of his miscarried baby's conception and its demise and an incident in which evil spirits attempted to deceive him into dying. He also spoke vaguely but at length at different points in the interview about an impending change or crisis, sometimes implying a personal change but at other times implying a worldwide change. He foretold that he would either emerge from his depression or it would continue to get worse until a "critical point." He spoke about preparing for the change by "separating" from his old self, and it was in terms of "separation" that he described his new disinterest in learning his Indian language, his lost desire to help his people or even to live on the reservation, and his discontinuance of war dancing.

Perhaps the most dramatic example of these "bizarre thoughts" was Earl's reason for refusing to leave his wife after her request that he do so. Earl explained his actions this way:

Well, another reason I didn't want to leave was I had a, I don't know, at certain times in my life, you know, there'll be a two-week span when I'll get the notion that I'm in danger. I don't mean danger for myself, but that that's a dangerous point in my life. I don't know if you know about the mathematics of the world, but that happens. So I told her [my wife] I couldn't [go], and said, "After this time [of danger], if you still want me to go, I'll go."

Earl described a two-month period of daily drinking after he left his second wife, four months prior to our talk. He also reported smoking marijuana and doing "some hard drugs, too, lately." Six weeks or so before the interview, Earl had confined his drinking to the weekends, although he reported "hard" drinking every weekend. At the time of the interview, Earl was ordered by the court to stay away from alcohol because he beat up another bar patron the previous Saturday. During the year or so before the interview, he had been able to secure only sporadic employment.

With the constellation of symptoms presented by Earl, a diagnosis of major depression with mood congruent psychotic feature and co-morbid substance abuse seems warranted. A closer look at the verbal and nonverbal symbols that Earl uses to communicate his current distress reveals, however, that their pathological significance emerges only in reference to local norms and idioms. For example, while Earl might not have appeared overly talkative or agitated to most clinicians, his volubility and occasional moving around were behaviorally atypical in the reservation setting, where a calm, sedate presentation is the norm. Earl provided a clue about this "agitation" when he noted how his father often got after him to stop pacing. Similarly, given what we have learned about men as the ones to bear and display much of the sadness of tribal and familial losses, the apparent pathology of Earl's description of himself as "crying easily" is reduced. We also know that suicidality is highly stigmatized among the spiritually oriented Flathead and that it tends to be associated with the impulsivity of youth and rejected lovers. Thus, despite Earl's denial of suicidal intent, his excessive brooding about his own death is a powerful indicator not only of distress but also of potential risk.

The specific content of some of his thoughts deserves contextualizing as well. Neither his foreknowledge of his wife's pregnancy and miscarriage nor his experience with spirits is culturally inappropriate in and of itself. However, the morbid character of these experiences and their pairing with the notion of the "mathematics of the world" make them quite unusual. Along this same line, Earl uses another very powerful idiom of distress (separation), but in the flatness of his affect, he does so in a culturally atypical way. His complaint about his lack of loneliness

for his children is a strikingly astute comment on the cultural inappropriateness of his response to this separation. Similarly, while complaints
of "not caring anymore" are not uncommon, they are usually delivered
in remorseful or angry tones. Again, Earl's affective distance in talking
about his lack of caring is strange. Thus while Earl uses the language of
interdependence to express his distress, he nonetheless uses it in such an
atypical fashion as to communicate his oddness.

The need to understand the cultural parameters of Earl's presentation extends beyond symptoms per se. As potential stressors, Earl's
lack of a job and his weekend drinking need to be understood within
the context of reservation life. While unemployment is not negligible as
a stressor, neither is a man's identity necessarily damaged by the condition. Similarly, for a man of Earl's age, weekend drinking, as long as it
has not become solitary or a drain on his family's resources, is not necessarily pathological and may instead indicate a strong network of
friends. As stressors, his separation from his second wife, his divorce
from his first wife, and his estrangement from his children need to be
assessed vis-à-vis the cultural value of interdependence and the corresponding view of deaths and other interpersonal disruptions as disruptions of the self.

These cases help to illustrate that DSM criteria are not a completely
accurate map for distinguishing normality and pathology in the experience of loneliness among the Flathead. Moreover, it is not simply a
matter of adjusting "upward" or "downward" for the normative experience of loneliness.[6] In fact, from the yardstick of pathological loneliness, DSM criteria are variably relevant. For example, in looking at the
first criterion attending to "mood," the presence of dysphoric affect
may not be a clear sign of distress. As we have learned, the Flathead
ideology of loneliness constructs selves as possessing a sentient awareness of human interdependence that develops naturally over time
through personal experience with grief and suffering. In this context, it
can be a mark of obedient maturity to express profound loneliness for
oneself when separated from loved ones, to express sorrow for the
pain one has caused others, and to express pity for those who have
nothing. In this setting, the pursuit of happiness, as Robert N. Bellah
and his colleagues (1985) describe for mainstream American society, is
often thought to indicate immaturity. Sadness, especially if cast in the
idiom of loneliness, can communicate awareness of the gravity of historical, tribal, familial, and personal losses. Loneliness, even when ac-

companied by the "symptoms" of tearfulness and sleep and appetite disturbances, can forcefully demonstrate one's connection to the Indian world.

Claims of loneliness can, thus, be positive expressions of belonging in this milieu. Yet they can also be the expressions of profound distress. As we saw in Part II, life within the community is characterized, ideally, by close affective ties of kinship and friendship as well as by expectations of generous sharing among one's group of family and friends. Daily life, however, is never ideal, and it is not uncommon for members of the community to report feelings of not being cared for, of having nothing, or, worst of all, of having been abandoned, of being left alone. Loneliness, then, can express an individual's sense of finding himself or herself outside expected relations of reciprocity. Among the Flathead people, loneliness can express the profoundly alienating experience of fear, confusion, loss, and righteous indignation when important affective and instrumental relationships seem to have become disrupted.

Loneliness and sadness can therefore be signs of pathological distress, but these internal signs are not what is likely to be presented to a clinician. Instead, it is far more likely that a Flathead individual will present with a dramatic story, or series of stories, about being neglected or abused by family members, a spouse, or a boyfriend or girlfriend. While the intense internal feelings associated with a mature loneliness are likely to be more notable to a clinician (seeming to indicate a greater depth of feeling), the recitation of such stories about disordered relationships (with comparably less emphasis on internal feelings) is a far more powerful sign of distress and one too often associated with the risk of unpremeditated suicide gesture or attempt.

Both normal and pathological loneliness are predicated in an understanding of the appropriately deep affective ties between and among family members and the demonstration of the ties in acts of material exchange and instrumental aid. Statements about one's own deep feelings of pity, compassion, and loneliness for others tend to be demonstrations of a profoundly sad but socially and psychically sound condition. In contrast, statements about the lack of appropriately compassionate feelings of others for oneself tend to be associated with a disordered condition—especially if those statements are accompanied by statements about feelings of worthlessness.

The most serious indications of pathology, however, are statements

about one's own lack of appropriately deep or compassionate feelings
for others. We saw such statements in Dan's narrative when he told me
about when his wife commented on his lack of grief over the deaths of
his mother and brother. In a similar way, Earl wondered about his lack
of "caring" about the various "separations" he was making and having to endure. "Not caring" is a far more serious indicator of pathology than profound dysphoric mood, and thus the second DSM mood
criterion (loss of interest) is far more likely to be associated with
pathological loneliness than is the first criterion (depressed mood).

With regard to the remainder of the DSM criteria for depression,
most can be found in both normal and pathological loneliness. Looking back at Nancy's recitation of her experiences, which included insomnia, poor appetite, fatigue, and indecisiveness, we can see that
these "symptoms" seem to possess little power to indicate pathology,
even when falling together in an apparent syndrome. Earl's pathological experience is marked by the presence of the same "symptoms," but
his experiences with insomnia, poor appetite, and fatigue are qualitatively distinct, possessing all the earmarks of true symptoms.

The pathological significance of the "symptoms" of depressive disorder can only be determined with the valid assessment of disturbed
mood. The two exceptions in the list include criterion 7, which
specifies feelings of worthlessness, and criterion 9, which specifies suicidal ideation, plans, or attempts. Neither of these criteria is found in
the narratives of normal loneliness. Correspondingly, each is only
found as an element of accounts of pathological experience.

Pathological loneliness and DSM criteria for depressive disorder are
distinct visions of distress and impairment that selectively attend to aspects of human experience. While there appears to be some overlap between the two visions, I have tried to demonstrate that DSM criteria
are not equally significant for understanding pathological loneliness.
Moreover, not all of the important signs of pathological loneliness can
be found among DSM criteria. At the forefront of these "missing"
signs is the absence of any reference to disordered or disturbed social
relationships. Also, there is a corresponding lack of reference to disordered or disturbed spiritual relationships.

If I had to mimic the DSM format to delineate the essence of pathological mood disturbance among the Flathead, it would look something like table 3. In summary, Euro-American criteria for depressive
disorder, as they appear in the DSM-III and the DSM-III-R, can be
heard in Flathead people's narratives of loneliness. They can be found

TABLE 3   CULTURE-SPECIFIC DIAGNOSTIC CRITERIA
FOR PATHOLOGICAL MOOD DISTURBANCE
AMONG THE FLATHEAD

A. A profound and pervasive experience of loneliness, separation, or fear of abandonment that colors the whole psychic life. The mood disturbance may be expressed by the client as (1) a feeling that specified others do not care for him or her; (2) a more generalized feeling that no one cares for him or her; or (3) a feeling that he or she no longer cares for others.

B. Evidence of relationship difficulties with family members, a spouse, or a boyfriend or girlfriend that may include isolation, stinginess, resentment, or jealousy on either side of the relationship.

C. Two or more of the following:
   (1) a crisis of faith
   (2) appetite disturbance or significant weight change
   (3) sleep disturbance
   (4) fatigue
   (5) difficulty concentrating; excessive preoccupation with misfortunes
   (6) high levels of help-seeking for oneself or by others for the self
   (7) suicidal ideation, plan, or attempt

individually and grouped, and in patterns that yield diagnoses of depressive disorder. However, with the exception of two criteria (feelings of worthlessness and suicidality), DSM criteria fail to reliably capture locally defined experiences of distress and disorder. Moreover, that DSM criteria are unable to accurately apprehend pathological experience among the Flathead is true at the level of individual criteria as well as at the syndromal level.

How are we to understand the similarities and differences between Flathead concepts and DSM criteria? Earlier I suggested that each comprises a distinct vision of distress and impairment. I can be more specific at this point. DSM and Flathead visions are distinct in the emphasis each places on internal feeling states of the disturbed individual versus the relational aspects of psychiatric disturbance.

But do differences such as these make a difference for understanding depressive disorder cross-culturally? After all, DSM criteria have emerged from decades of scientific observation, whereas Flathead concepts are folk concepts, loosely articulated at best.

Such differences *are* important for two related reasons. First, disorder can only be comprehended, only has meaning, as an alteration of the normal at the level of individual phenomenal experience. In other words, symptoms without implications for the whole self simply are not symptoms. To use the words of Georges Canguilhem, an eminent historian of medical science,

> To return once more to diabetes, it is not a kidney disease because of glyco-suria, nor a pancreatic disease because of hypoinsulinemia, nor a disease of the pituitary; it is the disease of the organism all of whose functions are changed, which is threatened by tuberculosis, whose supperated infections are endless, whose limbs are rendered useless by arteritis and gangrene. . . . It seems very artificial to break up disease into symptoms or to consider its complications in the abstract. What is a symptom without context or back-ground? What is a complication separated from what it complicates? When an isolated symptom or a functional mechanism is termed pathological, one forgets that what makes them so is their inner relation in the indivisible to-tality of human behavior. (1989: 88)

Just as with diabetes, depressed affect cannot be considered a symptom and depressive disorder cannot be considered a syndrome unless they hold pathological significance for meaningful human behavior.

Second, differences such as are seen between Flathead and DSM vi-sions of distress are also important because of what they imply for meaningful human behavior. Following Canguilhem's insights, the nor-mal and the pathological must be understood as concepts of value, rather than as concepts of objective reality susceptible to quantified sci-entific definition. Rather than by biochemical imperatives, the normal and the pathological are framed primarily by cultural definitions of the self.[7] An individual will perceive pathology, as an alteration of the nor-mal, according to value-laden qualities that have been constructed as important in his or her culture. Thus a teenage girl from mainstream American society in the 1980s or 1990s who is confined to a back brace because of a curvature of the spine might well experience her pathology in terms of a diminished sense of attractiveness—at a time in her life when personal attractiveness is emphasized for young women within her culture. For a Flathead person, pathology is apprehended, is felt at the phenomenal level, when he or she no longer feels connected to family and friends. And it is in those culturally emphasized terms that depressed affect may or may not be perceived as an alteration of the normal.

If pathology is inseparable from culturally constituted meaning sys-tems that define normality, how are we to proceed with the investiga-tion of depression cross-culturally, and how can clinicians proceed with treatment in cross-cultural encounters? These are the questions that propel the next, and final, section of this chapter.

CULTURE AND DEPRESSION

This book began with a detailed look at Flathead narratives of history and identity. Throughout those narratives, loss, Indian identity, morality, and feelings of sadness and loneliness were discursively linked in images of the Flathead people as enduring survivors whose pain has been transformed into compassion and generosity. In documenting the Flathead response to one hundred fifty years of domination and in describing the terms within which contemporary Flathead Indian identity is played out, Part I introduced one of the unique and powerful meanings of depressive-like affect in Flathead culture: as an embodied testimonial to the past and present losses endured by the Flathead people.

Part II continued to unpack the rich meanings of depressive-like affect among the Flathead through an analysis of the ideology and practices of loneliness and pity. In both ritual and mundane settings, loneliness is tied to the guiding image of the interdependent self. The linking of loneliness as motivator to gift giving, visiting, and proper manners reveals additional meanings for depressive-like affect among the Flathead: as an expression of one's sentient awareness of the interdependence of all human beings; and as an expression of the pain that one feels on finding oneself outside usual or expected relations of compassion and exchange.

Chapter 5 and the first two sections of this chapter explored the implications of the broad cultural meanings of loneliness for understanding normal and pathological experience in individual narratives of "depression." In uncovering the specific relational, historical, and moral meanings of loneliness among the Flathead people, I have been able to answer two of the puzzles that propelled my research from the start: What can it mean to say that 70 to 80 percent of the Flathead people are depressed? And why do Flathead narratives of depression seem to resonate as much with positive moral meanings as with ego-centered pain?

The answers to these questions lie in the finding that depression among the Flathead people encompasses much more than an individual affliction or illness. It derives its meaning from a morally charged vision of Flathead life in which loneliness is a natural and esteemed response to current and historical tribal losses, to the poignancy of inescapable human need for one another, and to disruptions of self-sustaining relationships. Flathead loneliness, in narratives of individual and collective depression, is a powerful plea for pity, respect, and a place to belong. It is an idiom that seeks to reclaim relationships and identities that it proclaims as lost. Flathead loneliness gives voice to the meaning of suffering in a way that ties individuals to the group and the present to the past. Flathead depression, thus, speaks not only to individual pathology but also to the sociohistorical processes of the demoralization and remoralization of all Flathead people.

One puzzle remains, however: Why did I have such a hard time finding the answers to the first two puzzles? In other words, why were the broader cultural meanings of depression among the Flathead so difficult for me to grasp?

As I suggested in the introduction, the answer to this final puzzle resides in the particular perspective I took on how to research depression, on the ways in which I decided what counted as evidence of "real" depression, on where I stood to view the issue. Where I first stood was dictated by my steadfast interest to speak to two distinct disciplines—social anthropology and cross-cultural psychiatry. Throughout my fieldwork, I clung tenaciously to the idea that I could respond clearly to the concerns of both branches of knowledge, to the idea that I could find a place to stand that incorporated the respective disciplinary insights into certain forms of human suffering. I wanted to stand on the mountaintop, on ground that unified psychiatric and anthropological perspectives, that could accommodate the visions of depression both from Main Street *and* from across the bridge.

Standing on Main Street, DSM criteria in hand, it seemed a straightforward task to diagnose depressive disorder among the Flathead and then to look for variations in its expression (i.e., somatization or a shorter course of illness). Similarly, it seemed a simple chore to select those who could be diagnosed with depressive disorder and then search for evidence of unique circumstances in the psychosocial context of Indian lives that would predispose Flathead people to depressive disorder (i.e., high levels of stress, alcoholism, or bereavement). However, after crossing the bridge at the end of Main Street to see life from the Flathead perspective, the task of diagnosing depression seemed far less straightforward. From that ground, the meanings of individual symptoms, even the syndromes themselves, were altered enough to call into question their status as symptoms and syndromes.

From the mountaintop, I saw the need to adhere to the psychiatric vision of depressive disorder as a biomedical condition of the individual, but my continued belief that it was only through DSM criteria that I could tap the essence of depression blinded me to the relational, historical, and moral meanings of Flathead "depression"—meanings that I now regard as essential to understanding normal and disordered affect among the Flathead. In my experience, the DSM encouraged a narrow understanding of disordered experience that reified the internal and protodisease aspects of psychiatric disorder, banishing most psychological, social, and cultural dynamics to the sidelines. It allowed questioning of the influence of nonbiomedical aspects of the illness process, but only in terms that did not question the validity of the diagnostic categories themselves.

My investigation of depression among the Flathead does, however, question the definition of depressive disorder as essentially a biomedical condition. In fact, the ethnographic material argues that depression is essentially a cultural condition—in that the symptoms and syndromes of depressive disorder are terms of value that rest on culturally distinct notions of normality and pathology. In that argument lies the hidden, but potentially threatening, suggestion that the biology of depression may be facilitating or predisposing to pathological mood disturbance, but may be neither necessary nor sufficient for the disorder.

So what does this signify for cross-cultural work, whether research or clinical practice? It means, basically, that psychiatric visions of disorder cannot be used naively in distinct cultural settings. Arthur Kleinman has already discussed the important risk of "category fallacy" that inheres in the exportation of Euro-American disease criteria into non-Euro-American settings (1977). At a more practical level, an uncritical reliance on DSM definitions of depressive disorder for cross-cultural research risks potential irrelevance, such as when esteemed Flathead elders like Nancy are prescribed antidepressants while others at far greater risk are not recognized. Worse, the unexamined use of DSM criteria for research purposes can lead to the medicalization or pathologizing of alternate visions of normality, or to the trivialization of profound human misery. Gannath Obeyesekere's (1985) playful yet profoundly persuasive example of the importation of the Ayurvedic disease category of "semen loss" into a Euro-American setting reinforces this point: each vision of human distress imagines the lines around normality and pathology in ways that may or may not work in other settings.

In clinical work, the same lesson applies. Despite the fact that diagnosis often assumes a secondary importance in clinical practice, the unscrutinized use of Euro-American ideas of normal and pathological functioning can have results similar to the naive use of the DSM in cross-cultural research. Importantly, there is the risk of compromised therapeutic efficacy. The therapeutic process can be compromised when clinicians misjudge the pathological implications of certain behaviors and statements. For example, a Flathead client whose life is structured by the values of the interdependent self may find himself judged as pathologically "dependent" or "enmeshed" by a clinician whose own life tends to be structured by the Euro-American value of the *independent* self. Similarly, a Flathead client who exhibits the value of endurance may be judged as pathologically "passive" by a clinician whose cultural heritage places much more value on a active revising of the world. In misjudging the normative meanings of a client's behavior, clinicians may jeopardize rapport when the client senses the discrepancy and reacts justifiably with resentment and distrust. Moreover, the clinician's failure to recognize the positive value of certain culturally grounded behaviors and attitudes can lead to his or her inability to forge with the client metaphors with the power to induce healthy change. Finally, by attempting to impose Euro-American values in a therapeutic encounter, the clinician may unwittingly perpetuate a powerful delegitimizing of Indian lifeways and values.

In this litany of dangers, it may seem that I am advocating the abandonment of the DSM for cross-cultural work. I am not. In fact, I am arguing for the opposite. Anthropologists and other researchers should use the DSM as a basis for their cross-cultural investigations. Ironically, while the protodisease formulations of the DSM reflect a very narrow vision of pathologically disordered affect, that vision nonetheless facilitates a more reliable and accountable framework for cross-cultural work than any previous vision within psychiatry. Using that document with a critical eye, researchers can evaluate the cultural relevance of DSM criteria separately as individual symptoms and together as syndromes. Throughout, of course, special efforts must be directed to uncovering local signs and symptoms that may not be included in DSM formulations. Unfortunately, while the DSM permits more precise cross-cultural investigations, it currently remains unable to incorporate the resulting knowledge in any meaningful way. Based in a scientistic framework that accords truth value only to quantifiable and universal "biological" processes, the medical model of psychiatric disorder represented in the DSM turns a deaf ear to the statement that culture matters in a fundamental way.[8]

I can envision a future psychiatry resting on an interpretive epistemology, in which disordered experience is always understood as expressed by an enculturated individual whose language of emotion and distress derives from cultural definitions of normality. In that future psychiatry, culture is of essential interest to the discipline of psychiatry. Anthropologists and psychiatrists alike will share the notion that disease, help-seeking, and healing are culturally constituted processes from which biological and psychological conditions derive their significance. At that point, depressive disorders as they are currently formulated will be seen as culturally meaningful syndromes that channel the expression of distress associated with certain biological, social, and psychological conditions *within* Euro-American settings. At that point, the DSM will include culturally meaningful syndromes from non-Euro-American cultures around the world—perhaps along the lines of the criteria I generated for pathological mood disturbance among the Flathead. Clinicians will be trained in techniques to elucidate the cultural context that provides the sense and meaning of their clients' presentations. Finally, cross-cultural researchers will have progressed beyond basic studies of different languages of disturbance and into more sophisticated investigations that explore the biological, social, and psychological correlates of locally defined syndromes.

That time has not yet come, however; and until it does, there can be no unified ground, no mountaintop on which to stand to view psychiatric disorder cross-culturally. For the time being, then, we must be cognizant of the vastly different ways that disciplines view depression and not be surprised when our communication is strained and seemingly antagonistic at times. The difficulty of communicating, however, is no excuse for not trying. Put explicitly, cross-cultural researchers must not be content to stay on Main Street, leaving unquestioned the primacy of the medical model of depression. Moreover, to question effectively the unstated premise of the universality of that model, we cannot stand only on ground across the bridge either. After learning a local language of normality and pathology, we must struggle to understand it from the view from Main Street. Only in this way will our findings and message about culture and psychopathology speak to the pertinent issues facing psychiatric researchers and clinicians.[9]

After gathering and distilling the expert opinions of leading scholars in history, anthropology, psychology, and psychiatry, Kleinman and Good called in 1985 for a multipronged program of research for investigating depression cross-culturally. Central to each of the directions they recommended, as well as to their entire vision, was the need to avoid simplistic monodisciplinary frameworks. Instead, they concluded with a plea for anthropologically informed psychiatric research and nosologically sophisticated anthropological inquiry. This book was designed, in part, to respond to Kleinman and Good's plea. As it turns out, in responding to that plea, this project develops a clearer picture of what a nosologically sophisticated anthropology might look like. In essence, my findings suggest that researchers interested in disordered emotion must not, at this point, contemplate standing atop the mountain but must instead be capable of running back and forth between Main Street and the spot across the bridge. In responding to Kleinman and Good's plea, this work also details a much-needed understanding of depression among an American Indian people. In leaving the mountaintop and even Main Street behind, *Disciplined Hearts* tells a story about historical loss, tribal belonging, and the cultural discourse of loneliness and pity that ties each Flathead person to others, to the past, and to the future.

Afterword

Conclusions are hard to write. The thought of bringing closure to a set of ideas that have preoccupied me for years makes it particularly difficult to draft an ending to this book. The conclusion, it seems, is my last chance to get it right, to pay homage to those with whom I have worked by writing the perfect denouement. The only escape is by sleight of hand, by taking this opportunity to reflect on some of the issues raised in this text rather than by writing a conclusion per se. In this way, I affirm that my engagement with the issues raised by Flathead loneliness is ongoing, that these ideas are simply my contribution to the ongoing dialogues about human experience within anthropology and psychiatry.

I begin by responding to two issues raised by reviewers of this manuscript. In responding to each of these queries I hope to clarify potential misreadings. First, one reviewer suggested that the manuscript skirts the question of whether Flathead depression is solely a colonial phenomenon, a form of suffering absent among precontact Flathead people. Second, this reviewer also questioned Dan's "representativeness," inquiring whether his experiences were "characteristically Flathead." The reviewer is right; this study does not answer either question. However, rather than the result of skirting around key questions, it seems to me that the absence of such answers relates to more fundamental issues. The first question—about depression as a colonial phenomenon—requires a different use of history than characterizes this investigation. The second—about Dan's "representativeness"—relies on

a vision of culture and the individual and the relationship between the
two that is at odds with my presentation. Let me explain.

To answer the question posed in the first comment, a researcher
would need to establish a description of "depression" that could
validly describe distress across pre- and postcontact Flathead people,
establish the levels or rates of such distress in the contemporary Flathead population, and devise a method to search the early written
record for evidence of the presence or absence of "depression" among
precontact people. This I do not do. Rather, the present study turns to
the history of contact and oppression in all its Flathead particularities
in order to understand its meaning and its use *among contemporary
Flathead people*. To paraphrase Marshall Sahlins, the significance of
history in this book is not to document whether the past occurred as
depicted, but rather to consider its contemporary construction as historically significant (1985: xiv).

A meaning-centered approach to history permits different kinds of
questions about the effects of colonialism, questions that lie at the
heart of the matter for many students of postcolonial life: Has oppression and domination had an effect on the psychological functioning of
this colonized people? And if so, how? On the basis of this study with
the Flathead, the answer to the first question is an irrefutable "yes."
For the Flathead, colonialism and domination have taken multiple
forms: early militaristic and economic threat; geographic displacement
and confinement; enforced cultural and educational assimilation; the
specter of legal annihilation and an increasing legalism in the definition
of community membership; the institutionalized barriers that keep
Flathead people out of the workforce; relative deprivation; and continued racism and hostility. In each of these manifestations and in their
totality, Flathead families and tribes have been fractured, rendered less
powerful in ways that have produced a sense of personal fragility
among Flathead individuals. The effects are witnessed most clearly,
perhaps, in the widespread comment by Flathead people about the
high rates of depression that can be found among their people. This
lament displays forcefully the effects of historical oppression on modern Flathead life.

My approach to history allows me to conclude that colonialism has
disrupted the lives of Flathead people in powerful ways. I cannot, however, answer the question about "depression" as a direct product of
colonial contact posed in the reviewer's comment. This book is even
less able to address the second comment, about Dan's "representative-

ness." Consonant with much of the recent writing about the ethnographic enterprise, this work avoids representing culture as timeless,
given, and completely coherent, and individuals as typical of their culture, or not. Instead, I seek to cast Flathead culture as a complex, historically situated process of reinvention—a view that seems better able
to capture the complicated indeterminacy of social life. Toward that
end, I focus on the contextual and negotiated nature of history, Indian
identity, family relations, and emotion. Within each of these realms,
I try to display the specific historical grounding of these meaning-
making processes, arguing that Flathead culture is always in the act of
being remade.

I attempt to represent what it means to be Flathead, not as inhering
in "typical" or universally shared experiences, but rather as an engagement in a set of conversations around issues of belonging and moral
worth. Flathead culture, in this presentation, reveals itself as a set of
discursive forms with which individuals and groups negotiate the significance of their lives. Along these lines, I focus primarily on the language of loneliness and its semiotic and practical structure. Through
Dan's story, however, I also attempt to reveal the positionality of any
use of the language of loneliness. As a male, in his middle adulthood,
and with claims to a certain degree of "traditionality," Dan's narrative
is positioned on a moral trajectory that could scarcely be said to be
"typical" of Flathead experiences. Within this framework, the question
of Dan's "representativeness" or the "characteristicness" of his experiences cannot be answered, despite the intelligibility of his story to his
friends and family. To attempt to reframe the relationship of culture
and individual so as to be able to answer the question moves us back
toward a monolithic view of culture that denies the complexity and indeterminacy of the flux of everyday social interaction.

If this book answers neither the question about depression as a
colonial phenomenon nor that about typical Flathead experience, then
what questions does it answer? Most simply, this book speaks to the
three puzzles that I raised in the introduction: Why is it commonly
held that a preponderance of Flathead people suffer from depression?
Why do Flathead narratives of depression resonate as much with positive moral meanings as with personal distress? Why did I find it so
difficult to grasp the historical, relational, and moral bases of Flathead
"depression"? In struggling to answer these three central puzzles, this
study has been able to speak to important issues confronting cultural
psychology and cultural psychiatry. By taking emotion as a meaningful

construction, it joins others in offering a vision of emotion not as the simple or sole product of "inner" processes but as a discursive product of the interaction between an enculturated individual and a social, cultural, and political world. Emotion thus moves from being enveloped within the body to being situated in the dialogue between persons, their social circumstances, and cultural interpretations that organize the self vis-à-vis those circumstances.

This account views emotion as culturally meaningful social action. In doing so, it raises the issue of the psychological actor with motives, desires, and intentions. As I noted in the first part of chapter 6, the retrieval of the psychological actor may pose one of the thorniest dilemmas for cultural psychology. Yet it seems essential to pursue if we want to move beyond cross-cultural explorations of the semantics of emotion and into studies of psychological functioning cross-culturally in ways that do not recapitulate the ethnocentrism of earlier culture and personality studies.

In reflecting on this exploration of Flathead loneliness in these terms, it appears to me that the study is rooted primarily in the realm of semiotics, despite forays into the everyday and ritual practices that are inextricably linked to loneliness and pity in contemporary Flathead life. In this detailed look at the language of Flathead loneliness, it has become increasingly clear, to me at least, that there is *within that language* a semiotic structuring of the pragmatic force of loneliness and that therein may lie a clue to how to proceed with a cultural psychology that can attend to psychological functioning and the psychological actor.

At base, this orientation is simply a recognition that emotion talk, like all talk, is both representational and pragmatic. In other words, emotion not only depicts a particular vision of the self and its relation to the world, but its usage actually defines or redefines that social reality. Significantly, however, the pragmatic potential of emotion to effect social action is embedded deeply in the symbolic structure of emotion within a culture. For example, by virtue of its role in the semiotic structuring of belonging and moral worth, Flathead loneliness currently has the potential for pragmatic force in three realms of contemporary Flathead life: in defining and redefining the moral worth of Flathead people as a tribal group through historical and current contact with whites; in negotiating and renegotiating the moral standing of individuals and their relatives and friends within the community; and in organizing and reorganizing intimate and familial relationships.

By shifting the focus onto what people are trying to do, and what they accomplish, in specific contexts in which selves are linked to emotion—by exploring the ethnopragmatics of how to do things with emotions—we can build up a picture of psychological dynamics unclouded by an uncritical importation of Euro-American ideas on intentions and motivations. This move helps, for one example, to illuminate the crucial role of tribal history or cultural activities or of an active association with tribal elders that characterizes many of the therapeutic efforts that emerge from American Indian communities. The by-product of this shift, however, is that we may end up with a cultural psychology that bears little resemblance to Euro-American psychology. In turning an eye to the culturally constituted domains within which emotion has an integral role in establishing agency and social action, we may discover a "psychological" dynamics that has as much to do with sociopolitical processes of history, ethnic identity, and family relations as it does with processes of autonomy, self-actualization, or self-esteem. In considering the semiotic and pragmatic bases of discursive acts that construct emotional experience, however, we will be rewarded with a language for understanding personal experience cross-culturally that does not disfigure the very terms of personal experience in other cultures and that positively attends to the complex social processes of emotional life.

Notes

ACKNOWLEDGMENTS

1. The Flathead Culture Committee is headquartered in the St. Ignatius Longhouse, a comfortable place where painted portraits of the elders line the walls, where community members drop in for a cup of coffee and to visit, where most wakes are held, and where visiting linguists, historians, and anthropologists check in. The committee was established in 1976 by the Confederated Salish and Kootenai Tribes in recognition and support of several tribal members who had banded together in the previous year to record and translate the stories of the elders (B. White 1994). Since the seventies, Flathead Culture Committee efforts have been directed toward the written documentation and preservation of tribal knowledge and tradition: cataloging the traditional uses of plants; compiling and publishing traditional legends and stories; and producing educational materials for teaching the native language. Equally important during my stay, however, were activities designed to teach aspects of Flathead tribal heritage through actual practice: teaching language classes; holding cultural encampments; and sponsoring traditional dances, ceremonies, and pilgrimages. The committee also served, and continues to serve in an increasing capacity, as a bridge between traditional tribal concerns and the exigencies of modern life: hosting monthly Elders Meetings at which issues before the tribal council are discussed by the elders and overseeing the activities of ouside groups whose business brings them in contact with matters of spiritual or cultural significance.

INTRODUCTION

1. Throughout this book I use the term "Flathead" to refer to people of the Salish and Pend d'Oreilles tribes. The Flathead Reservation is home to about

half of the approximately 6,000 enrolled members of the Pend d'Oreilles, Salish, and Kootenai—three tribes brought together when the reservation was created in 1855 by the Hellgate Treaty. The Salish and the Pend d'Oreilles share the same native language and many cultural practices. The Kootenai are linguistically unrelated to the Salish and the Pend d'Oreilles, and while all three tribes share the Flathead Reservation, the Kootenai remain socially separated, to a degree, from the other two tribes. My work was conducted primarily with the Salish and the Pend d'Oreilles and should not be generalized to the Kootenai.

2. See Roy, Choudhuri, and Irvine 1970; Shore et al. 1973; Sampath 1974.

3. See also Shore and Manson 1981, 1983.

4. See, e.g., Good and Good 1982; Good, Good, and Moradi 1985; Keyes 1985; Kleinman 1977, 1982; Kleinman and Kleinman 1985; Lutz 1985; Marsella 1978, 1980; Marsella et al. 1985; Sartorius et al. 1983; Scheifflin 1985.

5. See Kaplan and Johnson 1964; Johnson and Johnson 1965; Matchett 1972; Lewis 1975; Shore and Manson 1981; Manson, Shore, and Bloom 1985.

6. See, e.g., Johnson and Johnson 1965; Townsley and Goldstein 1977; Hammerschlag 1982; Shkilnyk 1985.

7. In "Peña in the Ecuadorian Sierra: A psychoanthropological Analysis of Sadness," Michel Tousignant suggests that peña, a Peruvian discourse of troubles and submission, "encompasses much more than an illness" (1984: 394). In particular, peña forms "a central element in a philosophy of life, a life of renunciation filled with concern for an uncertain future and remembrance of a humiliating past" (383). But rather than moral weakness, peña "indicates an honest . . . sensitivity. It is a kind of indicator of cultural identity and a mark of socialization and integration into the group" (384–385). Particular meanings aside, Tousignant's insights about the extension of peña into a general philosophy of life and its positive meanings might well have been written about depression among the Flathead people.

8. This perspective is built on the ongoing debate within anthropology around issues of rationality cross-culturally and relativity (Wilson 1970; Hollis and Lukes 1982). For a dramatic synthesis of these perspectives, see Tambiah (1990: 3), who writes, "How do we understand and represent the modes of thought and action of other societies, other cultures? Since we have to undertake this task from a Western baseline so to say, how are we to achieve 'the translation of cultures,' i.e., understand other cultures as far as possible in their own terms but in our language?"

9. The image-switching analogy has its limits, of course. The main drawback is that both images in the illusion are contained within the same frame, an assumption that cannot be made for cross-cultural investigations. Despite some family resemblance across cultures, complex constructs, such as depression, are likely to relate to various domains of life in distinct ways, thus fundamentally shifting the frame of the phenomenon in question.

PART ONE: HISTORY AND IDENTITY

1. This narrative perspective has a great deal in common with those of others within the field of ethnopsychology. See, e.g., Lutz 1988, 1990; White 1990, 1992a, 1992b; Lutz and Abu-Lughod 1990; Miller et al. 1990.

CHAPTER ONE: TELLING ABOUT WHITES,
TALKING ABOUT INDIANS

Much of the mateiral in this chapter appears in "Telling about Whites, Talking about Indians" (O'Nell 1994).

1. In this chapter and throughout the remainder of this book, the names of contemporary residents of the Flathead Reservation have been changed to protect their identities. At times, the circumstances of individuals and families have also been altered for the same purpose.

2. This story, like all stories I gathered about encounters with whites, was told in English. With the important exception of some ritual events, most public discourse is conducted in English rather than Salish. The reason most often given for the dominance of English in public settings is to protect the comfort of participants who do not speak the traditional language.

3. Although not addressed directly to the ethnicity literature, this examination is consonant with many of the issues of import in that field. Numerous authors trace the origins of the anthropological study of ethnic identity to the late 1960s, and most credit Frederick Barth (1969) with formulating the powerful view of ethnicity as a subjective process of group identification (Wright 1988; Smith 1982; Despres 1982; Cohen 1978). Early on Barth's formulations were criticized for their inattention to the fluidity of ethnic identities (Cohen 1978). Summarizing recent trends in anthropology, Maybury-Lewis (1982) argues that ethnicity is treated almost universally as a latent qualification to be contextually activated and as a social process whose analysis has as much to do with issues of meaning as with power. In line with this formulation, my analysis of Flathead storytelling contributes to an understanding of group formation as one historically informed element in the "continuing and often innovative cultural process of boundary maintenance and reconstruction" (Cohen 1978). As such, my study complements the work of scholars, such as Albers and James (1985) and Cornell (1988, 1990), whose analyses emphasize the economic and political structures that make certain forms of group organization probable. With my emphasis on the meaning of an American Indian identity in these storytelling contexts, my work falls more in line with the works of Basso (1979), Braroe (1975), Blu (1980), Clifford (1988), and Clifton (1989).

4. ACE came into existence only in the early 1980s. ACE's predecessor, MOD, or Montanans Opposing Discrimination, was active in the mid-1970s.

5. Tribal members and whites on the reservation generally concur that irrigators make up the bulk of ACE membership.

6. Under the Indian Self-Determination and Education Assistance Act of 1975 (25 U.S.C.A., secs. 450a–450n), the tribes currently administer programs

for child custody and welfare, housekeeping and meal assistance for the elderly, law and order, housing and heating assistance, commodity foods distribution, and various community health, mental health, and alcoholism services. About the act it has been written that "although the tribes complain that the BIA has been slow to implement the 1975 Act, it reflects a fundamental philosophical change concerning the administration of Indian affairs: tribal programs should be funded by the federal government but the programs should be planned and administered by the tribes themselves; federal 'domination' should end" (Getches, Rosenfelt, and Wilkinson 1979: 110–111).

7. In 1988, residents of the reservation could for the first time receive medical treatment from an Indian physician.

8. What follows in this section is a specific history of Indian-white relations as it is rendered in the dominant historical narratives of Flathead elders and leaders of the 1980s. What does not follow is a procedurally strict ethnohistory of Indian-white relations. I make no attempt to "validate," "correct," or "supplement" these native texts with more properly speaking historical texts. Those interested in other accounts of this history may want to read Teit (1928), Turney-High (1937), Fahey (1974), and Phillips (1974). For readers interested in the history of Jesuit involvement with the Flathead tribes, I recommend Schaeffer (1937) and Forbis (1951). However, readers should recognize that tribal elders have found fault with each of these accounts.

9. It is interesting that these "historical" events are not so distant in time from the lives of contemporary Flathead Indians. The now-elderly children of the last survivor from the march from the Bitterroot Valley are still living. And, as you will soon learn, so is the son of one of the victims of the Swan River Area Massacre, having been born a few months after his father was killed.

10. In these times of mass violence, when we often hear of hundreds killed and injured, the figure of two persons injured may seem unimportant. However, in the context of such a small group of related individuals, the injuries suffered by these two people were significant.

11. In the telling of the story of the Bitterroot Salish, proud parallels are sometimes drawn between their relocation and the relocation of a band of Nez Perce Indians led by Chief Joseph, a heroic and popular figure at the reservation. Chief Joseph and his people, mostly women, elders, and children, eluded the U.S. Calvary for months. They traveled hundreds of miles through winter wilderness, including parts of Flathead country, only to be captured and "removed" to a reservation when they were but a day's ride from freedom in Canada. In the end, Chief Joseph laid down the weapons he had used for the defense of his people and declared, "I will fight no more forever." Like Joseph, Charlo and the Bitterroot Salish continued to deal honorably and peaceably with the U.S. government, even in the face of extended mistreatment. The tragic coda of Chief Joseph's story in which he dies in poverty, separated from his wife and child in Canada, resonates with the cruel eviction of Charlo's widow from her home.

12. The jurisdiction of the regulation of hunting continues to be a major source of dispute between the tribes and the state of Montana.

13. The national context of Indian-white relations is of importance as well, and some of the ways that national trends were influential at the Flathead Reservation are documented in chapter 2. However, the essential denial of the basic rights of all American Indians by government agencies is an important aspect of the context within which Flathead people interpreted their treatment. The nature of tribal-federal relations are well-documented. An especially clear documentation of this relationship can be found in the history of treaty violations that characterizes U.S. involvement with most American Indian tribes. See *Rethinking Indian Law* (National Lawyers Guild 1982) for a set of critical readings of the history of the legal relationships between the federal government and tribes.

14. To say that the Flathead Indians have actively constructed the meaning of the treatment they have received at the hands of whites over history does not negate the fact that that treatment was, and still is, dehumanizing and oppressive. Whites are continually "telling" the Salish and Pend d'Oreilles people in racist acts and racist statements that they are not worthy of humane treatment, of trust, compassion, or respect. And Indians can hear that whites are telling Indians that they are not fully human and therefore not deserving of the respectful treatment that whites are due by virtue of their own full humanity.

15. The interdependence of the self is articulated not only in expectations of mutual aid but also in patterns of emotional expression. The overt expression of emotion among Flathead Indian people tends to be more muted than in mainstream American society because, it is held, family and friends understand one's feelings without being told. Storytelling is structured by this understanding to the extent that the feelings of the protagonist of the story are not usually described by the storyteller; they are simply self-evident to those who are listening. Also self-evident to listeners is the behavioral response of the protagonist of the story to the racist actions of whites. With the exception of Sam Dumont's story of his encounter with the highway patrolman, behavioral responses are notably absent from the stories, the assumption being that the protagonists responded maturely by adjusting themselves to the situation rather than attempting to alter it. While the absence of "action" might appear passive and weak to some non-Indians, the message for Indian listeners is one in which Indians and whites are once again contrasted, with Indians embodying a mature endurance.

CHAPTER TWO: THE MAKING AND THE UNMAKING OF "REAL INDIANS"

1. Of equal importance to the more visible manifestations of out-marriage is the diminishing number of full-blooded Indians among the Flathead tribes. Since the time of the earliest enrollment, full-bloods have made up an ever-smaller percentage of the total enrollment population, starting at 43 percent in 1905 and falling to approximately 5 percent in 1960 and 1.5 percent by the late 1980s (Trosper 1976). In a survey of two consecutive samples of 100 enrolled individuals from the 1985 enrollment records, only one-fourth of the 200 individuals had blood quantum measurements of 19/32 or above. Half of

the sample had blood quantum measurements of 11/32 or below. One-fourth of the sample had blood quantum measurements at or below 1/4.

2. Starting at the turn of the century with the enumeration of tribal members for the purposes of land allotment, tribal membership has been defined to some extent by formal enrollment on the tribal rolls. The history of this period for the Flathead people and its effects are discussed in more detail in the remainder of this chapter.

3. Readers unfamiliar with tribal enrollment practices are cautioned that the history of rules and regulations for enrollment vary considerably across tribes. The specifics of Flathead enrollment should not be generalized to other tribes.

4. Per capita payments, or "per capitas" as they are commonly referred to, are regular disbursements of tribal resources to enrolled members of the tribes. During my eighteen-month stay, per capitas consisted of two $500 payments each year: one in August to coincide with school expenses and one in December to coincide with Christmas. At the time of this writing, the tribes were distributing per capitas thrice yearly: on April 1, on August 1, and on December 1.

5. The exclusivity of contemporary enrollment policies is also reinforced by another factor—budget constraints. In recent years, the tribes have taken over the administration of various services previously handled by federal agencies and, in doing so, have come to face more fully the realities of limited budgets. Combined with the cuts in federal allocations to human and social services associated with the Reagan and Bush years, the tribes have reached a point where the pie is not big enough to provide even the most basic services for all tribal members. As a result, services that used to be provided for tribal members and their spouses and children are now limited to enrolled tribal members themselves. This reality was clearly evident in the area of health care, where most nonemergency services, including preventive work, had to be given the lowest priority.

6. Among some Indian people, this situation is referenced by the term "sleeping elders"—a term that acknowledges the break in the transmission of cultural knowledge but does so without assigning blame.

7. A more secretive reverence for the sweatlodge can also be related to maturation.

8. Fanon's insights are particularly remarkable in contrast to the work of his near-contemporary, Octave Mannoni, who, in his analysis of the anticolonial revolt of 1947 in Madagascar, framed the question of the link between identity and domination in terms of the confrontation between colonialism and the preexisting "dependency complex" of the Malagasy (Mannoni [1950] 1990).

9. Fanon wrote primarily about violence as the terrible but necessary conclusion to the dehumanizing forces of colonialism. Yet, perhaps in part because of the gruesome magnitude of the violence that he witnessed in Algeria, Fanon left unexplored other less absolute processes of dehumanization. In exploring how Algerians answered the question of identity under French rule, Fanon focused minimally on the "colonized personality" that emerges during the nonviolent phases of colonialism. Instead, he directed his attention to the

dramatic "reactionary psychoses" experienced by the victims and imple-
menters of revolutionary violence. So, despite the power of his analysis of psychotic symptomatology among psychiatric patients in the context of violent
revolution, his insights into the relationship between domination and identity
seem less developed for less brutal forms of oppression, such as what is currently found at the reservation.

10. For Foucault, the basic mechanisms of power do not reside in ideological consensus and violence but in sets of relations in which realms of action
and their control are created. Resistance, in Foucault's framework, is the com-
patriot of power, existing as an opposite potential in the created realms of actions and their control. Resistance cannot be understood as existing alongside
domination as "truth" to "ideology," since this division relies on the insup-
portable privileging of power and knowledge outside of existing social relations.

11. Analyzing the apparently opposite strategies by Indians to either assimilate Indian culture to British ideals or to define India as the obverse of the
West, Nandy concludes that colonialism has wreaked the "ultimate violence"
in these instances by forcing Indians to counteract negative "imageries" of
themselves within the parameters of Western thought. Nandy locates true resistance in certain Indian responses to colonialism, such as noncooperation,
passivity, and the refusal to value face-to-face fights, that on the surface seem
indicative of capitulation or acquiescence. For Nandy, what is paramount in
defining subjugation or resistance is the moral and psychological grounding of
Indian efforts to oppose the negative images promulgated by British colonialism.

CHAPTER THREE: SPEAKING TO THE HEART

1. Theories of death caused by the ill will of others are widespread, especially, it would seem, in societies that elaborate some kind of "sociocentric"
personhood (Frake 1980).

2. Increasingly, songs are sung in English. These are often religious folk
songs that became popular in the Catholic mass after the changes wrought by
Vatican II in the 1960s, in which the language of the mass shifted from Latin
to the vernacular.

3. For an in-depth examination of Flathead music and songs, see Merriam's excellent studies "The Importance of Song in the Flathead Indian Vision
Quest" (1965) and *Ethnomusicology of the Flathead Indians* (1967).

4. See Tambiah for a stimulating analysis of the formal properties of ritual
language in "The Magical Power of Words" (1985a).

5. Specifically, some speakers will exhort others not to get up and talk
about the evils of drinking. Nonetheless, others will talk about how drinking is
bad, using their own histories of recovery as examples. Throughout my stay,
the inappropriateness of using the setting of the wakes to talk about drinking
was an issue of concern to the more respected prayer leaders, to elders, to
members of the Culture Committee, and to members of the more traditional
families. The topic would be raised regularly at the monthly Elders Meetings as

well as in private conversations. Some of the speakers who regularly trans-
gressed this convention were directly confronted, a last resort, and still the
practice continued, much to the distress of concerned parties.

6. Despite the presence of some whites at the Rosary and funeral, separation of the Indian and white communities is nowhere more evident than in
death rituals and practices. Not only are some of the practices very different,
such as whites not holding wakes or not staying at the cemetery until the body
is completely buried, but there are separate cemeteries that are used primarily
by each community.

7. Ron's grave had been dug by the local cemetery caretaker. In the past,
the grave would have been dug by friends and then watched over until the time
of burial.

8. The adult children and grandchildren of some of the elders recall instances in which entire households were emptied of their belongings, including
beds, other furniture, clothing, and all kitchen utensils. Although this custom
is still in practice among some of the more traditional families, others often decide to disperse only the more personal items of the deceased, such as clothing
and sports or hunting equipment.

9. In previous times, according to a friend of mine, men and women used
to sit and eat separately, and the serving of the food would be done entirely by
young men and boys. I was never able to follow up on the specifics of this
practice. In current times, however, people tend to sit in sex-integrated groups
of family and friends. The exception to this is that prayer leaders, who are usually men, often congregate together.

10. See Nations and Rebhun's "Angels with Wet Wings Won't Fly" (1988)
for a fascinating discussion of dampened expressions of maternal grief in
Brazil.

11. While other kinds of rituals, particularly the Catholic rituals of baptism
and marriage or the traditional New Year Dance or sweatlodge ceremony, are
performed among contemporary Flathead people, none approaches Flathead
death rituals in ideological significance or in the number of persons involved.
Nonetheless, these more circumscribed performances enact very similar themes
of social responsibility and reciprocity as the basis for community and individual well-being. Traditional rites of passage for young men and women are rare
today; I only learned of one such celebration following the first kill of an ado-
lescent male hunter.

12. In an analysis of aboriginal and contemporary ceremonial integration
in the Plateau region, Brunton (1968) documents the nature and extent of in-
tertribal visiting at powwows and feasts.

13. As far as I could tell, visitors may bring gifts, but it is the hosts who are
expected to give the most, a style of exchange that appears to be structured by
the fact that a visit is, in itself, considered a gift. Traveling to visit a friend is a
significant gesture, given the dangers of accidents and illness, and one that
needs to be repaid.

14. In the Salish language, there is a complex and highly specified terminology encompassing the extensive relations of kinship, with titles that differed by
side of the family, gender, and generation and that changed after certain

changes in the relationship (i.e., the death of a spouse). Interestingly, many of the traditional kinship terms are reciprocal. For example, great-grandchildren and great-grandparents call each other *tupye*, a nongendered term. The similarity with Leenhardt's exploration of Melanesian thought in *Do Kamo* (1979) deserves to be played out in more detail.

Nowadays, some of the simpler Salish terms are still in use, but very often young people call their older relatives simply "Auntie" or "Uncle." When younger people are asked to explain the relationship, they frequently resort to a simplified explanation, such as "She's my mother's auntie." Similarly, relatives of the same generation are called simply "cousin," further distinctions not being made. Older people may give such simplified explanations as well but equally often will be able, and very interested, in detailing the exact nature of the genealogical relationship in question. In fact, older people often lament that the younger generations do not know who their relatives are.

15. See Caudill and Plath's "Who Sleeps by Whom? Parent-Child Involvement in Urban Japanese Families" (1974) for a fascinating analysis of Japanese sleeping patterns.

16. Parents have the right to discipline their adult children. In the past, this could mean physical discipline. Although I learned of several cases in which parents continued to physically discipline their adult children, it was far more common to hear about how this form of authority is breaking down. Today, for the most part, and in all likelihood in the past as well, discipline is verbal, with parents expressing disappointment in their offspring either in a lecture or through teasing.

17. The regulations surrounding the rental and ownership of these homes are complicated and have changed over time. At base, though, ownership of the land remains tribal, whereas the home becomes the property of the owner, who can either bequeath the house to an heir or sell it back to the tribes.

18. Brockman also used the family, or household, as the unit of study in his work on reciprocity and market exchange on the Flathead Reservation (1971a, 1971b). He concluded that reciprocity, as an economic strategy, was confined to the poorer families and households of the reservation. I argue instead that reciprocity characterizes most Indian household economies. The difference in opinion can probably be traced to definitions of the Indian community. Brockman appears to have included households that would, in all likelihood, not be thought of as belonging to the Indian community.

19. Raising cattle is, in fact, a relatively insignificant part of the contemporary economic life of the Flathead Indians, although from the stories of elders it appears that it used to play a more important role in people's livelihoods.

20. Hearing about this alternate way of conducting friendship must have had some impact on the woman who insightfully revealed that calling beforehand was not necessary. When I returned for a short visit during the summer after my fieldwork was completed, I ran into this woman and she told me about a dream that she had had during my absence. In it, she and her husband and several friends drove to Boston to visit me, but when they got there, they didn't know where I lived. They found a phone and gave me a call and then "set up a time" to come visit me later that evening. Her reaction to the dream

was a sense of confusion and anger at being treated in such an inhospitable way.

21. See Basso 1971 for a discussion of silence among the Western Apache.

22. "Indian time" is also patterned by belief in the Creator, in which a profound trust exists that whatever needs to happen will happen in its own time. For example, plants will ripen and be ready for gathering when they are ready, regardless of the human calendar. This fundamental trust is generally extended to humans as well. See Phillips 1974 for a description of "Indian time" among Warm Springs Indians.

23. This aesthetics of interpersonal interaction characterizes Indian-Indian interactions but is extended to Indian-white interactions as well, especially when white people are on Indian turf. So, for example, Elders Meetings were always conducted in English so that anyone who did not speak Salish would not feel excluded. Flathead manners rely on a relational style that seeks to acknowledge everyone but in a way that minimizes the possibility of excessive attention that might be embarrassing to individuals. Thus, for example, if a stranger is present at a gathering, introductions may or may not be made. If introductions are made, they will be done quietly and take place between dyads or triads. Rarely would someone be presented to an entire group or even taken around a room and formally introduced to everyone in turn.

CHAPTER FOUR: FEELING BEREAVED, FEELING AGGRIEVED, AND FEELING WORTHLESS

1. In rendering written versions of the Salish words that I learned in oral interviews, I have relied on the expert advice of the Flathead Culture Committee in the use of the International Phonetic Alphabet (IPA).

2. The expression "old lady" does not carry the same disparaging connotations among the Flathead Indians as it does in mainstream American discourse. In fact, there is an implicit respectfulness in the adjective "old," reflecting the authority of the elders of the tribe and the ways of the ancestors.

3. Lévi-Strauss also speaks about how cultural meanings are imputed to geography in his discussion of history among the Australian aborigines (1966: 243). In an intriguing analysis, Basso has described the moral meanings and uses of geographic places for the Western Apache (1984, 1988). See also Kirkpatrick 1985.

4. This cultural orientation to the land seems to extend back into history as well and can be seen in an excerpt from a congressional report from 1855:

> For years now has their country been the theatre where have been committed murders the most brutal, and robberies the most bold and daring, until *there is not left a spot but that is pointed out to the traveller* where some innocent and unsuspecting Flathead was put to the knife in cold blood, or where were shot down scores of friendly Indians, by these devils of the mountains [Blackfeet]. (Cited in Fuller 1974; emphasis added)

5. This loneliness for the land is part of the implicit story of grief in the forced relocation of Charlo's band from the Bitterroot.

6. Suicidality attributed to anger or manipulation of others is reported by a

number of researchers working with American Indian people (Miller and Schoenfeld 1971; Curlee 1969; Levy 1965), which is very much in line with early ethnographic accounts on the display of overt anger as a serious breach of cultural norms (Briggs 1970; Hallowell [1955] 1974). More globally, Levy has written on aggressive suicide among the Tahitians (1973); Rubenstein on the relations of anger to suicide in Micronesia (1983); Lutz on justifiable anger as a cause for suicide among the Ifaluk (1988); Hallon on indignant suicide among the Toraja in Indonesia (1990); and Malinowski on similar connections among the Trobriand Islanders (1929).

7. The transparency of emotions is traceable to three related ideas. First, as the idea of reading emotions on someone's face illustrates, individuals are not supposed to be able to hide or feign true feelings. Second, the feelings of an individual are known by others because others actually experience what the individual experiences by virtue of an intertwining of selves that is based in a sensitivity that human beings have for the feelings of one another. A third and very important idea related to the transparency of emotions is that emotional responses are natural; anyone would feel the same way in the same situation.

CHAPTER FIVE: SPEAKING FROM THE HEART

1. This point is entirely consistent with the point made repeatedly in anthropology of late about the variability and contestability of cultural meanings and the need to be wary of representations that are cast as global and static.

2. I conducted thirty-three such interviews in the course of my research. I began to collect the depressive experience interviews as early as five months into the research period, but I conducted most in the final six months, after I had attained a degree of familiarity with the culture and social practices of the reservation community. Ranging in length from 45 minutes to 3 1/2 hours, the interviews were rich, culturally informed accounts about the phenomenological realities of depression for the respondents. The accounts were also sufficiently informative to enable me to make diagnostic decisions about the presence or absence of psychiatric disorders for each respondent using DSM-III criteria (American Psychiatric Association 1980).

Interviews opened with a general invitation for the respondent to describe the worst depression he or she had ever experienced, and each episode was probed for additional detail, often with merely a period of silence that encouraged the respondent to elaborate. The open-ended style was guided at times, however, by particular research interests, for example, in specific symptoms, treatment efficacy, drinking history, marital history, participation in the Indian community, or childhood experiences. Overall, however, respondents were encouraged to talk about what was important about their experiences with depression from their own perspectives.

Interview respondents were solicited for the study in various ways. The majority were approached informally in private conversations at community events, such as at a conference for Adult Children of Alcoholics, or in public places, such as at a bar, at the local college, or at another of the community gathering spots. Others were longer-term acquaintances who agreed to be interviewed, and some were elders who were invited to participate in the study during visits I made to their homes. Although I make no claims as to the representativeness of my sample, an effort was made to achieve a balance in terms of age, sex, economic circumstances, and marital status.

3. As in preceding chapters, pseudonyms have been used for all persons who appear in this chapter. Moreover, certain aspects of Dan's social circumstances have been altered to protect his identity.

4. Here is an instance of the double bind of Indian identity that was described in chapter 3, in the discussion of the "real Indians."

5. Interestingly, in terms of the structure of the entire narrative, we will see that this message is mirrored in reverse in the final paragraphs, where Dan states his intention to learn the language, a sign of his increasing responsibility.

6. For elders, this type of statement is often followed by the claim that racism is a new phenomenon, a permutation of the discourse that sets up the present as a corrupted form of the past. I also believe that there is a persuasive element in Dan's narrative designed to impress me, the interviewer, with Dan's success in school and the white man's world. Interviewees often attempted to persuade me of their successes, their morality, their strengths.

7. Dan's story bears a certain similarity to an AA-style "drunkologue." This aspect of the structure of Dan's narrative is discussed further in the conclusion of this chapter, in which I note that Dan's voice in this story resonates not only with the moral and social authority of an AA-recovering alcoholic but also, and more profoundly, with the force of the "real Indians" that attaches to the Flathead narrative forms of the mea culpa lament and preaching. For readers interested in anthropological treatments of the narratives and practices of Alcoholics Anonymous, see Fainzang 1994, Cain 1991, Sutro 1989, and Slagle and Weibel-Orlando 1986.

8. This scene gains significance against the discursive backdrop of grief and mourning detailed in chapter 4.

9. It remains unclear to me whether Dan intended to represent his spending the money that his grandmother had given him as an act of irresponsibility. My guess is that "public opinion" on the reservation would be about evenly divided on the issue. In contrast, there would be near-unanimity on the irresponsibility of almost missing his mother's funeral and failing to grieve at the deaths of his mother and brother.

10. Another form of reciprocity inheres in Dan's presentation of the elder's words on the spiritual basis of health, in which the Creator can be called upon through prayer to take one's ills.

11. I derived this idea in part from an article by Victor Turner in which he argues that social dramas are the social ground or experiential matrix out of which narratives are generated. In his view, social dramas are organized by a four-part structure that constitutes the natural and empirical basis for many types of narratives. Turner describes the structure this way:

> A social drama first manifests itself as the breach of a norm, the infraction of a rule of morality, law, custom, or etiquette, in some public arena. . . . [A] mounting crisis follows, a momentous juncture or turning point in the relations between components

of a social field. . . . In order to limit the contagious spread of breach, certain adjustive and redressive mechanisms, informal and formal, are brought into operation. . . . The final phase consists either in the reintegration of the disturbed social group or the social recognition of irreparable breach between the contesting parties, sometimes leading to their spatial separation. (1980: 146–147)

12. Both intimacy and distance are implied in Dan's inclusion of me in the circle to whom he owes responsibility. As with all relationships at the reservation, the intimacy and distance of my relationships with Dan and other interviewees were patterned primarily by the relational logic of Flathead culture. Most centrally, I attribute our ability to relate with a degree of closeness in the interview context to the compatibility between my aims and research techniques and Flathead values and practices that equate affective closeness to a concern with the feelings of others and certain forms of reciprocity, that is, listening and visiting. Moreover, within Flathead society, these is a general ease with storytelling, as well as a general desire to help others through sharing one's own story. It was this motivation to help others, in fact, that brought Dan to me in the penultimate month of my fieldwork. Dan had known of my work since my arrival and had professed himself eager to participate in the study. We had met frequently over the ensuing months and had had several long conversations about his work and mine. However, it was not until I saw Dan at a community event 16 to 17 months into my research and was bemoaning my impending departure that Dan found the opportunity to tell me his story. By that time, Dan knew me as a white person who was willing to enter into meaningful and extended relationships with Flathead people. However, despite this basis for intimacy, distance was an inevitable aspect of our relationship—as it was to varying degrees with all my relationships at the reservation, whether with a friend, an acquaintance, or an interviewee. More than being white, it was the temporary nature of my involvement at the reservation that produced the distance manifested in Dan's double-edged inclusion of me into his network with the comment "Even you."

CHAPTER SIX: CULTURE AND DEPRESSION

1. I am grateful to one of the reviewers of this manuscript for pointing out that this critique of Mead's position does not extend to contemporary work among neo-Meadians or symbolic interactionists. Readers interested in recent literature on emotion in that subfield of sociology may want to start with the excellent volume of works edited by Franks and McCarthy (1989).

2. It can also be seen, for example, in Levy's judgmental assessment that Tahitians "*avoid* naming and labeling . . . the emotional significance of events" (1973: 304; emphasis added), rather than simply noting that the emotional significance is not a conventionally important aspect of an event in its retelling in certain specified contexts.

3. Hallowell, despite his phenomenological bent, is most similar in his position on emotion to the culture and personality position. Both aspects of his position can be seen in the following quotation:

Cultures may be said to be elaborated systems of meaning which makes the role of the human being intelligible to himself, both with reference to an articulated universe and to his fellow men. . . . [H]is emotional nature becomes structuralized in such a way that emotions become indices to the integrative level reached by the individual in relation to the symbolically expressed and mediated norms of his society. ([1955] 1974: 10)

4. The implications are contradictory for the ritual construction of affective life. On the one hand, messages about the ideal self and its relations are strengthened by the increased status of participants as morally correct traditionalists. On the other hand, the force of the messages is weakened for individuals who increasingly come to see the messages as not applicable to themselves or to contemporary life.

5. See O'Nell 1993 for a description of how these cases were selected.

6. This finding echoes the conclusion of Pollack and Shore (1980) in their assessment of the Minnesota Multi-Phasic Inventory (MMPI) for use with American Indian people. Given that MMPI profiles differed more by culture than by diagnosis for a group of 142 Indian patients, the authors concluded that it would be insufficient to simply modify the instrument's norms; rather, what is needed is "cultural research that identifies culturally appropriate instruments from the outset" (p. 950).

7. For a similar approach to pathological drinking among American Indian adolescents, see O'Nell and Mitchell, n.d.

8. The makers of the DSM-IV have taken an important step forward in acknowledging the role of culture in psychopathology. Their efforts have taken three directions: incorporating "cultural variations" under various DSM-IV disorders; including an alphabetical listing of "culture-bound syndromes" in an Appendix; and advancing an outline (also in an Appendix) to elicit the cultural identity of the patient, the cultural explanations for the individual's experiences, and cultural factors relating to the psychosocial environment and levels of functioning. The Complementary Cultural Formulation (CCF), as the outline is called, also lays out a set of questions to help clinicians assess cultural elements of the relationship between the patient and the clinician. In light of what has preceded the DSM-IV, these attempts are commendable. However, they fall short of the mark by relegating the role of culture to the experiences of "others," by exoticizing the role of culture in assigning such a central place to culture-bound syndromes, and by marginalizing the role of culture to psychiatric practice by incorporating the CCF only in a late appendix.

9. Many of the research findings about the biological, social, and psychological correlates of depression provide excellent hypotheses for cross-cultural work. For example, do tricyclics and monoamine oxidase (MAO) inhibitors show differential effectiveness for pathological mood disturbances among the Flathead according to signs of "atypicality," that is hypersomnia and weight gain (American Psychiatric Association 1993: 14)? Do the gender differences found in Euro-American samples, and others, hold up for pathological mood disturbance among the Flathead, especially since the culture-specific criteria may help to weed out the number of men who might appear as false positives with the DSM criteria (Weissman et al. 1991; Kessler et al. 1994)? Does the

finding by Brown and Harris (1978) about childhood loss of mother leading to a vulnerability to depression among working-class British women have a parallel for pathological mood disturbance among the Flathead, such as in the processes that contribute to a childhood characterized by "not feeling cared for"?

References

Abu-Lughod, Lila
1986   *Veiled Sentiments: Honor and Poetry in a Bedouin Society.* Berkeley, Los Angeles, and London: University of California Press.
1990   Shifting politics in Bedouin love poetry. In C. Lutz and L. Abu-Lughod (eds.), *Language and the Politics of Emotion,* 24–45. Cambridge: Cambridge University Press.

Albers, Patricia C., and William R. James
1985   On the dialectics of ethnicity: To be or not to be Santee (Sioux). *Journal of Ethnic Studies* 14: 1–27.

American Psychiatric Association
1980   *Diagnostic and Statistical Manual of Mental Disorders.* 3d ed. Washington, D.C.: APA.
1987   *Diagnostic and Statistical Manual of Mental Disorders.* 3d ed., rev. Washington, D.C.: APA.
1993   Practice guideline for major depressive disorder in adults. Supplement. *American Journal of Psychiatry* 150(4).
1994   *Diagnostic and Statistical Manual of Mental Disorders.* 4th ed. Washington, D.C.: APA.

Barth, Frederik
1969   Introduction. In F. Barth (ed.), *Ethnic Groups and Boundaries,* 9–38. Boston: Little, Brown.

Basso, Keith H.
1971   "To give up on words": Silence in Western Apache culture. In K. H. Basso and M. E. Opler (eds.), *Anthropological Papers of the University of Arizona,* no. 21, 151–161. Tucson: University of Arizona Press.
1979   *Portraits of "The Whiteman": Linguistic Play and Cultural*

Symbols among the Western Apache. Cambridge: Cambridge University Press.

1984   "Stalking with stories": Names, places, and moral narratives among the Western Apache. In E. Bruner (ed.), *Text, Play, and Story: The Construction and Reconstruction of Self and Society*, 19–55. 1983 Proceedings of the American Ethnological Society. Washington, D.C.: AES.

1988   "Speaking with names": Language and landscape among the Western Apache. *Cultural Anthropology* 3(2): 99–130.

Bellah, Robert N., R. Madsen, W. M. Sullivan, A. Swindler, and S. M. Tipton

1985   *Habits of the Heart: Individualism and Commitment in American Life.* New York: Harper and Row.

Benedict, Ruth

1934   *Patterns of Culture.* Cambridge, Mass.: Houghton-Mifflin.

Blazer, D. G., R. C. Kessler, K. A. McGonagle, and M. S. Swartz

1994   The prevalence and distribution of major depression in a national community sample: The national comorbidity survey. *American Journal of Psychiatry* 151(7): 979–986.

Blu, Karen I.

1980   *The Lumbee Problem: The Making of an American Indian People.* Cambridge: Cambridge University Press.

Braroe, Niels Winther

1975   *Indian and White.* Stanford: Stanford University Press.

Briggs, Jean L.

1970   *Never in Anger, Portrait of an Eskimo Family.* Cambridge: Harvard University Press.

Brockman, C. Thomas

1971*a*   Correlation of social class and education on the Flathead Indian Reservation, Montana. *Rocky Mountain Social Science Journal* 8: 11–17.

1971*b*   Reciprocity and market exchange on the Flathead Reservation. *Northwest Anthropological Research Notes* 5(1): 77–96.

Brown, George, and Tirril Harris

1978   *The Social Origins of Depression.* New York: Free Press.

Brunton, Bill B.

1968   Ceremonial integration in the Plateau of Northwestern North America. *Northwest Anthropological Research Notes* 2(1): 1–28.

Cain, Carole

1991   Personal stories: Identity acquisition and self-understanding in Alcoholics Anonymous. *Ethos* 19(2): 210–253.

Canguilhem, Georges

1989   *The Normal and the Pathological.* New York: Zone Books.

Carr, John E., and Peter P. Vitaliano

1985   The theoretical implications of converging research on depression and culture-bound syndromes. In A. Kleinman and B.

Good (eds.), *Culture and Depression*, 244–266. Berkeley, Los Angeles, and London: University of California Press.

Caudill, William, and D. Plath
1974   Who sleeps by whom? Parent-child involvement in urban Japanese families. In R. A. Levine (ed.), *Culture and Personality: Contemporary Readings*, 125–154. Honolulu: University of Hawaii Press.

Clifford, James
1988   *The Predicament of Culture*. Cambridge: Harvard University Press.

Clifton, Robert A.
1989   *Being and Becoming Indian: Biographical Sketches of North American Frontiers*. Chicago: Dorsey Press.

Cohen, Ronald
1978   Ethnicity: Problem and focus in anthropology. In B. Siegel et al. (eds.), *Annual Review of Anthropology* 7: 379–404. Palo Alto, Calif.: Annual Reviews.

Cohn, Bernard S.
1984   The census, social structure and objectification in South Asia. *Folk* 25: 25–49.

Cornell, Stephen
1988   The transformations of tribe: Organization and self-concept in Native American ethnicities. *Ethnic and Racial Studies* 11(1): 27–47.
1990   Land, labour and group formation: Blacks and Indians in the United States. *Ethnic and Racial Studies* 13(3): 368–388.

Curlee, Wilson V.
1969   *Suicide and Self-Destructive Behavior on the Cheyenne River Reservation*. Public Health Service Publication no. 1903. Washington, D.C.: National Institute of Mental Health and Indian Health Service.

Despres, Leo A.
1982   Ethnicity: What data and theory portend for plural societies. In D. Maybury-Lewis (ed.), *The Prospects for Plural Societies*, 7–29. Washington, D.C.: American Ethnological Association.

Downs Roll
1905   *Register of Indian Families, Flathead Reservation*. Seattle: National Archives.

Ekman, Paul, Wallace V. Friesen, and Phoebe Ellsworth
1972   *Emotion in the Human Face*. New York: Pergamon Press.

Ekman, Paul, Richard Sorensen, and Wallace Friesen
1969   Pan-cultural elements in facial expressions of emotion. *Science* 164: 86–88.

Eschback, Karl
1990   Boundary maintenance on American Indian Reservations. Oral report, Department of Sociology, Fall Talks, Harvard University.

Evans-Pritchard, E. E.
1976   *Witchcraft, Oracles, and Magic among the Azande.* Oxford: Clarendon Press.
Fahey, John
1974   *The Flathead Indians.* Norman: University of Oklahoma Press.
Fainzang, Sylvie
1994   When alcoholics are not anonymous. A research report. *Medical Anthropology Quarterly* 8(3): 336–345.
Fanon, Frantz
1963   *The Wretched of the Earth.* New York: Grove Press.
Finley, Mary Stousee
1956   Story of the shooting of four Flathead Indians in Swan River Area, Western Montana, 1908. 8-page manuscript.
Flathead Culture Committee
1975   Elders Tapes, no. 2.
1988   *A Brief History of the Flathead People.* St. Ignatius, Mont.: Char-Koosta.
Forbis, Richard
1951   The Flathead apostasy: An interpretation. *Montana: Magazine of History* 1: 35–40.
Foucault, Michel
1972   *The Archaeology of Knowledge and the Discourse on Language.* New York: Pantheon Books.
1973   *The Order of Things: An Archaeology of the Human Science.* New York: Vintage Books.
1980   *Power/Knowledge.* New York: Pantheon Books.
Frake, Charles O.
1961   The diagnosis of disease among the Subanun of Mindanao. *American Anthropologist* 63: 113–132.
1980   Interpretations of illness. In A. S. Dil (ed.), *Language and Cultural Description: Essays by Charles O. Frake,* 61–82. Stanford: Stanford University Press.
Franks, David D., and E. Doyle McCarthy, eds.
1989   *The Sociology of the Emotions: Original Essays and Research Papers.* Greenwich, Conn.: JAI Press.
Fritz, W. B.
1976   Psychiatric disorders and natives and non-natives in Saskatchewan. *Canadian Psychiatric Association Journal* 21(6): 393–400.
1978   Indian people and community psychiatry in Saskatchewan. *Canadian Psychiatric Association Journal* 23(1): 1–7.
Fuller, E. O.
1974   The Confederated Salish and Kootenai Tribes of the Flathead Reservation. In E. O. Fuller et al., *Interior Salish and Eastern Washington Indians,* vol. 3, 25–168. New York: Garland.
Getches, David H., Daniel M. Rosenfelt, and Charles F. Wilkinson
1979   *Federal Indian Law.* American Casebook Series. St. Paul, Minn.: West Publishing.

Good, Byron
1977   The heart of what's the matter: The semantics of illness in Iran.
            Culture, Medicine, and Psychiatry 1: 25–58. Also to appear in
            *Medicine, Rationality and Experience: An Anthropological
            Perspective.* The 1990 Lewis Henry Morgan Lectures. Cam-
            bridge: Cambridge University Press.
Good, Byron J., and Mary-Jo DelVecchio Good
1982   Toward a meaning-centered analysis of popular illness cate-
            gories: 'Fright illness' and 'heart distress' in Iran. In A. J. Mar-
            sella and G. M. White (eds.), *Cultural Conceptions of Mental
            Health and Therapy,* 141–166. Dordrecht: D. Reidel.
Good, Byron J., Mary-Jo Good, and Robert Moradi
1985   The interpretation of Iranian depressive illness and dysphoric
            affect. In A. Kleinman and B. Good (eds.), *Culture and Depres-
            sion,* 369–428. Berkeley, Los Angeles, and London: University
            of California Press.
Good, Byron J., and Arthur Kleinman
1985   Epilogue. In A. Kleinman and B. Good (eds.), *Culture and De-
            pression,* 491–506. Berkeley, Los Angeles, and London: Uni-
            versity of California Press.
Hallon, Douglas
1990   Indignant suicide in the Pacific: An example from the Toraja
            Highlands of Indonesia. *Culture, Medicine and Psychiatry*
            14(3): 365–379.
Hallowell, A. Irving
[1955] 1974 *Culture and Experience.* Philadelphia: University of Pennsylva-
            nia Press.
Hammerschlag, Carl A.
1982   American Indian disenfranchisement: Its impact on health and
            health care. *White Cloud Journal* 2(4): 32–36.
Hansen, Bert
1947   Minutes of meetings. Full Blood Flathead Indian Montana
            Study Group, Arlee, Montana.
Hollis, Martin, and Steven Lukes, eds.
1982   *Rationality and Relativism.* Cambridge, Mass.: MIT Press.
Johnson, Dale L., and C. A. Johnson
1965   Totally discouraged: A depressive syndrome of the Dakota
            Sioux. *Transcultural Psychiatric Research Review* 2: 141–143.
Kaplan, Bert, and Dale L. Johnson
1964   The social meaning of Navaho psychopathology and psy-
            chotherapy. In A. Kiev (ed.), *Magic, Faith, and Healing: Studies
            in Primitive Psychiatry Today,* 203–229. New York: Free Press.
Kessler, Ron C., K. A. McGonagle, S. Zhao, C. B. Nelson, M. Hughes,
M. Eshleman, H. Wittchen, and K. S. Kendler
1994   Lifetime and 12-month prevalence of DSM-III-R psychiatric
            disorders in the United States: Results from the National Co-
            morbidity Survey. *Archives of General Psychiatry* 151: 8–19.

Keyes, Charles F.
1985   The interpretive basis of depression. In A. Kleinman and B.
          Good (eds.), *Culture and Depression*, 153–174. Berkeley, Los
          Angeles, and London: University of California Press.
Kinzie, J. D., P. K. Leung, J. Boehnlein, D. Matsunaga, R. Johnson, S. Manson, J. Shore, J. Heinz, and M. Williams
1992   Psychiatric epidemiology of an Indian village: A 19-year repli-
          cation study. *Journal of Nervous and Mental Disease* 180(1):
          33–39.
Kirkpatrick, John T.
1985   Some Marquesan understandings of action and identity. In
          G. M. White and J. Kirkpatrick (eds.), *Person, Self, and Expe-
          rience: Exploring Pacific Ethnopsychologies*, 80–120. Berkeley,
          Los Angeles, and London: University of California Press.
Kirmayer, L. J., M. Malus, M. Delage, and C. Fletcher
1993   *Characteristics of Completed Suicides among the Inuit of the
          East Coast of Hudson Bay, 1982–1991.* Montreal: Institute of
          Community and Family Psychiatry, Jewish General Hospital.
Kleinman, Arthur
1977   Depression, somatization, and the new cross-cultural psychia-
          try. *Social Science and Medicine* 11: 3–10.
1978   Concepts and a model for the comparison of medical systems
          as cultural systems. *Social Science and Medicine* 12: 85–93.
1980   *Patients and Healers in the Context of Culture.* Berkeley, Los
          Angeles, and London: University of California Press.
1982   Neurasthenia and depression: A study of somatization and cul-
          ture in China. *Culture, Medicine and Psychiatry* 6: 117–190.
Kleinman, Arthur, and B. Good, eds.
1985   *Culture and Depression: Studies in Anthropology and Cross-
          Cultural Psychiatry of Affect and Disorder.* Berkeley, Los An-
          geles, and London: University of California Press.
Kleinman, Arthur, and J. Kleinman
1985   Somatization: The interconnections in Chinese society among
          culture, depressive experiences, and the meanings of pain. In
          A. Kleinman and B. Good (eds.), *Culture and Depression*, 429–
          490. Berkeley, Los Angeles, and London: University of Califor-
          nia Press.
Kondo, Dorinne K.
1990   *Crafting Selves: Power, Gender, and Discourses of Identity in a
          Japanese Workplace.* Chicago: University of Chicago Press.
Leenhardt, Maurice
1979   *Do Kamo: Person and Myth in the Melanesian World.* Chicago:
          University of Chicago Press.
LeVine, Robert
1982   *Culture, Behavior and Personality: An Introduction to the
          Comparative Study of Psychosocial Adaptation.* 2d ed. New
          York: Aldine.

Lévi-Strauss, Claude
1966   *The Savage Mind*. Chicago: University of Chicago Press.
Levy, Jerrold E.
1965   Navajo suicide. *Human Organization* 24(4): 308–318.
Levy, Robert I.
1973   *Tahitians*. Chicago: University of Chicago Press.
Lewis, Thomas H.
1975   A syndrome of depression and mutism in the Oglala Sioux. *American Journal of Psychiatry* 132(7): 753–755.
Lutz, Catherine
1985   Depression and the translation of emotional worlds. In A. Kleinman and B. Good (eds.), *Culture and Depression*, 63–100. Berkeley, Los Angeles, and London: University of California Press.
1988   *Unnatural Emotions: Everyday Sentiments on a Micronesian Atoll and Their Challenge to Western Theory*. Chicago: University of Chicago Press.
1990   Engendered emotion: Gender, power, and the rhetoric of emotional control in American discourse. In C. Lutz and L. Abu-Lughod (eds.), *Language and the Politics of Emotion*, 69–91. Cambridge: Cambridge University Press.
Lutz, Catherine A., and L. Abu-Lughod
1990   Introduction: Emotion, discourse, and the politics of everyday life. In C. Lutz and L. Abu-Lughod (eds.), *Language and the Politics of Emotion*, 1–23. Cambridge: Cambridge University Press.
McDermott, Louise
1904   Ethnology and folklore—Selish proper. Master's thesis, University of California, Berkeley.
McIntosh, John L., and J. F. Santos
1980/1981   Suicide among Native Americans: A compilation of findings. *Omega* 11(4): 303–316.
Malinowski, Bronislaw
1929   *The Sexual Life of Savages*. New York: Harcourt, Brace and World.
Malouf, Carling
1967   Historic tribes and archaeology. *Archaeology in Montana* 8(1): 1–16.
Mannoni, Octave
[1950] 1990 *Prospero and Caliban*. Ann Arbor: University of Michigan Press.
Manson, Spero, J. H. Shore, and J. D. Bloom
1985   The depressive experience in American Indian communities: A challenge for psychiatric theory and diagnosis. In A. Kleinman and B. Good (eds.), *Culture and Depression*, 331–368. Berkeley, Los Angeles, and London: University of California Press.

Marsella, Anthony J.
1978   Thoughts on cross-cultural studies on the epidemiology of de-
              pression. *Culture, Medicine, and Psychiatry* 2: 343–357.
1980   Depressive experience and disorder across cultures. In H.
              Triandis and J. Draguns (eds.), *Handbook of Cross-Cultural
              Psychology*, Vol. 6, *Psychopathology*, 237–289. Rockleigh,
              N.J.: Allyn and Bacon.
Marsella, Anthony J., Norman Sartorius, Assen Jablensky, and Fred R. Fenton.
1985   Cross-cultural studies of depression: An overview. In A. Klein-
              man and B. Good (eds.), *Culture and Depression*, 299–300.
              Berkeley, Los Angeles, and London: University of California
              Press.
Matchett, William F.
1972   Repeated hallucinatory experiences as part of the mourning
              process among Hopi Indian women. *Psychiatry* 35: 185–194.
Mauss, Marcel
1967   *The Gift: Forms and Functions of Exchange in Archaic Soci-
              eties.* New York: W. W. Norton.
May, Phillip A.
1990   A bibliography on suicide and suicide attempts among Ameri-
              can Indians and Alaska Natives. *Omega* 21(3): 199–214.
Maybury-Lewis, David
1982   Introduction: Alternatives to extinction. In D. Maybury-Lewis
              (ed.), *The Prospects for Plural Societies*, 1–6. Washington,
              D.C.: American Ethnological Association.
Mead, George Herbert
[1934] 1962   *Mind, Self and Society*. Chicago: University of Chicago Press.
Merriam, Alan P.
1965   The importance of song in the Flathead Indian vision quest.
              Ethnomusicology 9(2): 91–99.
1967   *Ethnomusicology of the Flathead Indians*. Chicago: Aldine.
Merriam-Webster
1993   *Merriam-Webster's Collegiate Dictionary*. 10th ed. Springfield,
              Mass.: Merriam-Webster.
Miller, Peggy J., Randolph Potts, Heidi Fung, Lisa Hoogstra, and Judy Mintz
1990   Narrative practices and the social construction of self in child-
              hood. *American Ethnologist* 17(2): 292–311.
Miller, Sheldon I., and Lawrence S. Schoenfeld
1971   Suicide attempt patterns among the Navaho Indians. *Interna-
              tional Journal of Social Psychiatry* 17(3): 189–193.
Mission Valley News
1988   Race issue? Commissioner candidates say it is, and isn't a cam-
              paign issue. News article, October 27, St. Ignatius, Montana.
1988   Tribal government is elitist. Editorial, October 20, St. Ignatius,
              Montana.
Morgan, Lewis Henry
[1877] 1974   *Ancient Society*. Gloucester, Mass.: Peter Smith.

Moyer, J. Michael
  1961   Missionary-Indian alienation at St. Mary's Mission, 1841 to
              1850. Unpublished student paper, Gonzaga University.
Nandy, Ashis
  1988   *The Intimate Enemy*. Delhi: Oxford University Press.
National Lawyers Guild
  1982   *Rethinking Indian Law*. New Haven, Conn.: Advocate Press.
Nations, Marilyn K., and L. A. Rebhun
  1988   Angels with wet wings won't fly: Maternal sentiment in Brazil
              and the image of neglect. *Culture, Medicine and Psychiatry* 12:
              141–200.
Obeyesekere, Gannath
  1985   Depression, Buddhism, and the work of culture in Sri Lanka. In
              A. Kleinman and B. Good (eds.), *Culture and Depression*, 134–
              152. Berkeley, Los Angeles, and London: University of Califor-
              nia Press.
O'Nell, Theresa D.
  1989   Psychiatric investigations among American Indians and Alaska
              Natives: A critical review. *Culture, Medicine and Psychiatry*
              13: 51–87.
  1993   'Feeling worthless': An ethnographic investigation of depres-
              sion and problem drinking at the Flathead Reservation. Special
              issue, Jack Maser and Norman Dinges (eds.). *Culture, Medi-
              cine, and Psychiatry* 16(4): 447–470.
  1994   Telling about whites, talking about Indians: Oppression, resis-
              tance, and contemporary American Indian identity. *Cultural
              Anthropology* 9(1): 94–126.
O'Nell, Theresa D., and C. M. Mitchell
  n.d.   Alcohol use among American Indians adolescents: The role of
              culture in pathological drinking. *Social Science and Medicine*,
              in press.
Philips, Susan U.
  1974   Warm Springs 'Indian time': How the regulation of participa-
              tion affects the progression of events. In R. Bauman and J.
              Sherzer (eds.), *Explorations in the Ethnography of Speaking*,
              92–109. London: Cambridge University Press.
Phillips, Paul C.
  1974   History of the Confederated Salish and Kootenai Tribes of the
              Flathead Reservation. In E. O. Fuller et al., *Interior Salish and
              Eastern Washington Indians*, vol. 3, 1–67. New York: Garland.
Pollack, David, and J. H. Shore
  1980   Validity of the MMPI with Native Americans. *American Jour-
              nal of Psychiatry* 137(8): 946–950.
Ray, Verne F.
  1939   *Cultural Relations in the Plateau of Northwestern America*.
              Los Angeles: F. W. Hodge Fund, Southwest Museum.

Rhoades, Everett R., et al.
1980   Mental health problems of American Indians seen in out-patient
            facilities of the Indian Health Service, 1975. *Public Health Re-
            ports* 96: 329–335.
Ronan, Peter
1890   *Historical Sketch of the Flathead Indian Nation.* Minneapolis:
            Ross and Haines.
Rosaldo, Michelle
1980   *Knowledge and Passion: Ilongot Notions of Self and Social
            Life.* Cambridge: Cambridge University Press.
Roy, Chanilal, A. Choudhuri, and D. Irvine
1970   The prevalence of mental disorders among Saskatchewan Indi-
            ans. *Journal of Cross-Cultural Psychology* 1(4): 383–392.
Rubenstein, Donald H.
1983   Epidemic suicide among Micronesian adolescents. *Social Sci-
            ence and Medicine* 17(10): 657–665.
Sahlins, Marshall
1976   *Culture and Practical Reason.* Chicago: University of Chicago
            Press.
1985   *Islands of History.* Chicago: University of Chicago Press.
Sampath, H. M.
1974   Prevalence of psychiatric disorders in a Southern Baffin Island
            Eskimo settlement. *Canadian Psychiatric Association Journal*
            19(4): 363–367.
Sartorius, Norman, et al.
1983   *Depressive Disorders in Different Cultures.* Geneva: World
            Health Organization.
Schaeffer, Claude E.
1935   *An Acculturation Study of the Indians of the Flathead Reserva-
            tion of Western Montana.* Washington, D.C.: U.S. Commis-
            sioner of Indian Affairs, Department of Interior.
1937   The first Jesuit mission to the Flathead, 1840–1850: A study in
            culture conflicts. *Pacific Northwest Quarterly* 28(3): 227–250.
Schieffelin, Edward L.
1985   The cultural analysis of depressive affect: An example from
            New Guinea. In A. Kleinman and B. Good (eds.), *Culture and
            Depression*, 101–133. Berkeley, Los Angeles, and London:
            University of California Press.
Schoenberg, Wilfred P.
1960   *Jesuits in Montana.* Portland, Oreg.: Daily Journal of Com-
            merce.
Schoenfeld, Lawrence S., and Sheldon I. Miller
1973   The Navajo Indian: A descriptive study of the psychiatric pop-
            ulation. *International Journal of Social Psychiatry* 19: 31–37.
Shkilnyk, Anastasia
1985   *A Poison Stronger than Love.* New Haven: Yale University
            Press.

Shore, James H.
1975   American Indian suicide—Fact and fantasy. *Psychiatry* 38:
            86–91.
Shore, James H., J. D. Kinzie, J. L. Hampson, and E. M. Pattison
1973   Psychiatric epidemiology of an Indian village. *Psychiatry* 36:
            70–81.
Shore, James H., and Spero Manson
1981   Cross-cultural studies of depression among American Indians
            and Alaska Natives. *White Cloud Journal* 2(2): 5–12.
1983   American Indian psychiatric and social problems. *Transcul-
            tural Psychiatric Research Review* 20: 159–180.
Shweder, Richard A.
1979   Rethinking culture and personality theory. Pt. II. *Ethos* 7(4):
            279–311.
1993   The cultural psychology of the emotions. In Michael Lewis and
            Jeanette M. Haviland (eds.), *Handbook of the Emotions*,
            417–431. New York: Guilford Press.
Slagle, A. Logan, and Joan Weibel-Orlando
1986   The Indian Shaker Church and Alcoholics Anonymous: Revi-
            talistic curing cults. *Human Organization* 45(4): 310–319.
Smith, M. G.
1982   The nature and variety of plural unity. In D. Maybury-Lewis
            (ed.), *The Prospects for Plural Societies*, 146–186. Washington,
            D.C.: American Ethnological Association.
Sutro, L. D.
1989   Alcoholics Anonymous in a Mexican peasant Indian village.
            Human Organization 48: 180–186.
Tambiah, Stanley J.
1985a   The magical power of words. In his *Culture, Thought, and So-
            cial Action*, 17–59. Cambridge: Harvard University Press.
1985b   A performative approach to ritual. In his *Culture, Thought, and
            Social Action*, 123–166. Cambridge: Harvard University Press.
1990   *Magic, Science, Religion, and the Scope of Rationality*. The
            1981 Lewis Henry Morgan Lectures. Cambridge: Cambridge
            University Press.
Taylor, Charles
1989   *Sources of the Self: The Making of Modern Identity*. Cam-
            bridge: Harvard University Press.
Teit, James A.
1928   *The Salishan Tribes of the Western Plateaus*. Annual Report
            no. 45. Washington, D.C.: Bureau of American Ethnology.
Termansen, Paul E., and J. Ryan
1970   Health and disease in a British Columbian Indian community.
            Canadian Psychiatric Association Journal 15(2): 121–127.
Todorov, Tzvetan
1984   *Mikhail Bakhtin: The Dialogic Principle*. Minneapolis: Univer-
            sity of Minnesota Press.

Tousignant, Michel
1984   *Peña* in the Ecuadorian Sierra: A psychoanthropological analy-
              sis of sadness. *Culture, Medicine and Psychiatry* 8(4): 381–398.
Townsley, H. C., and G. S. Goldstein
1977   One view of the etiology of depression in the American Indian.
              Public Health Reports 92(5): 458–461.
Trosper, Ron L.
1976   Native American boundary maintenance: The Flathead Indian
              Reservation, Montana, 1860–1970. *Ethnicity* 3: 256–274.
Turner, Victor
1980   Social dramas and stories about them. In W. J. T. Mitchell
              (ed.), *On Narrative,* 137–164. Chicago: University of Chicago
              Press.
Turney-High, Harry H.
1937   The Flathead Indians of Montana. *Memoirs* [American Anthro-
              pological Association] 48(4).
U.S. Bureau of the Census
1980   *Census of Population.* Vol. 1. *Characteristics of the Popula-
              tion, Chapter A, Number of Inhabitants, Montana, October
              1981.* Washington, D.C.
U.S. Congress
1953   *House Concurrent Resolution 108.* 83d Congress.
Vizenor, Gerald
1990   *Crossbloods: Bone Courts, Bingo, and Other Reports.* Min-
              neapolis: University of Minnesota Press.
Weissman, Myrna M., M. L. Bruce, P. J. Leaf, L. P. Florio, and C. Holzer
1991   Affective disorders. In L. N. Robins and D. A. Regier (eds.),
              Psychiatric Disorders in America, 53–80. New York: Free
              Press.
Weissman, Myrna M., P. J. Leaf, M. L. Bruce, and L. Florio
1988   The epidemiology of dysthymia in five communities: Rates,
              risks, comorbidity and treatment. *American Journal of Psychi-
              atry* 145: 815–819.
White, Betty L.
1994   Flathead Reservation. *Montana Magazine* (July–August): 11–23.
White, Geoffrey
1980   Conceptual universals in interpersonal language. *American An-
              thropologist* 82(4): 759–781.
1990   Moral discourse and the rhetoric of emotions. In C. Lutz and
              L. Abu-Lughod (eds.), *Language and the Politics of Emotion,*
              46–68. Cambridge: Cambridge University Press.
1992a   Ethnopsychology. In T. Schwartz, G. M. White, and C. A. Lutz
              (eds.), *New Directions in Psychological Anthropology,* 21–46.
              Cambridge: Cambridge University Press.
1992b   *Identity through History: Living Stories in a Solomon Islands
              Society.* Cambridge: Cambridge University Press.

Wilson, Bryan, ed.
  1970   *Rationality*. Oxford: Basil Blackwell.
Wright, Robin M.
  1988   Anthropological presuppositions of indigenous advocacy. In
              B. Siegel et al. (eds.), *Annual Review of Anthropology* 17: 365–
              426. Palo Alto, Calif.: Annual Reviews.
Young, L. T., E. Hood, S. E. Abbey, and S. E. Malcomson
  1993   Psychiatric consultation in the Eastern Arctic, II. Referral pat-
              terns, diagnoses and treatment. *Canadian Journal of Psychiatry*
              38: 28–31.

Index

AA. *See* Alcoholics Anonymous
Abandonment: in feeling aggrieved, 121–122, 125; in feeling bereaved, 81, 116; in feeling worthless, 127–128, 132, 134; in Flathead ethnopsychology, 110–111, 137, 179; in pathological loneliness, 203. *See also* Belonging; Economic system; Family; Reciprocity
Abu-Lughod, Lila, 186, 187, 219n1
ACE. *See* All Citizens Equal
Adams, Myrna, ix
Adams, Pierre, 27, 43
Adams, Sophie, ix
Affect: in family life, 94–95, 155, 201; normal and pathological, 9, 191–204; proper affect and Indian identity, 73, 77–78, 85, 91–93, 138–139, 187; as separate from cognition, 182. *See also* Anger; Depression; Emotion; Feeling aggrieved; Feeling bereaved; Feeling worthless; Loneliness; Peña; Pity
Albers, Patricia, 219n3
Alcohol. *See* Alcoholics Anonymous; Drinking
Alcoholics Anonymous, 64, 152–153, 174
Algeria, 68
All Citizens Equal, 22–23, 219n4. *See also* Montanans Opposed to Discrimination; Racism
Allotment Act, 48, 54
Anger: cultural sanctions against, 85, 92–93, 106, 174; and drinking, 131; in feeling aggrieved, 122–123, 125–126;

in feeling worthless, 132, 136; as a primary emotion, 183; and suicide, 59–60, 125–126
Apache. *See* Western Apache
Azure, Kim, ix

Bakhtin, Mikhail, 145–147, 174, 185
Barth, Federick, 219n3
Basso, Keith, 20, 21, 219n3, 226n3, 226n21
Beadwork, 103–104
Beaverhead, Pete, 28, 43
Bellah, Robert, 200
Belonging: and Indian identity, 138; and loneliness, 108–109, 110, 137–138, 177–178, 201; and practices of reciprocity, 77–78, 93–94, 99–100, 108–109; and its ritual construction, 77–78, 91–93. *See also* Abandonment; Family
Benedict, Ruth, 182
Bereavement. *See* Feeling bereaved; Death rituals
BIA. *See* Bureau of Indian Affairs
Big Ignace, 27–28. *See also* Blackrobes
Bitterroot, 26, 58, 89; annual feast, 64, 91
Bitterroot Salish: forced relocation of, 29–32, 35, 220n9, 220n11, 226n5. *See also* History
Blackrobes, 26–29, 35, 81, 220n8; St. Louis delegations, 27
Blazer, D. G., 4
Blood pressure, and loneliness, 117, 128, 133

247

Designer:	U.C. Press Staff
Compositor:	Com-Com, Inc.
Text:	10/13 Sabon
Display:	Sabon
Printer & Binder:	Haddon Craftsmen, Inc.